SO-BSK-676

Ephemeral Territories

Ephemeral Territories

REPRESENTING NATION, HOME, AND IDENTITY IN CANADA

Erin Manning

University of Minnesota Press   Minneapolis / London

Chapter 2 has been reprinted from *Alternatives: Social Transformation and Humane Governance* 25, no. 1; copyright 2000 by Lynne Rienner Publishers, Inc.; reprinted with permission of the publisher.

Copyright 2003 by the Regents of the University of Minnesota

All rights reserved. No part of this publication may be reproduced, stored in a retrieval system, or transmitted, in any form or by any means, electronic, mechanical, photocopying, recording, or otherwise, without the prior written permission of the publisher.

Published by the University of Minnesota Press
111 Third Avenue South, Suite 290
Minneapolis, MN 55401-2520
http://www.upress.umn.edu

Library of Congress Cataloging-in-Publication Data

Manning, Erin.
　　Ephemeral territories : representing nation, home, and identity in Canada / Erin Manning.
　　　　p.　　cm.
　　Includes bibliographical references (p. 　) and index.
　　ISBN 0-8166-3924-8 (acid-free paper) — ISBN 0-8166-3925-6 (pbk. : acid-free paper)
　　1. National characteristics, Canadian.　2. Nationalism—Canada.
　3. Canada—Politics and government—1980–　.　4. Political culture—
Canada.　5. Canada—Intellectual life.　6. Discourse analysis—Canada.
　7. Human territoriality—Canada.　8. Canada—Ethnic relations.
　9. Home—Social aspects—Canada.　10. Regionalism—Canada.　I. Title.
　　F1021.2.M36 2003
　　305.8'00971—dc21

2002013119

Printed in the United States of America on acid-free paper

The University of Minnesota is an equal-opportunity educator and employer.

12 11 10 09 08 07 06 05 04 03   10 9 8 7 6 5 4 3 2 1

For my mother, Margaret McCullough

Contents

Preface
Unmoored

What does it mean to be at home?

This text, which crosses boundaries both national and disciplinary, is about home. Through the figure of the home, I tell a story of the nation: *Ephemeral Territories* is my attempt to explore the unhomeliness within the familiar contours of the discourse of the nation-state. In a critical engagement with territory, identity, racial difference, immigration, separatism, multiculturalism, and homelessness, I delve into the question of what it means to belong.

This is both my history and that of others. It is mine insofar as it charts my discomforts in the face of the specter of home. It is mine insofar as it draws from the concept of the *Unheimlich*, an unhomely haunting that has accompanied me throughout my travels, both here and there. It is mine in the sense that I want to believe that not being "at home" in the traditional sense does not necessary belie the possibility of being accommodated. It is the story of others insofar as *Ephemeral Territories* delves into experiences beyond my grasp: stories of displacement, of immigration, of war, of separation. It is also the story of others insofar as its political inspiration is based on cross-cultural texts. I choose these texts not only because of their infinite read-ability, but because these texts-in-the-making are ephemeral gestures toward response-ability.

With any attempt to write a genealogy comes the risk of rewriting a history fraught with exclusions. In the case of *Ephemeral Territories,* what remains occluded is a reading of the native presence in Canada. This was brought to my attention in Hawai'i, where the native presence cannot be divorced from the politics "at home." In Canada, this should be the case as well. Unfortunately, the sheer distances that separate people in Canada make it difficult to speak of any experience other than that of proximity.

In my case, this means having little firsthand experience of what it is to be "native" and "at home."

I recognize that history, as a Western construct, has rarely been able to accommodate a native presence. In my attempt to articulate a Canadian cultural politics without delineating the vicissitudes of the native presence in Canada, I run the risk of perpetuating this tendency. This is not my aim. Rather, I hope the inroads traced by *Ephemeral Territories* will permit others to continue to ask troubling questions concerning gender discrimination, racial inequality, and territorial integrity, maintaining an important and necessary dialogue between native peoples and settlers to Canada.

My own trajectory spans Quebec and Ontario. Born of bilingual parents (a child of the Trudeau generation), I was encouraged to "belong" both here and there. From the outset, I have questioned what it means to be at home, a question that has followed me through two referenda on Quebec sovereignty and many travels abroad. I have come to think that, in most cases, "to be at home" is to belong to a system that has always already been written in the name of an exclusionary system of governance. The notion of "being at home" suits those who are not at odds with the parameters of belonging and the limits of inclusion perpetuated within the discourse of the nation-state. *Ephemeral Territories* is a challenge to this notion of "home," a challenge that resists at every turn the encroachment of a naturalized understanding of the concept of home that feeds the exclusionary narrative of the nation.

This is not to say that solutions have been garnered. My attempts at a rearticulation of the political are ephemeral gestures directed toward a "now" that involves accommodating myself in a globalizing world. I do not seek a stable political construct to "re-place" the home. This would negate my experience of being-in-between and the wealth I have encountered in the notion of a practice of accommodation that resists stultifying narratives of identity and belonging. I currently live between Ottawa and Montreal, traveling weekly between two transitory spaces, cognizant of the fact that tensions have not abated at the border.

As I travel between here and there, I register the growing apathy in Ontario with regard to Quebec sovereignty politics and the stubborn allegiance to separatism in Quebec, where the specter of Anglo-Canadian oppression remains palpable. I say little, aware that the complexities in these arguments have taken on lives of their own. But I do ask myself questions. I ask what is at stake when a "people" recognizes itself as such. I ask who "belongs," here and there. I ask what stories are told and who tells them. And I attempt, at all costs, not to immerse myself in a suf-focating narrative that celebrates the home as the light at the end of the tunnel.

Bearing these questions in mind, *Ephemeral Territories* is an explo-ration of the exclusionary practices inherent in the discourse of home, identity, and the nation. It is written from a perspective indebted to an experience of being in-between. This is not everyone's story, nor does it claim to be a parchment on which all of Canada will see itself reflected. Canada is too large, too multifaceted, too regional to be one place from which one discourse could emerge. *Ephemeral Territories* is therefore both much less than a national text and much more. It is a text that celebrates cultural works "made in Canada" that appeal to a polity that extends far beyond the reaches of the Canadian nation. Thought-provoking cultural texts incite me to ask difficult questions of the political, questions that exceed the space of the nation. In turn, I am encouraged to imagine an errant politics that celebrates encounters of difference that are not de-fined through the vocabulary of the nation-state.

Acknowledgments

Ephemeral Territories has taken me from Ottawa to Berlin to Honolulu to Montreal and back to Ottawa. Along the way, I have greatly benefited from the generosity and intellectual acuity of Barry Rutland, Ben Jones, and Michael Shapiro. Heartfelt thanks are also due to Sankaran Krishna, Nevzat Soguk, Manfred Henningsen, Rob Wilson, Mick Dillon, Patricia Molloy, Simon Dalby, François Debrix, Rob Shields, Peter Harcourt, and Will Straw.

For ongoing support and encouragement, I thank Carrie Mullen at the University of Minnesota Press. For the film stills, I thank Peter Harcourt. For financial support in the forms of doctoral and postdoctoral research grants, I gratefully acknowledge the Social Sciences and Humanities Research Council of Canada. I am also grateful to those who have allowed me to reprint passages or chapters already published: I thank *Alternatives* and *Space and Culture,* which both published earlier versions of my second chapter, and *Theory and Event,* in which a version of my first chapter appeared. I also acknowledge Jin-me Yoon and Jamelie Hassan, who granted permission to reproduce copies of their artwork in the book, and Mary Knox, who permitted reproduction of the work of Lawren Harris.

Many personal thanks are due to those who stood by me in the process of writing and rethinking this book. Thank you, Paul, for giving me a place to stay, think, and enjoy fresh ahi during the early part of the process. For living with me across time and space, and for giving me a sense that I can indeed be accommodated, *merci,* Maman. Thank you to all my separatist friends whose views continue to leave me unmoored. *Merci,* Patrick, for understanding the implicit connection between my art and my writing, and *merci,* Francis, for allowing me to express the complex webs of identity through dance.

Introduction

Close to Home: Canadian Identity, Nationalism, and Errant Politics

> Those who give way to the demand for sense (which by itself already seems to make sense and to provide some reassurance . . .) demand of the world that it signify itself as dwelling, haven, habitation, safeguard, intimacy, community, subjectivity; as the signifier of a proper and present signified, the signifier of the proper and the present as such.
>
> **—Jean-Luc Nancy, *The Sense of the World***

There are many ports of entry into the discourse of nationalism. Indeed, nationalism by its very nature depends on policed ports of entry from whence enunciation is limited by the vocabulary of the nation, a language that determines which bodies are qualified to speak. Accordingly, those who have curtailed access to the vocabulary of the nation—due to their renunciation of, expulsion from, or incomprehension of the nation's semantics—are invariably politically disqualified: as a noncitizen, I am denied access not only to your passport but also to your language, guaranteed nothing more than the amorphous vocabulary of homelessness and statelessness.

The vocabulary of the nation can be understood as the structuring of a language that produces the distinction between qualified and unqualified bodies, where qualification within the identity and territory of the nation presupposes an attachment to the nation in its linguistic, cultural, and political incarnations. This language of the nation is characterized, alternately, by a desire to naturalize a cohesive sense of identity and territory through official cultural and political texts that depict the nation as a harmonious entity, and by the lawful enforcement of the discourse of state sovereignty as the guarantor of liberty, equality, and fraternity. Harmony and liberty come at a high price, however, as is apparent when we examine the ways in which the vocabulary of the nation excludes and oppresses those it deems unqualified. A subversion of the language of the nation is called for to better understand the ways in which the nation's very semantic structures work to define liberty, fraternity, and equality as discourses to which only a select few have access.

In my study of the nation and its vicissitudes, I undertake a critical reading of the language of the nation to demonstrate the ways in which nationalism and the discourses of exclusion it generates are contained within and contaminated by this vocabulary of (dis)qualification. To do so, I resist embarking on a straightforward voyage into the nation's locus of enunciation. This would deny the complexities inherent in the construction and dissemination of vocabularies, be they languages of containment or resistance. I opt instead for a perusal through the obstacle-ridden and dis-eased entrails of the nation and its (in)secure vocabularies, acknowledging, at every juncture, that all language potentially turns on itself.

This voyage begins by borrowing concepts that exceed and transgress the language of state sovereignty. These concepts range from "ontopology" to "deterritorialization" to "errant politics." Ontopology is a useful concept with which to begin a rearticulation of the bounds of the nation, for Jacques Derrida's notion of "ontopology" allows us at the outset to better understand the implicit connection, in the language of the nation, between ontology (being) and topos (territory, native soil, city, or body). When we consider the nation's locus of enunciation as ontopological, we become cognizant of the limitations and exclusions always already at work within the nation's vocabularies, where "political possibilities have been limited by the alignment between territory and identity, state and nation, all under a sign of 'ethnicity,' supported by a particular account of history" (Campbell 1998: 80).

To adequately subvert the language of the nation, we must develop an awareness of the conjunction between ontopology and the manner in which we negotiate time and space. It is only then that we begin to appreciate the ways in which we reproduce the vocabulary of the nation within our personal circles of existence. For instance, even as many of us provisionally assume a political stance that refutes nationalism, we often design our homes to mirror the exclusionary aspects of the nation's mandate on belonging, forgetting, perhaps, that the notion of the home (or homeland) remains one of the nation's most powerful ontopological enunciations. If we refrain from questioning the validity of the political structures that guarantee our "safety" within the discourse of the home, we are blinded to the ways in which the home mirrors the politics of state-sovereignty, offering protection from the outside by condoning an ethics of exclusionary violence on the inside. We must therefore develop an awareness that, as we mortgage our lives and construct fences and walls, install security systems and guard dogs, we are offering unwavering support to a vocabulary that is at the heart of the imaginary of the nation.

In the work to follow, the image of the home as an extension of the nation surfaces often. The home provides not only a tangible example of how we perpetuate the vocabulary of the nation in our daily utterances, it offers also a visceral instance of our desire for attachment and belonging. In *Ephemeral Territories,* I challenge the naturalization of the concept of home, drawing attention to the fact that "home" is not a stable entity, but rather another of modernity's constructions. As Witold Rybczynski writes, the concepts of domesticity, privacy, and comfort that characterize the concept of home are achievements of the bourgeois age (1986: 7).

When we begin to pay attention to the ways in which "home" is constructed as a modern discourse that parallels the discourse of the nation-state, we begin to subvert the imaginary of the nation. The notion that the home is an uncanny aspect of national life is a tenet of my own experience. As a Canadian who has always felt at odds with the nation and has never felt "homed" in the traditional sense, I have often wondered about the exigencies of the discourse of belonging. Like most in my situation, I have secretly held onto a tenuous desire to "belong," all the while knowing that this very lack of belonging—or homelessness—affords me intimate insight into my own alterity, alerting me to the danger of propagating a cohesive discourse of national identity based on a homogenous notion of what it means "to be at home." Ironically, my personal sense of a certain territorial homelessness is not necessarily at odds with "being Canadian." "Being Canadian" has always presented itself to me as somewhat coterminous with homelessness, if one can gauge a nation by its incessant preoccupation with its own sense of elusive identity.

However, the obsession with "Canadian identity" perpetuates a violent discourse of national exclusion that is masked in the myth of Canadians as a harmless, open, and generous people. For despite that the discourse of generosity and benevolence prevails within the Canadian national imagination, the categories of "us" and "them" remain standard practices at ports of entry, where the language of the nation has not become polyvocal. I am not suggesting, of course, that benevolent Canadians do not exist. Rather, I am proposing that by delving into these questions with respect to Canada—which seems to most an unlikely place to undertake such an exploration—we may be better prepared to envisage the ways in which all cultures of the national perpetuate a vocabulary from which certain people are disqualified.

An emphasis on the politics "at home" serves to highlight that issues concerning the home, state sovereignty, and nationalism are not limited to certain geopolitical territorialities. Every nation carries within its vocabularies semantic politics that delimit its understanding of what it means to house "a people." As I have already emphasized, we cannot adequately rethink the political without first deconstructing[1] the vocabulary of the home, since the language of the nation informs the very enunciations we employ to "comprehend" both the home and the political.

Since vocabulary is what is at stake, it is useful—at the outset of a rethinking of the limits of the political—to turn to Jacques Rancière's formulation of the difference between *politics* and *the political*. Throughout the work to follow, *the political* refers to a category that distinguishes itself from *politics* by alluding to the creative process of the enactment of politics. In Rancière's terminology, *politics* (or policy) involves that which is concerned with government and "relies on the distribution of shares and the hierarchy of places and functions," whereas *the political* concerns that which is engaged with questions of equality or emancipation, defined as "the encounter between emancipation and policy in the handling of a wrong" (1992: 58–59). A marked differentiation between politics and the political allows us to better appreciate the ways in which the discourse of the nation infiltrates our understanding of politics through an emphasis on policy.

"Political activity," according to Rancière, "is whatever shifts a body from the place assigned to it or changes a place's destination. It makes visible what had no business being seen, and makes heard a discourse where once there was only place for noise . . ." (1999: 30). Rancière argues that it is only when we emphasize the heterology within the very notion of subjectivity on which the political is construed that we can begin to undermine the process of self-identification that attempts to turn the techniques of governance into the natural laws of the social order. Through a focus on the heterology of the political, the encounter with "the political community" becomes an encounter not with the community as self, but with the impossibility of community as a homogeneous political entity. The question then becomes not simply "How are we to face a political problem?" but "How are we to reinvent politics?" (Rancière 1992: 64). In the work to follow, this challenge to reinvent politics resounds as the basis for a rethinking of territory and identity in the name of the deconstruction of the nation.

Postnational Deterritorializations

Arjun Appadurai underscores the complexity inherent in the current relationship between territoriality, sovereignty, and nationalism when he states that, despite that territorial sovereignty became the foundational concept of the nation-state after the agreements associated with the Westphalian peace settlements of 1648, there is very little the state can realistically monopolize today other than the *idea* of territory as the crucial diacritic of sovereignty (1996a: 41). Appadurai argues that as fissures appear between and among local, translocal, and transnational spaces, territory as the ground of loyalty and national affect is increasingly divorced from territory as the site of sovereignty and state control of civic society. Territorial tropes for the imaginary of the nation persist, however, due to our allegiance to an unproblematized understanding of territory. As Appadurai writes, "The idea that cultures are coherent, bounded, contiguous, and persistent has always been underwritten by a sense that human sociality is naturally localized and even locality-bound" (1996a: 53). Following Appadurai, then, territory can be recognized as the crisis in the relationship between the nation and the state (1996a: 54).

Territoriality is a key geopolitical component in understanding how society and space are interconnected. In his introduction to *Human Territoriality,* Robert Sack defines territoriality as a spatial strategy that is intimately linked to the ways in which people use the land, how they organize themselves in space, and how they give meaning to place. Sack's definition of territoriality emphasizes that human spatial relationships are not neutral. Rather, they are the results of influence and power. If we combine Sack's and Appadurai's definitions of territoriality as a starting point in a rearticulation of the political, it becomes apparent that what is at stake in the rethinking of the nation's territorial imperatives is a renegotiation of the link between territory and power. This is one of the tasks undertaken by the geophilosophy of Gilles Deleuze and Félix Guattari, who invite us to move beyond hierarchized structures of territoriality to a milieu where space incorporates territoriality's strange doubleness, and where what is of concern is not the stability of origins but the creative possibilities produced by interconnection and alignment.

Deleuze and Guattari propel state sovereignty toward a moment of deterritorialization, unsettling the regulation and dissemination of the vocabulary of the nation by opting for attachment not to the hierarchical limitations of what they call the *plane of organization,* but by transgressing the institution of state philosophy through an emphasis on the *plane of consistency*. The departure from the plane of organization through the re-nunciation of the vocabulary of state philosophy underscores the inextricable link between the state, philosophy, language, and nation. As Derrida writes, "The affirmation of a nationality or even the claim of nationalism does not happen to philosophy by chance or from the outside; it is essentially and thoroughly philosophical, *it is a philosopheme*" (1992a: 10).

Focusing our attention on the nationalizing impulses of philosophy, we become attentive to the ways in which the national experiments of state philosophy are articulated through a language that is invariably violent and restrictive. It is here that the plane of consistency becomes useful as a metaphor for the interruption of the discourse of state philosophy and, by extension, of state sovereignty. In contrast to the rigid demarcations of state philosophy and its plane of organization, the plane of consistency facilitates deviation from the strict codes of territoriality and governmentality. It does so by foregrounding a becoming-deterritorialization that takes into account distributional articulations rather than anchorages, compositions rather than unities, emphasizing a rhizomatic relationship to both territory and identity rather than a rooted, arboreal one.

Deleuze and Guattari's theory of the plane of consistency is at the forefront of my renegotiation of the nation through cross-cultural Canadian texts. A focus on deterritorialization involves a desire on my part not to act once and for all, but to evoke a continual rewriting of the political through a multiple and rhizomatic movement of territorialization, reterritorialization, and deterritorialization. This shifting between the different states of territoriality is what assures me that we continue to be in a state of flux whereby the homes we construct remain ephemeral.

This is not to imply, however, that deterritorialization negates the possibility of home as such. Deterritorialization is not involved in such ultimate pronouncements. Deterritorialization simply subverts the notion that territory and identity can be adequately policed so as to create an entity called "home" that will indefinitely protect us from the exigencies of our existences. Deterritorialization is but one step in an ongoing practice of a reterritorialization that attempts to restratify errant spaces.

A vigilance is called for in the name of deterritorialization to prevent errant spaces from becoming sedentary. When we begin to think of the home as rhizomatic rather than arboreal (as a multiplicity rather than a rooted structure), we expose arborescent territorializations—such as the nation-state—as the dichotomous, hierarchized systems they are. To offer a transgressive alternative to the nation and its politics, it is necessary to invent a vocabulary that departs from the certainties of arboreal ontopologies, shifting instead to a vocabulary of the rhizome that under-mines stable notions of identity and territory through its uncompromis-ing tubular propagations across boundaries and ideologies.

It is through cross-cultural texts that I expose the rhizomatic elements within the vocabulary of the nation. I do so by turning to the moments of enunciation, within the nation's cultural narratives, that speak against the hierarchized and dichotomized limitations propagated in the name of the imaginary of the nation. Through cross-cultural texts from artworks to film *to* literature, I emphasize ways in which culture can talk back to the nation. The texts I foreground effect a rhizomatic deterritorialization with respect to the discourse of "national identity" in Canada, question-ing what it means to "be at home" within the discourse of the nation. Here, culture operates as a complex utterance that resonates within and beyond the nation, where "culture is the distinctive element that allows us to avoid conflating the nation with the state, even as, in practice, indi-viduals 'encounter' the nation through the state" (Balibar 1995: 177).

Placing culture at the forefront, I delineate ways in which cultural texts are capable of subverting the nation, concurrently drawing attention to the manner in which the language of the "culture" of the nation-state can itself perpetuate exclusions based on race, gender, and citizenship. Culture plays a double-edged role within the nation. On the one hand, culture is often the name given to the "essential nation" (Balibar 1995: 178), while on the other hand, culture is also potentially that which is in conflict with the assimilatory politics of the nation-state's institutions and practices. As Étienne Balibar writes, culture can "either anticipate the state, resist it, or figure the 'ultimate' goal of its constitution" (1995: 178). If we are to employ culture as an instance of a countercoherence to the nation's vocabularies of exclusion, we must locate within cultural texts the promise not of a stable language, but of an alternative that retains its ephemerality.

In the work to follow, I situate culture as the stuttering voice of "na-tional identity,"[2] where culture is figured both as that which echoes and sustains the nation and as that which refutes and deconstructs the nation. I begin with the specter of the nation as a central character, placing em-phasis on Benedict Anderson's suggestion that "nation-ness is the most universally legitimate value in the political life of our time" (1983: 3). I suggest that to understand the effects of culture on the nation requires a keen awareness of the manner in which the nation has come into histori-cal being, in what ways the nation has changed over time, and why, today, it commands such profound emotional legitimacy. For regardless that the term "nation" holds far less historical "meaning" than many would expect, all states today are officially "nations." It would therefore be blindness to conclude that the "nation" is historically unimportant and powerless, or even in decline. On the other hand, the nation's epithelium is increasingly showing symptoms of its inner ravagings. This hemorrhaging is being exposed due to rearticulations of the political that exceed the vocabulary of the nation: the nation-as-state philosophy is becoming the product of its own inevitable disarticulation.

A Short Genealogy of the Nation

The word "nationalism" does not come into wide general use until the end of the nineteenth century, when it emerges due to the distillation of a complex crossing of discrete historical forces. At this historical juncture, three fundamental cultural conceptions—all of great antiquity—lose their axiomatic grip on peoples' minds. The first of these cultural conceptions of antiquity cast aside by the modern age is script language; the second, the demise of the belief that society is naturally organized around and under high centers/monarchs who are apart from any other human beings and who rule by some form of cosmological (divine) dispensation; and the third, the conception of temporality in which cosmology and history are indistinguishable. Combined, as Anderson writes, "these ideas rooted human lives firmly in the very nature of things, giving certain meaning to the everyday fatalities of existence and offering, in various ways, redemption from them" (1983: 36).

The uneven decline of these interlinked certainties, under the impact of economic change, social and scientific "discoveries," and the development of increasingly rapid communications, drives a wedge between antiquity's understanding of time and space and that of the incumbent modern age. As well, the onset of print-capitalism makes it possible for rapidly growing numbers of people to think of themselves and to relate themselves to others in profoundly new ways: print-capitalism creates languages of power through the inception of unified fields of exchange and communication. This, Anderson suggests, lays the basis for national consciousness. People who otherwise found it impossible to understand one another in conversation become capable of comprehending one another via print and paper. These fellow-readers, to whom they are connected through print, form in their secular, particular, visible invisibility the embryo of the nationally imagined community.

The concept of nation-ness as linked to private-property language has a wide influence on nineteenth-century Europe and on subsequent theorizing about the nature of nationalism. As Edward Said writes in *Orientalism*, "Language became less of a continuity between an outside power and the human speaker than an internal field created and accomplished by language users among themselves" (1979: 136). Out of these semantic mutations comes philology and its study of comparative grammar and classification of languages into families. If all languages now shared a common (intra)mundane status, then all were in principle equally worthy of study and admiration. Since none was the language of God, they now belonged to their new owners, that is, to each language's *native* speakers. Hence, the activities of grammarians, philologists, and litterateurs are central to the shaping of nineteenth-century European nationalisms. As Tom Nairn writes: "The new middle-class intelligentsia had to invite the masses into history; and the invitation-card had to be written in a language they understood" (1977: 340).

World War I brings the age of high dynasticism to an end. In place of the Congress of Berlin comes the League of Nations, from which non-Europeans are not excluded. According to Anderson, from this time on, the legitimate international norm is the nation-state. In addition to a new understanding of territoriality, the "national" awareness of being embedded in secular, serial time, with all its implications of continuity, engenders the need for a narrative of "identity." However, since there was no Originator, the nation's biography could not be written evangelically through a long, procreative chain of begettings. It was thus from the outset apparent that articulating a vocabulary of the nation that would facilitate a national imaginary would depend on a certain historical amnesia wherein the inconsistencies that did not serve the narrative purpose had to be forgotten. "How could it be otherwise," Eric Hobsbawm asks, "given that we are trying to fit historically novel, emerging, changing, and . . . far from universal entities into a framework of permanence and universality?" (1990: 6).

Since World War II, and especially since the 1960s, the role of "national economies" has been displaced by the major transformations in the international division of labor, whose basic units are transnational or multinational enterprises, and by the corresponding development of international centers and networks of economic transactions, which are, for practical purposes, outside the control of state governments. In step with the processes of globalization, the sovereignty of nation-states, while still effective, has progressively declined. The primary modi of production move with increasing ease across national boundaries; thus the nation-state is less capable of imposing its authority over the economy.

Accordingly, some historians suggest that the twenty-first century "will have to be written as the history of a world which can no longer be contained within the limits of 'nations' and 'nation-states,' either politically, economically, culturally or linguistically" (Hobsbawm 1990: 191).

In light of these transformations, "[e]ven the most dominant nation-states should no longer be thought of as supreme and sovereign authorities, either outside or even within their own borders," despite that "the decline in sovereignty of nation-states . . . does not mean that sovereignty as such has declined" (Hardt and Negri 2000: xi). Following this hypothesis, the twenty-first century will see "nations" and "nation-states" or ethnic/linguistic groups as "retreating before, resisting, adapting to, being absorbed or dislocated by the new supranational restructuring of the globe" (Hobsbawm 1990: 191). Despite the substantial evidence backing these proliferating forays into globalization, however, it is nonetheless important to be attentive to the pungent desire in the late twentieth and early twenty-first centuries to continue to secure time and space as the investment in identity, an investment based on territorial imperatives.

Nationalist resurgences are not necessarily in conflict with globalization. Although throughout *Ephemeral Territories* I often use the metaphor of the container when speaking of the nation, I do so not to suggest that the nation-state *as such* is a unified spatiotemporality, but to highlight the manner in which the nation-state imagines itself. My theorization of the vocabulary of the nation as one that is politically contained is based on the awareness that no container can be completely airtight. In the current era, the nation-state often merges politically with institutions and ideologies of globalization. In many cases, as Saskia Sassen points out,

> [g]lobal processes are . . . strategically located/constituted in national spaces, where they are implemented usually with the help of legal measures taken by state institutions. The material and legal infrastructure that makes possible the global circulation of financial capital . . . is often produced as "national" infrastructure—even though it is increasingly shaped by global agendas. (2000: 218)

This complicity between national and global projects results in a diversification of national space within a global arena and vice versa, alerting us to the fact that national space as such is never completely unified.

Whether in the name of the nation-state or under the heading of globalization, resurgent nationalisms are powerful and dangerous, their forms diverse and complex. Roger Brubaker urges that we develop a perspective that, while attending to these resurgent nationalisms, does not lead us to reify nations. He argues that

> [n]ationalism can and should be understood without evoking "nations" as substantial entities. Instead of focusing on nations as real groups, we should focus on nationhood and nationness, on "nation" as practical category, institutionalized form, and contingent event. . . . To understand nationalism, we have to understand the practical uses of the category "nation," the ways it can come to structure perception, to inform thought and experience, to organize discourse and political action. (1996: 7)

Following Brubaker, the nation—and, by extension, nationalism—must be understood not as a substantial entity but as a terminology of modernity that appears through idioms, practices, and possibilities endemic to modern cultural and political life. Within this conceptual framework, nation-ness is a variable rather than a "real" collectivity or community.

The question thus shifts from "What is a nation?" to "How is nationhood as a political and cultural form institutionalized within and among states?" For the growth of nationalism as the process of integration of the masses into a common political form, presupposing the existence—in fact or as an ideal—of a centralized form of government over a large and distinct territory, has been shown not to be a natural phenomenon, but rather a product of the growth of social and intellectual factors at a certain stage of history. This is the focus of a recent debate between Jürgen Habermas, Arjun Appadurai, and Timothy Mitchell in *Public Culture* (1998).

In Habermas's piece "The European Nation-State: On the Past and Future of Sovereignty and Citizenship," he explores the current challenges to the nation-state, notably globalization and the politics of subnational cultural identity. What Habermas seeks is a model of transformation for the nation-state where supra- and transnational forms of governance would rely on "constitutional patriotism," a concept that Habermas offers as an alternative to nationalism. "Constitutional patriotism" is defined by Habermas as the instance in which the constitutional order reflects a particular national interpretation of constitutional principles such as popular sovereignty and human rights, linking citizens irrespective of ethnic bonds or national identities.

One of the shortcomings of Habermas's argument is the manner in which he arrives at the postnationalist discourse he proposes. As Mitchell and Appadurai point out, Habermas seeks the postnational by rearticulating the vocabulary of the nation. Mitchell observes: "To embark on a postnationalist politics we must revisit the history of nationalism. But must we retell it as a history of the nation-state?" (1998: 417). To begin with the nation-state and to become uncritically captive in its linguistic, conceptual, and territorial imaginaries is, invariably, to reinforce nationalism by condoning the notion that the nation-state "exists." We must instead speak of the nation as an institutionalized category and a conceptual contradiction. Following this argument, Appadurai suggests that

> we may need to abandon precisely the idea that space, cultural identity, and distributive politics need to be contained in formally equal, spatially distinct, and isomorphic envelopes, the design which undergirds the architecture of the modern state. (1998: 448)

It is time, instead, to conceptualize a

> global politics that admits of a heterogeneity of *overlapping* forms of governance and attachment (some national, some statist, and others neither), rather than one that requires a homogenous set of interacting units. (449)

However, we must take care not to reinvent globalization in the image of the nation or, conversely, to place globalization as completely outside the realm of the nation's narratives of exclusion. As Mitchell reminds us, rather than being incidental to the history of nationalism as Habermas claims, imperialism and, by extension, globalization (as the postnational form of governance Habermas emphasizes), is a concept that shapes nationalism and defines its vocabulary. Mitchell argues that the political integration that globalization enables must be understood also as a potential process of exclusion. Globalization follows in the shadow of imperialism: the nineteenth century's focus on imperialism was already a globalization that encompassed the relationships of production as well as trade. In this vein, Mitchell warns that "we need to be careful not to treat globalization (or neo-imperialism) as a teleology. Not all recent history has been a process of increasing integration" (1998: 421).

The subversion of the nation-state, as both Mitchell and Appadurai emphasize, requires a deconstruction of the historical, political, and cultural legacies of the nation. This task can initially be broached through close scrutiny of the ways in which the political has been "nationalized" through the normalization of the discourse of state sovereignty. As Bernard Yack writes: "By breaking down and integrating local communities and overlapping jurisdictions, state sovereignty has in effect 'nationalized' political communities" (1996: 194). Such a conflation of the national with the political has been achieved, Yack suggests, through a marked differentiation between "civic" and "ethnic" nationalisms, creating a rift between nationalisms that correspond to "civilized" attachments to modern states and "uncivilized" attachments to ethnic origins. We must recall that ethnic and civic nationalism are inextricably intertwined, and that it is the depiction of ethnic nationalism as an atavistic and racist enterprise that encourages civic nationalists to bask in the myth that, among the civilized, nationalism is a choice, not a prescription.

If we resist adhering to civic nationalism on the basis that all nationalisms contain within their vocabularies the seeds of oppression, we are perhaps ready to admit that another language of the political must be sought. In the work to follow, I attempt to compose such an adjacent vocabulary, using as a drawing board various contemporary Canadian artworks, current cross-cultural Canadian films, and a recent Canadian novel. My choice of Canadian texts for this purpose does not represent a desire to limit a rearticulation of the political to Canada and to Canadian politics of national identity, nor does it promise an overarching reading of Canadian culture. Rather, my focus extends beyond the nation-state: I turn to certain cross-cultural texts that, albeit "Canadian," demonstrate symptoms of a world in flux, where culture operates as a creative voice that speaks out against the violence of territorial cohesion and enforced homogeneity. Canada is but a case in point.

Throughout the chapters that follow, cross-cultural, counternational threads are explored in the context of identity, territory, immigration, gender, race, and the politics of home. Each of these themes is taken up in an effort to reconceptualize what it means to live with one another across time and space, in Canada as elsewhere. The image I propose to accompany such a rewriting of the nation is that of errant politics. In errant politics, the political is not envisaged as the organizational element of the state apparatus, but becomes, rather, a mobile vehicle that acts as a hinge between time and space, rearticulating our understanding of the political through nomadic vocabularies of resistance.

Errant Politics

Errant politics subverts attachments that depend on the stability of territory and identity, rewriting the national vocabulary of belonging into a language of movement. To err within politics is to initiate a dialogue that transgresses monologic state sovereignty. Such a dialogue prizes the ephemeral rather than the static. Errant politics is a politics that seeks to instantiate a vocabulary of incommensurability, maintaining a critical stance toward all discourses that offer the promise of homogeneity and cohesion. Rather than comfortably residing within a territoriality that can be measured and policed, errant politics demands a continued re-negotiation of the terms of containment. Errant politics is a recasting of the politics of space and time as ephemeral, inciting us to question the terms of inclusion and exclusion that define our access to narratives of home, identity, and territory.

The errant journey is a roaming that seeks, where the finding does not first of all mean "to find" in the sense of a practical or scientific result. As Maurice Blanchot suggests, "To find is to turn, to take a turn about, to go around. . . . No idea here of a goal, still less of a stopping" (1993: 25). To take a turn around is to err, to be a curious drifter who yearns for move-ment. Such a voyage cannot be thought of as linear, for it does not return to itself, completing a circle. Rather, to err is "to seek in relation to the center that is, properly speaking, what cannot be found" (Blanchot 1993: 26). To seek the center, then, is always to err in search of the ephemeral. Searching and error are akin, both turning and returning to sacrifice themselves to the detour.

To err is to take a voyage, to wander. In French, *erre* signifies the track of an animal, left for us to discover in the sand, in a trace on the snow, on the earth. To err is to travel along these traces, barely perceptible to some, of memory—reminders that lead in all directions, left by a mul-titude of species, wandering across the land. Erring, I advance on a path that corresponds to no opening. Errant politics is this movement within unbounded space that is invested neither in veiling nor in unveiling, re-siding neither on the inside nor on the outside. Errant, I seek a space of encounter that shifts between the center and the periphery, wandering through the margins. "To err is probably this: to go outside the space of encounter" (Blanchot 1993: 27).

The encounter of the political errant is an encounter that seeks what it finds, traveling along the fringes of the adventure that displaces the text, bringing to the fore elements that lie forgotten on the fringes of the center. Errant politics seeks to locate the world differently, trying to find through language a deferred text, an aberrant landscape, a configuration of the other that alters the boundary of the configuration itself, of space as configuration. Errant politics speaks to the *différance* of space through language, reveling in an etymology that explores the facetious play of the text: I write my own erring as I depart from all directions and paths, crossing all lines, resignifying the impossible, the immobile. Erring, I effect a curvature of space. Errant politics is the writing of this spatio-temporal curve that refutes and resists the politics of state sovereignty.

Errant politics attempts to undermine every hierarchy, tying and untying the knots of accepted systems, simultaneously entangling them and setting them loose. Through such a practice of tying and untying, errant politics draws our attention to the liminal site of the intermingling of exteriorities and interiorities, to the moment when inside and outside turn toward each other, when everything is suspended in a state of redefinition. This process of and against denouement is at the heart of errant politics. For errant politics refuses to contain itself within a coherent and homogenous matrix of intelligibility. Instead, errant politics foregrounds instances when articulations of subjectivity, territoriality, and belonging are at odds with the official imaginary of the nation.

Instances of errant politics can be observed in countercoherences to the nation, such as cultural texts that decry the nation's exclusivity by emphasizing counterarticulations that serve to undermine national narratives of attachment. These counternarratives provoke a politics that does not seek a deepening of attachments, but rather navigates within the uncertain vistas of a spatiotemporality that refuses to adhere to the policy-ordained limitations of the nation-state and its adjacent discourses of territory and identity. To err toward the wor(l)d is to be willing to wander along these tangled landscapes, to become enmeshed in the disparate lines of communication that call forth new political associations and commitments.

The political, as I imagine it throughout the work to follow, can be articulated through the concept of errant politics. Within errant politics, the political remains ephemeral, subject to continual change and redefinition. As an instantiation of the ephemeral, errant politics acts as a reminder that we must err in our thinking to resist tying the knots of knowledge and comprehension that potentially imprison us in the stultifying, encapsulated world of the nation through which we navigate, not necessarily by choice but often by habit. By imagining the political as a transitory movement, we are capable of participating in a deconstruction of the icons through which national imaginaries are composed. Here, deconstruction reveals itself not as a critical method but as a movement of and within the text (a gesture of reading), which engenders new textual possibilities that encourage us to rewrite the politics of space and time.

The contingency of language and representation underscores the ephemeral quality of the political, reminding us that errant politics is not an invention superimposed on a system of governance, but is, rather, the illumination of the incommensurability always already written within the concept of the political. Errant politics is not dissimilar to the concept

of deterritorialization: like deterritorialization, errant politics is continuously subject to the reterritorialization of political lines of flight. What
must be sought, therefore, if we seek to expose the ephemerality of the
political, is a widening of the breadth of the incommensurable with
respect to political practices. In order that errant politics retain claims
to ephemerality, errant politics must be articulated beyond the limits of
ontology and territorial containment, resisting at every turn the reterritorialization of its vocabularies.

This is achieved through a "seizure of speech" *(prise de parole),* where
language itself becomes the insubstantial tie. Such a seizure (cor)responds
to language, speaking back to the myth of the nation by drawing attention to the policing of all enunciations that diverge from those of the
nation. Errant politics can thus be thought of as a (re)writing, a praxis of
response-ability—without resolution—addressed to the injunction of
having to establish ties. As Nancy writes:

> Idioms must be possible that resist the bloody idiocies of identities indi-
> cated by blood, soil and self. Identities must *write* themselves, that is, they
> must know and practice themselves as non-identifiable (k)nots of sense.
> (1997: 122)

In the chapters that follow, an errant and erring rearticulation of the
political provisionally clears a path that departs from the nation's all-
encompassing narratives of containment and exclusion. This provisional
rewriting of the political does not guarantee a new language in competi-
tion with that of the nation, however. Rather, it emphasizes the emergent
vocabularies always already spoken within the nation's articulations of
space and time. This is achieved through a focus on the transgressive
potential of cultural texts. Through cultural texts, I reflect on the ways in
which the nation is subject to an inner hemorrhaging to which we must
attend if we seek new forms of governance.

Any exploration of new forms of governance by necessity involves a
rearticulation of the discourses of time and space. While this is not explicitly outlined as a primary focus in *Ephemeral Territories,* my analysis
of contending forms of cultural enunciation in Canada does necessitate
a shift from the manner in which space and time are defined and located
within the politics of modernity. The narrative of the nation-state is a
powerful modern enunciation that defines the ways in which we configure
space and time. Put simply, within the narrative of the nation-state, space
is delineated as a stable modus of containment while time is located as a
linear organization of the events that take place within this receptacle.

In *Ephemeral Territories*, I explore the manner in which space and time are written as pillars of the modern discourse of the nation. I do so through a focus on the landscape and its role in the visualization of national identity in Canada. I then turn to the figure of the home, suggesting a link between the construction of space within the discourse of the nation-state and that of the home. Shifting to a focus on time, the third and fourth chapters underline the necessity to challenge the writing of linear state-centric histories.

The final chapter returns time to space. Here, I turn to enunciations of the global within local politics to delineate the manner in which space and time must be rethought if we are to accommodate ourselves outside the exclusive habitations of modernity. *Ephemeral Territories* can therefore be located as an erring and errant journey into the possibility that adjacent discourses of space and time can narrate different modes of being incommon.

1. An Excess of Seeing: Territorial Imperatives in Canadian Landscape Art

> Landscapes can be deceptive. Sometimes a landscape seems to be less a setting for the life of its inhabitants than a curtain behind which their struggles, achievements, and accidents take place.
>
> **—John Berger and John Mohr, *A Fortunate Man***

Robert Racine's artwork *Page-Miroir: Terrir-1950-Test* demonstrates an engagement with the deterritorialization of the landscape in contemporary Canadian art by calling forth a rewriting of the assumptions within the notion of territory. Racine's work is marked by the specificity of Quebec culture and its linguistic tensions, as well as by his necessary affiliations within the sovereignty movement and the resultant political implications, within his work, of territory and identity. In *Page-Miroir*, Racine employs the French-language *Dictionnaire Robert* as his canvas, imposing the landscape onto the (missing words of the) dictionary, inviting the viewer to read critically the accepted meanings of territoriality. Against the (absent) signifier territory, Racine simultaneously superimposes onto language the symbols of the musical score, producing a cacophony of language and music that resists internal, territorial specifications.

Replaced by the gaze of the other and undermined by their lack of a secure signifier, words like *territory* begin to evade meaning. Signifieds such as "qui consiste en un territoire, le concerne. Intégrité territoriale" (that consists of a territory, that concerns it. Territorial integrity) lose their bearings on a landscape that refuses to adhere to referentiality. As we familiarize ourselves with Racine's *Page-Miroir*, we become aware that the lost signifiers are nowhere to be found, deterritorialized by the disengaged definitions that now stand on their own.

Rather than offering the term "territory" as a given, Racine's artwork divests itself of that signifier, leaving us instead with stranded definitions of the term, inciting us to reflect on the ways in which we construct languages that hold captive accepted understandings of time, space, and governance, alerting us to the fragility of such territorial languages. The distortion of light caused by the reflection of the mirror that functions as the "background" to the impossibility of territory[1] further confuses the direct relationship between signifier and signified, playing with the possibility of reflection as "meaning." What the work elicits is not so much what the landscape represents (or, in this case, what "territory" means), but what a definition without a signifier does to the very idea of territory or landscape itself. Left to invent its own music, the public becomes involved in the orchestration that is the re(de)territorialization of the deterritorialized landscape. In a maze of lost definitions and missing signifiers, floating musical notes and reflections, national affiliation is subverted through a transgressive politics of (de)territorialization.

Racine explores the link between nation, landscape, and territory, creating work that both corresponds and responds to a tradition of landscape painting in Canada. The traditional vocabulary of landscape painting in Canada stems in large part from the work of the Group of Seven.[2] In the landscape paintings of the Group of Seven, territory is imagined as a window into national identity, where the national is conceived on the basis of a homogenous notion of culture and belonging. Through art, the Group of Seven sought to create a vision of Canada that would be a departure from their colonial roots, claiming that it was only through a relationship to the land that Canadians could become acquainted with their "true" nature. Despite that the landscapes of the Group of Seven were virulently criticized during their formative years,[3] upon later recognition and subsequent national acclaim, there was little lasting critique of the nationalism espoused by the members of the Group:[4] while critical voices have emerged over the past forty years, even today the landscapes of the Group of Seven are widely described as an "invention of Canada" (Murray: 1984).

Generations of Canadians have grown up seeing Canada through the paintings of the Group, taught the link between territory and identity as a window into "their" landscape, where "[t]he great purpose of landscape art is to make us at home in our own country" (Hill 1995: 83). The landscape, foregrounded as the "true" image of Canada, is understood as an essential proponent in the nationalizing attempts to relegate the discourse of "Canadian identity" to notions of vastness and emptiness, where the nation represents the ideal image of an ordered universe, its limits fixed and identities secured. "Canadian identity" emerges within this discourse as the glue that is called upon to paste together the disparaging inconsistencies of a land that nonetheless never quite succeeds in representing itself as homogeneous.

Robert Racine's artwork *Page-Miroir: Terrir-1950-Test* addresses this complexity within the Canadian spatial and political imagination. Exploring the effects of a deterritorialization of the concept of territory, Racine undermines the accepted image of Canada as a land that defines itself according to an uncomplicated notion of territory, where the language of the (empty) landscape informs the coherence of a people. Instead of ascribing to the homogenization of identity and territory, *Page-Miroir* delves into the complexities of language, asking us to rethink our definitions not only of territory, but of language and representation. Racine solicits us to deterritorialize our imagined nation(s), offering not simply a countercoherence but an opportunity to rewrite and relocate territory in our political imaginations. What is particularly striking about *Page-Miroir* is not only the self-reflection of the political through the (absent) notion of territory, but the suspicion that the "need" for territory as a signifier must now be questioned. "When is the signifier 'territory' relevant," Racine seems to ask, "and how must it be reencountered?"

In this chapter, I suggest that contemporary renditions of the landscape in Canadian art evoke a deterritorialization of the nation-state that subverts the conflation of identity and territory celebrated in the work of the Group of Seven. This deterritorialization is accomplished by transforming the landscape into a critical apparatus that foregrounds territory as the contested hyphen between the nation and the state and deconstructs identity as the stable signifier of the nation's imaginary. Such a deterritorialization foregrounds not only the continuous movement between territorialization and deterritorialization in the depiction of the landscape within the national imagination, it also highlights the ways in which no rendition of the landscape stands still in time and space, no matter how idyllically it promises to define the ideological and natural surroundings of a "people."

The artworks I discuss offer a vocabulary that consists of counterhistories and counteridentities, inviting us to reorganize maps of allegiance and affiliation constructed around counternational cartographies. This is not to suggest that counternational cartographies can be packaged neatly as complete solutions, thus claiming nationalism as "passé" in the face of transnational and global concerns. Such a sweep of history would ignore that, even while Canada actively attempts to invent itself as a global player, the current language of "the Canadian landscape" continues to be written in the nationalist vocabulary that is the legacy of the Group of Seven. Hence, even while I turn extensively to recent attempts to traverse and displace the conflation of territory and identity in contemporary Canadian art, I do not claim that a departure from the conflation of territory and identity (or nationalism) is straightforward. Quite the contrary: to seriously engage with the limits of territoriality, a critical engagement with the bounded landscape as envisioned through art must remain both nuanced and contested, inciting us to ask ourselves at every juncture how "we" are involved in defining what it means to belong, and how such apparently secure notions of territory and identity contribute to "our" relationship to a landscape we recognize as "our own."

The venture into the vocabulary of nationalism is further complicated by the fact that, in many areas of the world (including northern Canada), the indigenous people's response to the perils of imperialism and Western pilfering of land, nuclear testing, militarization, human-rights abuses, sexism, racism, nonindigenous settlement, mining, industrialization, imposed economic dependency, and colonization increasingly results in the quest for a sovereignty that mirrors the dynamics of the nationalist ventures of the Western world. This raises a question that pursues me throughout my work: must we think of the conflation of identity and territory—or nationalism—as a necessary evil in some cases? At this point, I would suggest we approach the question with extreme trepidation, for the crisis of modernity I refer to in my exploration of the sublation of identity into territory seems always to carry within its thrust for freedom an intimate relation to racial subordination and colonization.

This paradox is emphasized by Michael Hardt and Antonio Negri:

> Whereas within its domain the nation-state and its attendant ideological structures work tirelessly to create and reproduce the purity of the people, on the outside the nation-state is a machine that produces Others, creates racial difference, and raises boundaries that delimit and support the modern subject of sovereignty. (2000: 113)

No matter from whence sovereignty is spoken, my suspicion is that it cannot but serve to regulate two-way flows between the inside and the outside. As Hardt and Negri write, "Colonial sovereignty is another insufficient attempt to resolve the crisis of modernity" (113). Sovereignty, whether in the name of a western understanding of territory and identity or in the name of a defection from these terms of engagement, is, it seems, about expressing a relationship to power that involves the imposition of binary structures and totalizing logics on social subjectivities, repressing their difference.

Geography Encounters Art History: Re-Visioning the Landscape

It has been argued that, while the land provides food and shelter, the landscape provides ideologies. This is certainly the case in Canada, where the country's "true north strong and free" asserts itself in the national imaginary as the link to "Canadian identity." This coupling for many continues to be associated with an empty, vivid, and unproblematic landscape reminiscent of those painted by the Group of Seven. In recent years, however, the view that representation not simply conceals but constitutes ideological interests has become prevalent, inciting a renewed engagement with what has been perceived as the silent subject: the landscape. This approach to the landscape considers the active role the representation of the landscape plays in shaping the identities of the dominant and the dominated, a stance that would support the theory that the Group of Seven's approach to painting occurs in tandem with the Canadian colonial enterprise.

If the cultural landscape is envisioned critically in the late twentieth century, it is not uniquely because of its morphologies, but also because the landscape is itself increasingly recognized as a "concept in high tension" that reflects multiple and competing claims regarding the constitution of the social order. I conceptualize this shift as a tenuous renegotiation of the ephemerality of the landscape. As an introduction to the concept of ephemerality, I turn to Antoine de St.-Exupéry's *Le Petit Prince*. I draw your attention in particular to the following brief exchange between the geographer and the little prince:

> "I also have a flower," says the little prince. "We do not record flowers," responds the geographer. "Why is that? The flower is the most beautiful thing on my planet!" "We do not record them," says the geographer, "because they are ephemeral." ... "What does 'ephemeral' mean? ..." "It means 'that which is menaced by imminent disappearance.'" (St.-Exupéry 1946: 56)

The little prince's journey is one that reflects the contingencies of the ephemeral, even as it engages with the tactile; hence his desire to have his rose recorded by the geographer. For the little prince, there is no question that the ephemeral is worthy of critical thought, nor is it difficult to visualize critical thought as ephemeral. However, in accordance with a discourse that still beckons at the center of much academic thought, the geographer looms as the figure of reason who asserts that the ephemeral cannot be recorded.

An engagement with the ephemeral represents all that is anathema to rationalist discourses that attempt to confine knowledge within prescribed disciplines and systems of understanding. The shift toward an exploration of the ephemeral implies a certain confrontation between the landscape as bounded territory and the landscape as that which cannot be contained. And yet, as the little prince had the foresight to understand, a critical engagement with the ephemeral is the only way we can begin to relocate ourselves so that we can appreciate the density of the texts that surround us, not so that we may "comprehend" them, but so that we may begin to be sensitive to the ways in which we assimilate and dissimulate the images we cultivate and repress. The ephemeral offers not the promise of an all-encompassing geography, but the magic and wisdom inherent in all that is plagued by imminent disappearance. The promise of the ephemeral *is* the very fact of its disappearance, and with this disappearance the inevitable rearticulation of its vocabularies.

By its very nature, the disciplinary resists the ephemeral. It is impossible to master the ephemeral. It is much more simple to transform the ephemeral—be it an artistic, literary, or textual landscape—into a detail that can be classified, thus divesting it of its ephemerality. A critical account of the landscape as an ephemeral text that at once inaugurates and defies a discourse of territoriality involves taking into consideration both the process by which the landscape effaces its own readability as well as the process through which the landscape is naturalized in the name of identity and territory. The landscape is a dynamic representation that is itself in motion from one place and time to another, circulating in a "medium of exchange, a site of visual appropriation, a focus for the formation of identity" (Mitchell 1994a: 2). Hence, the landscape must be read according to the "specificity of effects and spectatorial work solicited by a medium at a particular historical juncture" (Mitchell 1994a: 2–3). In addition, the landscape is an ephemeral representation that is, in some sense, intractable, tyrannizing the eye and the senses while it placates them, remaining problematic even as it seems to define itself as the stable locus of time and space.

These many facets of the landscape are undervalued within the art historical tradition, where the landscape is often viewed unproblematically as a western European and modern phenomenon that emerges in the seventeenth century and reaches its peak in the nineteenth century, originally and centrally constituted as a genre of painting associated with a new way of seeing. Within this traditional art historical trajectory, it is presumed that "the appreciation of natural beauty" begins with the inven-

tion of landscape painting (Clark 1949), a claim that is further substantiated by *The Oxford Companion to Art,* which states it was in the European
atmosphere of the early sixteenth century that the first "pure" landscape
was painted, until which time nature was conceived as an assemblage of
isolate subjects. If the ephemeral were renounced, nature could be considered unified and whole and the landscape could be conceptualized as
"a particular historical formation associated with European imperialism"
(*Oxford Companion to Art* 1994: 5).

The landscape as theorized through the tradition of landscape art remains a tool for the duplicitous political motivations of the West, where
"[the discourse of the landscape] is not only a matter of internal politics
of national or class ideology but also an internation and global phenomenon, intimately bound up with the discourse of imperialism" (Mitchell
1994: 9). The ephemerality of the landscape is cast aside here. Imperialism
is an injunction to see, not to look, evoking images of perfected prospects
in an attempt to silence unresolved ambivalences and unsupervised resistance. The lure of the landscape in early-twentieth-century painting in
Canada depends on this obfuscation of the ephemeral and the resultant
continuity between the landscape and imperialism. With the conflation
of identity and territory comes not only the promise of a spiritual one-
ness of nature and self,[5] but also the covenant of the mythical unity of a
people who are defined by the landscape they inhabit.

This is the certainly the case with the landscape paintings of the Group
of Seven: the depiction of the land as well as the nationalist rhetoric that
accompanies the work of the Group of Seven propagates a language of
territory and identity that is borrowed from the ideological assumptions of imperial Britain for which the colonial landscape existed to be
consumed, identified, and ruled. Despite that the Group of Seven sought
to escape these colonial roots through depictions of the Canadian landscape, one must surmise that their claim that the landscape could offer a
national coherence for Canadians follows directly on the heels of Western
imperialism. This quest for national identity through the image of the
landscape recalls the modern desire for authenticity, where the unity of
states and citizens is constructed on the putative ethnic or racial identity
of a nation, which, in turn, is anchored to the representation of the landscape of the motherland as a nostalgic longing for a lost, presumably less
alienated culture.

That the landscape is already artifice in the moment of its behold-
ing is rarely emphasized in this tradition of landscape painting. Rather,
the landscape is conceptualized as a representation that emanates only

in the moment of its artistic composition. The landscape thus becomes a "social hieroglyph" that works as an "emblem of the social relations it conceals" (Mitchell 1994a: 15).

> We say "landscape is nature, not convention" in the same way we say "landscape is ideal, not real estate," and for the same reason—to erase the signs of our own constructive activity in the formation of landscape as meaning or value, to produce an art that conceals its own artifice, to imagine a representation that "breaks through" representation into the realm of the nonhuman. (Mitchell 1994a: 16–17)

Such normative readings of the landscape correspond to the discourse of imperialism, which conceives of itself both as an expansion of landscape (where expansion is understood as an inevitable, progressive development in history) and as an expansion of "culture" into "civilization," where the usurping of "natural" space is itself narrated as natural. Increasingly, however, the landscape that held the promise of national unity and identity, and that symbolized unbounded and endless appropriation and conquest, is admittedly threatened, among other things, by imperialism's environmental shortsightedness; thus, the landscape is, ironically, often figured as an endangered species that is relegated to and kept safe in parks, museums, and shrinking "wilderness areas." This usurpation of the imperial landscape draws attention to the limitations of a territorially sanctioned concept such as that of the nation-state, which relies on a notion of identity that sustains itself through the image of the land. That this is not necessarily a recent realization is substantiated by W. J. T. Mitchell's assertion that:

> [w]e have known since Ruskin that the appreciation of the landscape as an aesthetic object cannot be an occasion for complacency or untroubled contemplation; rather, it must be the focus of a historical, political, and [...] aesthetic alertness to the violence and evil written on the land, projected there by the gazing eye. We have known at least since Turner— perhaps since Milton—that the violence of this evil eye is inextricably connected with imperialism and nationalism. What we know now is that landscape itself is the medium by which this evil is veiled and naturalized. (1994a: 29)

The desire for something akin to a "national art" based on the myth of the origin of Canadian identity as linked to the vastness and purity of the land paves the way for the reception of the work of the Group of Seven. While the landscape paintings of the Group of Seven do not *create* the type of nationalism that is based on an ideology of the land, they do play a role in supporting the myth of the "great white north," a myth that imagines Canada as a land with unmediated landscapes peopled by those of strong, pure character. These myths are upheld even today, despite that they risk obliterating the native presence to perpetuate the image of vastness and emptiness.[6] As Rob Shields notes, these are harmful myths "enshrining (despite its entirely past nature) a gendered opposition of nature versus civilization as the enduring rule of Canadian daily life" (1991: 182–83).

The myth of the north as the window to Canadian identity persists, as is apparent in the preface to the recent publication *The Group of Seven: Art for a Nation,*[7] where Tomlinson writes:

> In the seventy-five years since the first public exhibition of the Group of Seven's work, much has changed. What remains, however, are the images of a group of talented artists who defined how Canadians view their land. Their paintings are timeless and represent the collective strength of a nation and its people. (in Hill 1995: 5)

Tomlinson further suggests that, through a retrospective of the work of the Group of Seven, "we will again understand the role that our geography plays in the development of the Canadian identity" (in Hill 1995: 5), a stance substantiated by the fact that the Group of Seven remain the artists most celebrated in Canadian history (15). Underlining the implicit link between identity and the representation of the landscape, Joan Murray writes: "From the Group we gain inspiration about our own country" (1984: 23).

Through the assertion of the primacy of Canadian subject matter for a Canadian audience, and with the invention of a distinctive visual style and language, the Group of Seven sought to capture the "essence" of Canada. This is demonstrated in many of their slogans, one of which asserts that "[a]rt must grow and flower in the land before a country will be a real home for its people" (in Reid 1973: 146). This impulse toward nationalism and the colonization of a space for the identity of its people can be understood as one of the explicit goals of the landscape paintings of the Group of Seven. Read uncritically, this expansionist drive is depicted by one critic as

> a Northern people's growth during three centuries of evolution from colony to nationhood. It shows how a highly sophisticated European culture has been imported into and adapted for the New World. It is thus a demonstration of how people will struggle to achieve a sense of identity. (Russell 1966: 356)

If these views were to be transplanted into a contemporary transnational or postnational milieu, a rejection of the Group of Seven's work might seem justified. However, a simple dismissal of the Group's work is both unwarranted (given the complexity of the artworks themselves) and unwise (given that the discourse of territoriality for which we are indebted to the Group remains entwined in the political imagination). The Group of Seven's landscape art defies a simple reading in no small part *because* "no single event in the story of Canadian art has made the mass of our people as aware of painting as did the struggle of the Group" (Russell 1966: 288). Any discussion concerning the foregrounding of "national identity" in the Group's landscape art must therefore take into consideration the *public* importance of a body of work that celebrated a rift between European art and the quintessentially "Canadian" landscape, (re)presenting the land as a promise of a unique and united Canada.

For many years the quintessential Canadian landscape painting was an image of an unpopulated wilderness, with Tom Thomson's ancient pine tree or Lawren Harris's icebergs at the forefront. Only sporadic attention was paid to the conflicts already deeply entrenched in Canada at

Lawren S. Harris, *North Shore, Lake Superior,* 1926. Reproduced by permission of the family of Lawren S. Harris.

the beginning of the twentieth century with respect to territory and the nation, be they the exclusions within the public sphere of migrant and immigrant populations, racial oppression, or the attempted annihilation of native lands and customs. Alongside the eager cultural reception of an image of Canada as a vast emptiness, one might therefore suggest that the empty landscapes of the Group of Seven were indeed empty, reflecting none of the contradictions of the white/native/other Canadian populations. Within the landscapes of the Group of Seven there was no reference to native peoples, nor was there much reference to agricultural uses of the land, nor to the fact that—as Jackson, one of the key members of the Group, attests to in journal entries dating from the thirties and forties—finding pristine landscapes for painting was becoming increasingly difficult as pollution levels were rising.

What I call for is not a dismissal of the Group of Seven, but a critical engagement with the political and cultural legacy of their images of the land. My approach focuses on what I name an "excess of seeing," that is, an exploration of that which exceeds the visible. To exceed vision is to displace the disciplinary contours of thought to engage with the ephemeral. It is a conscious attempt to question the parameters of a discipline, any discipline, that would attempt to orchestrate the protocols of vision. An emphasis on an excess of seeing or representation draws our attention to the fact that the practice of art holds in abeyance a certain resistance to the protocols of vision. By exploring the limits of vision, what is not represented becomes as important as what is perceived.

Charles Harrison writes, "[P]ainting is not just a 'visual art,' the effects are not just visual effects, and . . . no interpretation can be adequate if it does not recognize what it is that any given painting significantly *withholds* from vision" (1994a: 204). Contemporary artists in Canada foreground this invisibility through renegotiations of the Canadian landscape that complicate the sublation of identity into territory and the assumption of vastness and emptiness. Contemporary Canadian landscape art refers to outside influences, assimilating both internal and external otherness in its creation of and transformation of the landscape. Although in 1970 R. H. Hubbard claimed that the "national landscape now seems a dead issue," this is clearly not the case, as attested to by such important contemporary pieces as Racine's *Page-Miroir: Terrir-1950-Test* and recent exhibitions such as *Out of Place* (Vancouver, British Columbia), *The Postcolonial Landscape* (Saskatoon, Saskatchewan), and *Crossings* (Ottawa, Ontario).

The vitality of the landscape and its potential to keep alive a dialogue concerning the (de)territorialization of the (political) landscape, as well

Lawren S. Harris, *Maligne Lake, Jasper Park,* 1924. Reproduced by permission of the family of Lawren S. Harris.

as the landscape's ability to respond critically to the question of Canadian identity and nationalism, is demonstrated through these recent exhibitions and artworks as a persistent concern of contemporary artists. In its reincarnation as a critical locus of enunciation, the deterritorialized landscape becomes a tool that challenges accepted configurations of space and culture, reinforcing the fissure in the perceived hyphenated continuity between the nation and the state. In Harrison's words:

> What may be of sharpest critical interest about the legacy of the genre of landscape ... lies ... in the precedents that the genre provides for a continued engagement, in the context of the visible, with that which is contingently excluded from the possibility of being seen and represented. (1994a: 234)

Dialogic Deterritorializations: Contemporary Landscapes

To recognize the harmful aspects of the territorialization of the Canadian landscape while concurrently addressing the ways in which the landscape carries within its own vocabulary the seeds of its transgression, it is important to recall that representation is not an image derivative of, subordinate to, or distortive of an underlying or more basic reality. Representation always involves a creative recombining and reconstructing of the world that potentially challenges hierarchies of truth and sovereignty. For the landscape to be envisioned critically, one must locate it as a *representation* whose vocabulary is as indebted to the language of the nation-state as it is to the subversion of such territorial imperatives. An awareness of the link between the landscape and its self-representation allows us to employ a vocabulary for the landscape that departs from the articulations of "national identity." This vocabulary would rely instead on such theoretical tools as the Bakhtinian notion of the chronotope, which highlights the dialogical movement between space and time inherent in all representations.

In his definition of the chronotope, Mikhail Bakhtin suggests that time and space are interdependent. Every entry into the sphere of meaning is accomplished via the gates of the chronotope, which results in the construction of timed-places and placed-times. As Bakhtin writes, in some chronotopes "a locality is the trace of an event, a trace of what had shaped it. Such is the logic of all local myths and legends that attempt, through history, to make sense out of space" (1981: 189). Landscapes can be regarded as chronotopes: they are places and representations where social, historical, and geographical conditions alert us to the political implications of an encounter between history and geography. Located as a chronotopic event, the landscape assumes a vocabulary that focuses on the *effects* of its representation in time and space—that is, on the ongoing historical developments that alternately anchor and destabilize the "natural harmony" of a given landscape.

Bakhtin's concept of dialogy is at the heart of his notion of the chronotope, since the politicization of the discourses of space and time instigates a critical engagement with the other. In Bakhtin's work, dialogy is understood as the constant interaction between meanings, with connotations of open-ended possibilities generated by the discursive practices of a culture. Dialogy conceives knowing as the effort of understanding "the active reception of the speech of the other" (Bakhtin 1973: 117). Chronotopes are dialogic because the oscillation of time and space requires a mediation between self and other, whereby the limits of territory and identity are exceeded. Dialogy is what introduces alterity into the concept of the chronotope, rendering time and space problematic by raising the question of the constitution of the subject of discourse with respect to the world of others. By critically combining time, space, and alterity, Bakhtin places the content of cultural expression into a context from whence a cultural manifestation cannot be definitively located solely in aesthetic terms, but must, rather, be reencountered within a social and political setting.

When we recognize the dialogical aspect of the landscape, we begin to notice the biases, ethnocentricities, and exclusions inherent in the notion of territoriality. This is not to suggest that we situate one tradition of envisioning the landscape against another, thereby creating a dichotomy between "national" and "postnational" landscapes. Such a strategy would be an attempt to naturalize the monologue of linear history on which the tradition of landscape painting depends, a tradition that seeks to write a progression from emancipation to naturalization to unification. Through a dialogical reading of the landscape we can instead begin to negotiate the fissures inherent in the territorial imperatives of the discourses of time and space, where the landscape is key. Within such a dialogical reading of the landscape, what becomes apparent is that the ephemeral is constructed and read on many levels and strata of time and space through a continual negotiation between self and other, inside and outside.

The art of the Group of Seven offers a primarily linear rendition of space, inviting us to enter into an apparently coherent construction of the Canadian landscape. Conversely, contemporary artworks such as Racine's *Page-Miroir* ask us to engage with the concept of territoriality as that which bears many definitions, thereby disrupting time and forcing us to reacquaint ourselves with a concept of territoriality that is as ephemeral as it is political. Contemporary landscape art such as that of Racine thus encourages a chronotopic reading of the landscape, permitting us to engage with the complexities within the discourse of the landscape, while at the same time inciting us to explore a production of locality that challenges the order and orderliness of the nation-state.

Racine's *Page-Miroir* encourages us to understand an engagement with the landscape as a "way of seeing." Through the figure of the chronotope, seen as a dialogic event, we become aware of the dilemmas of representation through which debts and departures are negotiated. Taking into consideration the legacy of the Group of Seven, we become attuned to the timeliness of their project while at the same time observing the importance of the deconstruction of the national brought to bear in contemporary landscape art. While the art of the Group of Seven was a critical response to what it perceived as colonial hegemony, contemporary landscape art is vital as a voice that seeks to alert us to the ways in which the national is increasingly complicated by indigenous, diasporic, migratory, and other nonnational groups who require us to undergo a serious rethinking of our existing images of the land.

Subject to a Bakhtinian reading, the landscapes both of the Group of Seven and of contemporary artists in Canada are expanded beyond strict relegation within visual and cultural fields to include their representation within the social and political realms. A dialogical/chronotopic reading of landscape art alerts us to the limits of cultural exchange, drawing our attention to the ways in which the language of art is a political utterance. This relationship between the cultural and the political is often swept aside, however, as is apparent in the continued resistance in art circles to the adoption of a critical stance concerning the nationalism surrounding landscape art in Canada. Such reticence on the part of curators, academics, and journalists, among others, ironically takes place in conjunction with a widespread desire by artists to extend the breadth of the discourse of landscape painting in Canada, a movement that can be traced back to the 1940s when artists such as Painters Eleven began to participate actively in a renunciation of a vision of the landscape that sought to conflate identity and territory,[8] emphasizing instead the importance of dispelling the myth of a unified, territorially bounded notion of space.

The manner in which contemporary landscape artists such as Racine negotiate time and space via the landscape can be further theorized through the work of Gilles Deleuze and Félix Guattari. Sometimes identified as geophilosophy, the work of Deleuze and Guattari provides a vocabulary of deterritorialization that emphasizes not origins but the creative possibilities produced by interconnection and alignment. Deterritorialization draws our attention to the multiplicities and contingencies inherent in any social interaction, reinforcing the notion that territoriality functions as a system of horizontal and complementary re(de)territorializations. Understood as a rhizomatic movement toward multiplicity, deterritorialization is the dialogic encounter with the rhizome that exposes arborescent territorializations for the dichotomous, hierarchized systems they are, reminiscent of state apparatuses, expansionist notions of territoriality, and grids of intelligibility. Combined with Bakhtin's concept of dialogy, deterritorialization offers a link to a vocabulary that facilitates a discussion of the ways in which contemporary Canadian landscape art seeks to undermine territorial imperatives and staid notions of national identity.

Deterritorialization is a concept in flux that is always already motivated by a dialogical current. Conceptualized as the movement of dialogy, deterritorialization could be seen as the *effect* of the chronotopic dialogue.

In other words, de(re)territorialization ensues due to the dialogic nature of the chronotope, which encourages a continual oscillation between time and space, self and other. In accordance with the dialogic aspect of the chronotope, whereby space and time are engaged in a dialogue that is continually deferred through a vocabulary that is at once social, cultural, and political, deterritorialization, before it is even defined or applied, is already in the process of re(de)territorializing itself as a concept that is always subject to redefinition. As Deleuze and Guattari remind us, nothing is ultimately deterritorialized; the dialogue must continue.

To think of holding a concept such as deterritorialization captive is to rigidify and ultimately render meaningless a field that must continue to draw on its uneven and sporadic re(de)territorializations. Hence the coupling here of deterritorialization and dialogy, where dialogy is concerned with the nature of polyglossia with respect to the social and political implications of the utterance. Deterritorialization occurs in tandem with reterritorialization, enacting a continuous dialogue with territoriality, where "reterritorialization must not be confused with the return to a primitive or older territoriality" (Deleuze and Guattari 1987: 174). Deterritorialization is not an ultimate event, but an opening for the dialogic. Deterritorialization is a moment when discourses collide and transform themselves outside the vocabulary of state philosophy.

Out of Place, an exhibition staged at the Vancouver Art Gallery in 1993, conceives of a coupling of dialogy and deterritorialization as its mandate, operating from the premise that a deterritorialization of the state apparatus encourages us to respond critically to the nationalist landscape tradition in Canada. In a show not dedicated solely to Canadian artists, *Out of Place* reflects upon measures of difference by acknowledging diverse cultural traditions, histories, and locales:

> The seven artists represented here each situate their work beyond emotionally charged rhetoric or antagonisms and invite each of us to consider our own hybrid identity in a world simultaneously divided and interconnected—a world that is at once local and global. (Brooks Joyner in Dufour 1993: 6)

Out of Place is the result not of a territorial imperative, but of a commitment to "defining and presenting contemporary art without regard to the limitations of national boundaries" (Joyner in Dufour 1993: 6). *Out of Place* articulates a desire to contribute regionally, transnationally, and internationally to the evolution of the concept of the territorial landscape in the awareness of the role contemporary art plays in shaping cultures.

An exhibition that explicitly reaches beyond the confines of the national, thereby critically disrupting any notion of a national art, *Out of Place* relies on the notion that radical changes to economies and systems of exchange and communication throughout the world have resulted in a disruption of borders and a redrawing of boundaries. Geographic distance no longer ensures the social coherence of unique identities. "The flux and energy of life paradoxically produces both a plurality of isolations and communities, irrespective of boundaries," writes Gilles Dufour, the senior curator (1993: 10). Dufour emphasizes the attempt in *Out of Place* to cross geographical and state borders, thereby intensifying the often invisible traditions and cultural patterns of locales, while at the same time resisting simple appropriations of otherness and difference. It is the complexity of the heterogeneous process rather than the simplistic categorization of landscape, place, and otherness that is at stake: "Where do our *externally* constructed images of elsewhere meet or miss another's *internally* constructed realities?" Dufour asks (11).

Out of Place calls for a dialogue conceived as a deterritorialization rather than an acknowledgment or a sympathetic "understanding" of a familiar vision of the landscape. Working to displace the mythologization of the other as unified in time and space, *Out of Place* engages in a plurality of strategies that speak to a transnational urban practice across historically, culturally, and geographically diverse situations. When seen in combination, the works of the various artists participate in an active deterritorialization of the landscape-art tradition in Canada, dislocating a nationalist emphasis based on the homogeneity and synchronicity of experience, revealing instead "a level of sophistication that embraces the movement of artists and multiple cultural identities in single locations at this moment when cultures are increasingly deterritorialized" (Dufour 1993: 11).

The deterritorialization of both the local and the national is apparent in Panya Clark's installation *Re Appearances*. Clark's installation restages an encounter with the home, bringing together mementos displaced in the passing of time, such as the works of her grandmother, Paraskeva Clark, reorganized within the configuration of contemporary artifacts. Panya Clark plays with the possibility of locating the home in a shifting time and space, drawing our attention to the conceptual transformation that goes hand in hand with any attempt to locate the landscape within a dialogical chronotope as opposed to a strict territoriality. Clark's work escapes the bounds of territoriality by foregrounding a staged "home" that is always on the move, transported from one artistic location to the next, where the home becomes the metaphor for the manner in which art is always already entangled in the dynamics of cultural translation and political enunciation.

The challenges of deterritorialization can be extrapolated beyond Clark's work to the larger picture of state sovereignty and nationalism. Clark's work acts as a mirror to the dilemma of the state apparatus, which, similarly to Clark's figure of the home, vacillates between ethnic diversity and its attempt to impose a structured coherence. Like Clark's figure of the well-kept home that hides within its fissures a hint of the spatiotemporal dissonance that accompanies any attempt at re-placing the past with the present, the state apparatus also carries within its narrative of spatiotemporal containment the seeds of its own unraveling in the guise of the always impending deterritorialization it must never publicly reveal: the dialogical threads of polyvocality that threaten to expose leaks in its apparently airtight receptacle.

To maintain its image as a territorial, bounded, and stratified entity, the state apparatus offers itself in the image of a coherence, policing its bounded territories by overlaying space with grids of intelligibility, thereby enforcing a codification of, among other things, the *effects* of the landscape. This results in the dissemination of a range of discourses that substantiate the state's hegemony vis-à-vis the landscape, whereby the landscape is exploited as the territorial trope that guarantees state sovereignty. Within this self-serving matrix of state sovereignty, the *effect* of the landscape becomes the articulation of the mode of articulation that binds the state apparatus and territoriality.

The landscape effect enables us to visualize the modern, offering us a visual vocabulary adjacent to the practices of modernity. As Harrison writes, "[It] transpired at various moments of development of the modern tradition that one way to signify the different disposition of the relatively modern viewer was to conceive of him or her as a viewer of the landscape" (1994a: 217). A naturalization of ideology prevails within the discourse of effect that constrains and limits the visible to contain the discourse of modernity. Within this discourse the land can only represent identity and territory; that is, the landscape can never exceed the visible. This is exemplified in the way Canada celebrates the work of the Group of Seven as the "natural" voice of the people without asking why or how the land came to signify such unity and homogeneity. To broach such necessary questions, we must initiate a dialogical reading of the landscape that exceeds and transgresses the effects of the landscape.

This reading must not only subvert the naturalization of ideology through a deterritorialization of the discourse of effect, it must also emphasize the fact that the effects of painting are neither fully apparent nor completely translatable: any given painting also withholds from vision. At best, deterritorialization renders the invisible visible, exposing what was considered "naturalized," thereby undermining the jurisdiction of the law of territoriality, which is also the law of vision and effect, and, by extension, the law of state sovereignty. Such a deterritorialization of the landscape alerts us to the dialogical aspects of vision, drawing our attention to *how* we view the landscape and inciting us to make the connection between imperialist structures of the sublation of identity and territory and a modernist conception of time and space.

Deterritorialization is the mandate of *Out of Place*. Through their artworks, the artists resist locating themselves within a bounded territory, preferring instead to respond to the continuous re(de)territorialization effected through the medium of the landscape-as-surface within their work. In addition, through a blatant combining of the notion of deterritorialization with Bakhtin's concept of the dialogical, *Out of Place* seeks to rewrite and enact a deterritorialized dialogue in which the notion of territory itself is at stake. As Dufour writes,

> a third zone that is neither *here* nor *there* is created by the artist's engagement with a hybrid sense of place, a dialogic zone where [t]here is neither a first nor last word. The contexts for dialogue are without limit. They extend into the deepest past and the most distant future. . . . For nothing is absolutely dead; every meaning will someday have its homecoming festival. (Bakhtin in Holquist 1990: 39, quoted in Dufour 1993)

Inherent in much of the work in *Out of Place* is the sense of being *out of place* as a participant in a dialogue that has not yet come to fruition. The contemporary landscapes in *Out of Place* leave us not only with a sense that the possibility of representing the (Canadian) landscape is being thought and translated differently, but also with the impression that art *can* dismantle a binary system of territorialized boundaries by engaging in a dialogic encounter with the landscape. Consequently, one might suggest that the artists in *Out of Place* not only deconstruct the language of the border, they also reconfigure the discourse that promises the cohesion of the land through art.

The Postcolonial Landscape, mounted in Saskatoon in 1993, is another instance of the potential for art to effect a dialogical deterritorialization. This is achieved in *The Postcolonial Landscape* through an exposition of the ways in which the discourse of imperialism seeps into the representation of the landscape in Canada. Set up as a "billboard exhibition," *The*

Postcolonial Landscape followed a mandate by the Mendell Art Gallery to find four artists who would develop work that would take as its subject the land and its representation for demonstration on a billboard in the center of Saskatoon's downtown business district during the summer of 1993. Each work was to be shown for a period of four weeks. The exhibition's focus was the fundamental and highly visible difference in the use of land by native peoples throughout Canada's early history, the appropriation of the landscape by European colonizers, and the land-scape's current, widespread use as an ideologically defined resource. The billboard itself was conceived as a strategic intervention into the urban landscape—the dialogical medium that could incite a dialogue between art, viewers, and the landscape.

Three of the four landscapes featured in the exhibition will be dis-cussed here. Each of the three billboards is critical of the landscape effects commonly accepted around the turn of the century and perpetuated even today. Through their art, the artists acknowledge the contemporary territorial dependence on the imaginary of the nation and respond criti-cally to the racial exclusion, (in)security measures, and ecological short-sightedness inherent within the governing model of the nation-state.

Edward Poitras's piece *1885* raises questions concerning the histori-cal interests of métis and native peoples. Showing massive clear-cutting and ecological destruction, Poitras uses an altered archival photograph taken in 1885 of a group of natives and métis overlooking the Lebret Indian Residential School by Mission Lake in southern Saskatchewan. Consistent with Poitras's project, the second piece—Grant McConnells's *Partly Cleared, Partly Cultivated*—considers the politics of topography, examining the romanticized narrative of the nation as unfettered ex-panse and undisturbed nature. This billboard draws from immigration posters, government literature, archival photographs of immigration exhibitions at fairs, and government survey manuals.

Jamelie Hassan's *Linkage* takes as its point of departure a more inter-national concern, looking at the environmental effects of the war waged by the United States on Iraq. In this artwork, both image and text refer to Iraq's precarious position in a globalized economy of state-sanctioned security, alluding to the complex webs of interaction and exchange that codify our relationships in time and space, alerting us to the dangers of sovereign control over the environment. To demonstrate the paradoxical and potentially deadly conjoining of the state apparatus and the land-scape, Hassan superimposes onto a photograph of a forest of palm trees in a marsh region of southern Iraq in 1979 a line of text that originates

40 TONS of nuclear waste was fired by the coalition forces into Iraq during the Gulf War...

Adam's tree

palm forest

leukemia

children

mysterious disease

Jamelie Hassan, *Linkage*, 1993, billboard.

from a report in the *London* [Ontario] *Free Press* (27 March 1993) by Eric Hoskins, who states that forty tons of nuclear waste was dropped onto Iraq by the coalition forces during the Gulf War. Through her artwork, Hassan empathizes with those who are culturally displaced and whose connection to a familiar environment is under attack while also responding critically to state-sanctioned practices of controlling the effects of the landscape.

The Postcolonial Landscape reflects on the problematic ways in which the landscape is conceptualized in the work of artists such as the Group of Seven. By turning to early immigration documents and by foregrounding narratives of war and displacement, all three artists engage in a rewriting of the landscape, both Canadian and international, thus creating an adjacent representation of the land that resists the apparent coherence of the nation-state's territorial imperatives and grids of intelligibility. Their work emphasizes not only the necessity to displace art from the museum to speak publicly about contested notions of territory and identity, it also addresses the ways in which minority discourses—the language of the migrant, the refugee, the native—reformulate accepted notions of territory as these "others" slip into "our" bounded polities.

The Postcolonial Landscape draws our attention to the exclusions propagated by a nationalist artistic discourse that demands a homogenous representation of the land. Each of the artists confronts the manner in which the landscape effect is naturalized and policed within the chronotope of the nation. In so doing, they remind us that, while "all modern ideologies of rights depend on the *closed* (enumerated, stable, and immobile) group of appropriate recipients of state protection" (Appadurai 1996a: 56), contemporary art *can* educate the public about the complex ways in which difference informs our narratives of coherence. Art such as that represented in *The Postcolonial Landscape* serves as a reminder that, when we are willing to attend to the exclusions encapsulated within our state-sanctioned discourses of identity and territory, we can begin to see beyond the nation's imaginary landscapes to loci of contention and possibility that refrain from perpetuating the discourse of effect propagated by the nationalization of landscape art.

As demonstrated by artworks such as Panya Clark's *Re Appearances,* Jamelie Hassan's *Linkage,* and Robert Racine's *Page-Miroir: Terrir-1950-Test,* for deterritorialization to be useful as a concept that alerts us to the shortcomings of territorialized discourses that perpetuate the myth of national identity, deterritorialization must not stagnate into an aggregate that stands in opposition to or beside territoriality. Rather, deterritorialization must remain in a dialogic relationship that defies any notion of the identical or the original. In other words, a de-re-deterritorialization must continually take place, inciting us to adapt ourselves to the continual movement between territorialization and deterritorialization, which, in turn, foregrounds the fluidity of constructions of identity practices. What is useful and interesting about the Deleuzo-Guattarian concept of deterritorialization is precisely the breadth of discourses it invites, paving the way for a breach within a state-centric conception of the political. Deterritorialization is a concept in motion that seeks to dispel the logocentric myth of the nation in order to speak against such binaries as nation/internation.

The impulse toward deterritorialization in contemporary landscape art does not preclude, however, that there continues to be a strong emphasis on national boundaries in Canada's political and cultural spheres. Given the limits of the state apparatus, this cannot come as a surprise, since deterritorialization implies acknowledging the other of the other rather than the other of the same, thereby foregrounding a smooth, rather than a striated, conception of space. Whereas striated space is heavily coded with normative boundaries that "produce a tightly controlled ascription of identity to those who enter and traverse them" (Shapiro 1997: 200), smooth space encourages errancy and nomadism. Contemporary landscape art in Canada introduces a tension within the striated space of state-centered national politics. Through a defiance of statist parameters of identity and territory, an encounter with the other is staged that resists domesticating the other or condemning the other to live on the outskirts of the nation. Consequently, through art the exclusionary vision of the nation is altered within the political imaginary.

Hence, one of the ways of conceptualizing a departure from a state-centric imaginary is to focus on the reworking of the discourse of territoriality as envisioned in the work of contemporary landscape art. These artworks alert us to the ways in which exclusions are propagated by an imperialist modern tradition, inviting us to explore critically the resistances within the nation-state caused by a growing political imaginary that encourages diasporic pluralism. These contemporary renditions of the landscape highlight the current crisis of the modern nation-state. This crisis is defined by Appadurai not as ethnic or cultural pluralism as such but as "the tension between diasporic pluralism and territorial stability" (1996a: 57).

Ethnic plurality within the nation-state results in the violation of the sense of isomorphism between territory and national identity on which the modern nation-state relies. One response to the "infiltration" of the nation-state by ethnic plurality is the stringent regulation and policing of borders (be they internal or external) in an attempt to monitor dissent and distribute entitlements within a finite conception of territory. Complete containment is impossible, however, as the delimitations between inside and outside are increasingly blurred by the complexities of difference. What emerges, as a result, are postnational geographies that engage with the spatializing contests between diasporic populations and the efforts of nation-states to accommodate them without reneging on the principle of territorial integrity.

For postnational geographies to be articulated within our political vocabularies, we must think of the landscape not as an object to be seen or a text to be read, but as a process by which social, political, and subjective identities are both territorialized and deterritorialized according to dialogical tropes of time and space. It is important to think beyond what landscape *is* and ask what landscape *does,* exploring the ways in which landscape works to create resistance as both a cultural and a political practice. The landscape does not merely signify or symbolize power relations. It is, rather, an instrument of cultural power that can strengthen a conflictive and diversified imaginary that responds critically to the homogenizing tendencies of state powers. Like the little prince, who knows his flower is worth recording, we must attend to and engage with these cultural and political landscapes—be they artistic, cinematic, or literary—not as peripheral instances of deterritorialization, but as living examples of an engagement with the other who is not the same. For contrary to the geographer's response to the little prince, we do have the tools to record ephemeral phenomena, especially when its ephemeral quality is what gives it consistency.[9]

Visible Difference: Deterritorialized Lines of Flight

In response to the call for an engagement with the ephemeral as the plane of consistency, I turn, in conclusion, to a recent exhibition entitled *Crossings,* presented at the National Gallery of Canada in the fall of 1998. The mandate of *Crossings* was to explore the ephemeral quality of the landscape to displace and reconfigure the symbiotic relationship between identity and territory. To achieve its mandate, *Crossings* featured the work of fifteen artists, most of whom live away from their countries of origin and all of whom consider the themes of migration and exile. The exhibition foregrounded displacement as "an important motif in cultural theories that seek to understand a world in which the old national and imperial certainties have come unmoored" (Nemiroff 1998: 13). In addition, *Crossings* sought to "explore some of the multiple intersections of place and identity encountered in the world of art at the end of the twentieth century" (Nemiroff 1998: 14–15) through an emphasis on the notion that

> the separation of people from their native culture either through physical dislocation (as refugees, immigrants, migrants, exiles or other expatriates) or the colonizing imposition of a foreign culture ... is one of the most formative experiences of our century. (Bammer 1994: xi)

In a marked departure from the nationalist mandate of the Group of Seven, where art functions as the representation of the cohesive link between identity and territory, the art represented in *Crossings* complicates the relationship between the land and the nation. This is achieved in part through the metaphor of the passage, where the passage refers to a conceptual transformation from the notion that identity is pure and fixed, located territorially. A diasporic articulation of the political is evoked rather than one of national attachment. By focusing on transnational and/or postnational networks rather than nationalist territories, the artwork in *Crossings* encodes practices of accommodation with, as well as resistance to, nations and their norms. This critique of the nation is centered on a renegotiation of the space of the home/land, where dwelling is conceived as

> a mobile habitat, as a mode of inhabiting time and space not as though they were fixed and clear structures, but as providing the critical provoca-

tion of an opening whose questioning presence reverberates in the movement of languages that constitute our sense of identity, place and belonging. (Chambers 1994: 4)

Through a refutation of the sublation of identity into territory, an
alternative experience of time and space is envisioned. In this altered
ephemeral chronotope, the other's entry into the territory is no longer
restricted, for there is no stable inside to protect from a dangerous outside. Rather, alterity is figured as the pivot around which the imagining
of chronotopes of accommodation takes place, where dwelling is always
subject to mutation and redefinition. From this perspective, there can be
no coherent representation of identity or territory since the acknowledgment that all dwelling occurs through the medium of representation
results in a reassessment of the very idea of attachment.

Among the artworks, the tension between place, cultural homogeneity,
and national identity is developed most clearly in the work of Jin-me Yoon,
who emigrated as a child to the Canadian west coast from Korea. Yoon focuses on the migrant, suggesting that the migrant exceeds the space of the
nation-state because the movements of the migrant remain in-between:
the migrant neither fully departs, nor fully arrives. Cultural, temporal, spatial, and political displacements complicate the space in-between, "resisting the neat containment of multiculturalism's ethnic categories as well as
generalized notions of nomadism" (Nemiroff 1998: 28). Through her work,
Yoon provides an embodied, critical response to nationalist mandates such
as that of the Group of Seven, taking into account issues of family and gender while bringing to the fore a historically grounded examination of race
in the context of the construction of the nation.

Yoon's *A Group of Sixty-Seven* (the installation featured in *Crossings*)
subverts the unitary and naturalized narrative of Canadian nationalism
by bringing back to life two icons of Canadian art, *Maligne Lake, Jasper
Park* (Lawren Harris 1924) and *Old Time Coast Village* (Emily Carr c.
1929–1930). Yoon achieves a subversion of the norms of the landscape
through a critical reversal of the modes of representation foregrounded
in these seminal works by Harris and Carr. Through an engagement with
Derridean deconstruction, where deconstruction refers to an attempt to
read the text to put it into play, Yoon affirms, countersigns, and makes
possible the singularity of early Canadian landscape painting while at the
same time challenging it by exposing it to its own internal violence.

Yoon's *A Group of Sixty-Seven* explores not only the nationalist appropriation of the landscape in the work of the Group of Seven, it also critically

Jin-me Yoon, *A Group of Sixty-Seven*, 1996. Copyright Jin-me Yoon.

assesses the acceptance within the contemporary Canadian imaginary of such nationalist rhetoric as that generated by the Group. Yoon achieves this critical stance by superimposing onto the familiar empty "Canadian" landscape (the paintings of Carr and Harris) the unassimilated images of immigrants who populate this very landscape: Yoon uses Harris's and Carr's paintings as frames for the portraits of sixty-seven members of Vancouver's Korean community, creating a "contentious *internal* liminality" (Bhabha 1994). This internal liminality displaces the external narrative of the nation, addressing its complexities from within, thus undermining its apparent stability and cohesion.

Yoon underscores this effect through her title, *A Group of Sixty-Seven*, which refers at once to the art of the Group of Seven, to Canadian confederation (1867), and to 1967, which is the year that marks the lifting of certain restrictions based on race for immigration to Canada (resulting in significant immigration from Asia). By crossing and overlapping these events, Yoon draws our attention to the complexities and confluences of these incidents. Confederation becomes a vehicle for the nationalism espoused by the members of the Group, which, in turn, affects the "Canada" faced by the subsequent waves of immigration. Yoon plays with these

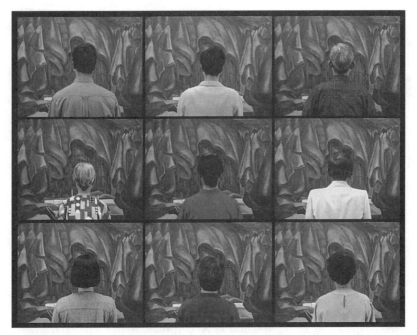

Jin-me Yoon, *A Group of Sixty-Seven,* 1996. Copyright Jin-me Yoon.

confluences by referring to the mosaic of official multiculturalism[10] through the colorful gridlike format of her photographs while simultaneously complicating simplified definitions of multiculturalism by foregrounding a dissonance within the photographs themselves, thus hinting at unresolved differences within both the representation of and the encounter with Asian immigrants in Canada.

As with her other installations, such as *between departure and arrival* and *Souvenirs of the Self,* Yoon's *A Group of Sixty-Seven* pays attention to the features of representation that ordinarily promise a condensation of identity. Through the subversion of the norms of engagement in these representations, she explores the state of suspension within the hyphen that identifies her as an immigrant. This hyphen operates both as that which denies her entry into the myth of the nation and that which transcends and transgresses a unified imaginary, giving her access to alternate notions of belonging. As a hybrid who navigates in the transitional interstices of space and time, Yoon displays the transparency of nationalist claims such as those propagated by the Group of Seven, demonstrating the ways in which any nationalist agenda is always implicated in the myth of the fixed identity and territory upon which the language of colonial violence rests. As Yoon writes with reference to *Souvenirs of the Self*:

> I am interested in appropriating the genre of landscape photography to question the constructed "nature" of Canadian identity. Imaged in the heroic setting of the Canadian Rockies, can I as a non-Western woman enjoy a "naturalized" relationship to this landscape? (1991: 5)[11]

In *A Group of Sixty-Seven*, a similarly ironic gesture takes place, wherein all "subjects" are posed twice, once facing the landscape, once with their backs to it—or, if seen from their perspective, once facing us with their backs to the landscape and once with their backs to us looking onto the landscapes of the Group of Seven. Through such a reversal, Yoon incites viewers to re-view the landscape as envisioned by the Group of Seven and to turn their backs on it, looking out at the world beyond territorial affiliations. Contrary to the tradition in Canada that celebrates the landscape as the unproblematized link to national identity, Yoon's reworking of the landscape attempts to reveal the "invisibilities" inherent in the conflation of identity and territory. In Yoon's work, these invisibilities refer to the immigrant population that continues to be excluded from the discourse of the national landscape. Yoon incites us to explore the ways in which the immigrant, superimposed onto the landscape, prevents us from seeing the "true" picture, where the truth of the landscape continues to be synonymous with the nation's connection to the landscape as envisioned by the Group of Seven.

In *A Group of Sixty-Seven*, Yoon mars "our" relationship to what has been represented as "Canada," as a result of which "Canada" becomes undone, repositioned, as it were, by the superimposition of the immigrant whose presence within "our land" causes us to re-view our naturalized images of the landscape. In an attempt to negotiate a deterritorialization of territory and identity, Yoon follows in Racine's footsteps, refuting the notion that territory can be defined according to a nationalized reflection into the landscape, introducing instead a complex repositioning of the figure within the landscape. Consequently, the landscape itself calls for sustained reflection on the nature of national affiliation.

A Group of Sixty-Seven is a challenge to the homogenizing tendencies of the national imaginary. Yoon constructs a postnational cartography within which various dialogical chronotopes emerge that do not correspond either to the organization or to the self-representation of the sovereign nation-state. Yoon's art thus alerts us that translocalities can be composed of migratory dynamics, thereby instantiating a relationship of translocality to the quotidian production of locality. Translocality, in this case, involves a conflict between national imaginaries, state-sanctioned practices, and transnational representations where territory is envisioned and represented as the contemporary crisis between the nation and the state.

Contemporary landscape art such as that of Yoon, Racine, and Hassan challenges us to reenvision the landscape, formulating for us a critique of the national and exclusionary practices of state sovereignty via the unstable figure of territoriality. Within this work, whether implicitly or explicitly, territory is represented as that which lacks a stable signifier. For as much of contemporary landscape art contends, territory's meaning falters when its hegemony is displaced by an influx of minority discourses that enter and subvert existing polities. By drawing our attention to the effects of such displacements, contemporary renditions of the landscape incite us to visualize and participate in dialogical (de)territorializations on a small scale, inviting us to adjust our territorial vocabularies. Through such adjustments our entry into ideologies of ethnic coherence is complicated; therefore, the ephemeral gains consistency in our political imaginations. Ephemeral nodes along the plane of consistency not only reply to the nation's exclusionary practices, they also undermine and subvert the nation's fictional narrative of territorial integrity and homogenous identity.

Art's capacity to identify and propagate something as problematic and elusive as "national identity" also gives it the power to deconstruct the codes of territoriality and state sovereignty; therefore, contemporary landscape art is capable of transgressing the policed borders of the nation-state. While I am encouraged by contemporary art's desire to transcend racial and national boundaries, I would not like to imply that the oppressions associated with the discourse of the nation-state are completely curtailed by an artistic renegotiation of the political and visual vocabulary of the land. Torn between the exciting and important transgressions of the art world with regard to the political scene, and politics' tightening of its oppressive and exclusive territoriality in the name of the nation-state, we find ourselves at the heart of the contemporary crisis of the nation-state, where the notion of territory is both maintained as the link to the elusive dream of national identity and undermined by the reality of ethnic diversity.

Through the evocation of a counternational cartography, work such as that of Jin-me Yoon reminds us that we must vigilantly attend to the ways in which culture re-presents itself as a suturing of convention rather than a homogenous terrain. As Mitchell suggests, we must be attentive to the manner in which "[a]rt, culture, and ideology explore and exploit the gap between representation and responsibility" (1994b: 421). A renegotiation of territoriality elicits a response-ability from the landscape that calls for a double reading, or, in Derridean terms, a reading that is a writing that responds to the exclusions potentially crystallized within nationalist imaginaries. *A Group of Sixty-Seven* can be read as one such disturbance of the national imaginary: Yoon composes a countercoherence, keeping alive a dialogue that responds critically to the use of the land as a common denominator for identity. In so doing, her work points toward a new tradition of landscape art emerging in the contemporary Canadian imagination, one that blurs the edges of identity and territory, responding politically to the notion of the other who exceeds the bounded Canadian landscape.

The subversion of the Canadian landscape is not limited to artworks, however, as attested to both by Anne Michaels's *Fugitive Pieces* and Atom Egoyan's *The Adjuster*, a text and a film I discuss in the following chapter. Via Michaels's *Fugitive Pieces* and Egoyan's *The Adjuster*, I shift the emphasis from the landscape to the figure of the home to undertake an exploration of the manner in which the discourse of the home is positioned in modern political philosophy. Identity politics are at the center of the sublation of identity into territory in the discourse of the landscape. Is this also the case with the figure of the home? The following chapter addresses this query in an effort to ascertain whether the figure of the home as theorized in modern political philosophy facilitates or complicates the passage into an errant politics of difference.

Rather than giving in to the representation of the landscape as the vehicle for national identity, Michaels and Egoyan follow in the wake of contemporary artists such as Racine, Hassan, and Yoon by responding critically to a rereading of the landscape as home. Michaels and Egoyan envisage the land not as a passive recipient of the nation's already semanticized articulations, but rather as the chronotope of *différance,* where *différance* refers to the injunction to "look attentively" without being certain of our capacity to recognize that which we seek. For the landscape, like the home, must both differ and be deferred as an invention that we must take pains to encounter, again and again, to be certain it hasn't calcified within our imaginations.

2. Beyond Accommodation: National Space and Recalcitrant Bodies

We children of the future, how can we be at home in this world of today!
—**Friedrich Nietzsche, *Werke in Drei Bänden***

According to Nietzsche, "German philosophy as a whole—Leibniz, Kant, Hegel, Schopenhauer, to name the greatest—is the most fundamental form of romanticism and homesickness there has ever been" (1968: 225). In response to the gnawing homesickness that characterizes modern thought, where the unity destroyed in Greek life must achieve realization at a higher level in modernity, modern philosophy writes the discourse of state sovereignty and national coherence as the organization of the political, thus perpetuating the notion that the *polis* is the homelike structure that organizes democratic political community. The thinker most concerned with the consequences of this adamant return to the home as the house of modernity is Friedrich Nietzsche.

Nietzsche attempts to rethink modern versions of the wish to find a home in the world, arguing that the error of modern philosophers is not their desire to find a home in the world as such, but their insistence that there be a way of life or afterlife that synchronizes with this urge to reside within a coherence that successfully keeps alterity at bay. The desire to erect a home that serves as protection against homesickness results in a politics of inclusion wherein the promise of home becomes the vessel for the perpetuation of racial, gendered, and state-centered exclusions, due in large part to the stringent security measures enforced to keep homelessness—or the discourse of the other—at bay.

Modern philosophy's desire to create a stable home is synonymous with modernity's attempt to render state sovereignty incontestable. Both rely on national cohesion to provide a sense of the lost home. State sovereignty and the discourse of the home are naturalized as normative

31

features of the political and domestic structures of our time. Political community becomes spatialized, resulting in "an understanding that necessarily gives priority to the fixing of processes of historical change in space" (Walker 1997: 172). If we adhere to the teachings of modern philosophy, we are forced to locate the home as the governing metaphor of the nation, based on the assumption that state sovereignty is inviolable as the spatiotemporal model of political governance. This discourse emphasizes the dichotomy of the homed and the homeless, classifying the homed as citizens in the citizen/nation/state triad.

Any deconstruction of the principle of state sovereignty must therefore be envisaged as the deconstruction figure of the home, where

> challenges to the principle of state sovereignty cannot be understood only as challenges to a historically specific account of what it means to engage in political community. They must also involve a questioning of the grounds on which that account of political community has become reified within a historically specific understanding of space-time relations. (Walker 1997: 175)

It is important to attend to the ways in which the principle of state sovereignty is informed by the philosophical resolutions constitutive of modernity, and to ask how these resolutions are articulated by the sovereign borders of the nation-state.

In this chapter, I intend to subvert the discourse of security, where security is that which is intent on confining us to a center from whence identities are stabilized, providing us with a homelike structure that promises to protect us against the invasion of the other. I suggest that there are texts in the making—among them Anne Michaels's novel *Fugitive Pieces* and two films, Atom Egoyan's *The Adjuster* (Canada 1992) and Bruce Beresford's *The Fringe Dwellers* (Australia 1987)—that attempt a critical rewriting of the discourse of security through a different engagement with the concept of home. These texts not only rethink the implications of the link between security and the political, they also ask how identities are constituted and deconstructed by the securing of habitable spaces. Questioning the principles of accommodation, these cultural texts alert us to the ways in which the bounded discourse of the home involves a politics of inclusivity where human mastery is foregrounded and sovereign subjects are organized to fit into spatial, homelike communities while the other is forced to abide in a labyrinth of exclusions. Within such a politics of inclusion, "those defined as other become subversive, others become perverse, others yet become sick, and still others become terrorists" (Connolly 1988: 140). What results is "a politics in which every-thing always remains to be done because each new triumph breeds a new set of enemies to be conquered" (1988: 140).

The discourse of security that undergirds the home and/as the nation is born of "a primal fear, a natural estrangement, and a condition of an-archy which diplomacy, international law, and the balance of power seek yet ultimately fail to mediate" (Der Derian 1993: 97). The desire for secu-rity is manifested as a collective fear and a resentment of difference—fear of that which is not us, not certain, not predictable. The quest for protec-tion against the unknown results in a tightening of the borders of the nation, the home, and the self. As a consequence, we are faced with a truncated life that conforms to the rationally knowable and the caus-ally sustainable. Ironically, what such a stronghold on security unveils is often security's opposite: the more unwavering the desire for security and conformity, the more apparent the fact that nothing is certain and fixed. Even the etymology of security is uncertain. As James Der Derian dem-onstrates, security has not always represented the accepted definition of that which keeps us safe. In fact, only a few hundred years ago, security's connotations led to the understanding of security as a condition of false or misplaced confidence in one's person. To assume, then, that security securely offers protection against the contingencies of the world is to forget that, not very long ago, it was from security itself that we were at-tempting to secure ourselves.

The link between security, the home, and the politics of inclusion in-forms a modern political imagination that rests on the assumption that state sovereignty offers the only viable form of political governance. In this vein, R. B. J. Walker argues that

> complaints about the complicity of modern accounts of security with practices of intolerable violence in the modern world must be harnessed to an attempt to work through more persuasive answers to those ques-tions about the character and location of political life to which the state and states system have seemed such a natural response for so many for so long. (1997: 63)

Since any discussion of security is inescapably reliant on the discourse of modernity and of the modern nation-state, a critical engagement with the character and location of political life must take as its point of de-parture the configuration of security, modernity, and the practice of state-sovereignty. We must critically reconsider the notion that states are our only source of security, for this state-centered discourse reinforces the notion that only homelike spaces provide the coherence necessary to understand and inhabit our worlds: modern accounts of state sovereignty assert that it is only through a spatial understanding of the home as state, nation, or domestic enclosure that the insecure can be conceptualized and conquered.

The subversion of a state-centered discourse of security involves rethinking the character and location of the political claims of state sovereignty that compose a coherence around the figure of the home. In addition, a rethinking of security involves critically reenvisioning the ways in which modernity is implicated in a discourse of homesickness that solidifies the relationship between the home and the nation and their adjacent discourses of inclusion and exclusion. Within the spatial discourse of state sovereignty, a boundary is always erected between the historical politics inside and the merely contingent nonpolitics outside. As Walker writes:

> Much of the history of the last half-millennium can be written as an account of the energy and violence required to ensure that the monopolistic claims of states be respected. Whether through appeals to the nation, the flag, or the national interest, states continue to deploy immense resources on an everyday basis to ensure that this monopoly is maintained. (1997: 73)

State sovereignty reifies the limits of what is understood as secure, naturalizing the notion that any bounded structure represents the needs of those located within. As one such bounded structure, the home is conceptualized as that which keeps the other at bay, offering the promise of safety in the wake of potential insecurities. In conjunction with this discourse of (in)security, modern philosophy warns us that it is only within the bounded structure of the home, nation, or state that politics can be imagined, thus relegating the homeless other to the realm of the apolitical.

Within the discourse of state sovereignty, the home extends itself metaphorically to the notion of the *polis*. As the microcosm of the *polis*, the home is involved both in the inclusion of the citizen (the nuclear family) and in the exclusion of the noncitizen (the homeless other). These blatantly exclusionary tactics are based on the configuration of the citizen/nation/state triad that forms the foundation of the discourse of the nation and, by extension, of the home. Despite this discourse of exclusion, however, the home continues to be portrayed as the secure entity that presides justly over domestic, racial, gendered, and sexual containment, placing itself as the locus of protection and inclusion. Hence, the home continues to be represented as the emblem of security even while it conceals a silenced matrix of terror within its bounds. Accepting the figure of the home at face value without concerning ourselves with the manner in which the home mirrors the exclusionary and potentially violent discourse of the nation, we risk emulating the state's affirmations of self-constituting danger, perpetuating the notion that the other must be excluded to ensure safety.

Through the notion of belonging, the home is foregrounded as the mimetic account of the nation: to "belong" within the parameters of the nation-state implies being "homed." Within the vocabulary of the nation, the home is theorized as a repository for cohesion and similarity, safety and territoriality. As Freud points out, however, the home is also the place of the uncanny, the infiltration of the *Unheimlich* within the *Heimlich*. Focusing on representations of the home, both through cultural texts and philosophy, it is therefore important to keep in mind that any conceptualization of the home depends on a desire to be blind to the strangeness, the uncanniness, and abject terror of the home as stable entity. As Freud stresses, the secret (wish) of the home, *das Geheimnis,* is always located within the strange, the unwieldy: the *Heimlich* takes place *within* the *Unheimlich,* always residing within its bounds.

The figure of the home occupies the discourse of political philosophy from its inception. Within the early writings of political philosophy, the home is conceptualized as both the policed enclosure that mirrors the *polis* and the unwieldy construction that houses the abject work of women, who are often excluded from the *polis.* From the outset, then, the discourse of the home plays a double-edged role within political philosophy, drawing attention to the ways in which the home is threatening as well as comforting, safe as well as dangerous. In light of such apparently contradictory renditions of the politics of home, analogies to the nation are sought to repress the insecurity within the figure of the home. The family operates as one such analogy to the nation, presenting itself as a binding vehicle for the discourses of the *Heimlich* and the *Unheimlich,* offering the promise of continuity and order within a disordered narrative. The family, as one representation of the home in political philosophy, follows the directives of the nation's cohesive imaginary to secure the representation of the home as an organized and secure *polis.* As Elshtain writes: "The family analogy, a theoretical argument based upon the presumption that familial and political authority, governance, and order were analogous one to another, dominated political discourse for centuries" (1982: 4).

Within the discourse of the family, Aristotle and Rousseau are two thinkers who attempt to negotiate and organize the link between the home and the *polis*. For Aristotle, the domestic home—the seat of the family—is a necessary though not integral condition of the *polis*, where the *polis* is defined as the creation of a space wherein the activities of free citizens take place. As a necessary condition, the household is located within the nonpublic sphere since the home is seen as the woman's site, and the woman is not a citizen of the *polis*. In an effort to depoliticize both the notion of the domestic and the figure of the woman, Aristotle opposes the public (politics) and the private (home).[1] For Rousseau, on the other hand, the household and the domestic role of woman are figured as a historical precondition for a modern society. As Nicole Fermon elucidates, "[i]n the eighteenth century Rousseau proposed a political program for the reform of politics through a reform of the household, the family and gender roles" (1994: 431).

The home emerges in political thought as a repository for both assimilatory and contestatory modes of governance. However, within the politics of state sovereignty, any contestatory reading of the home is disregarded, lest the home desist from providing the nation with a living example of its coherence. Hence, although representations of the home differ greatly, the reading of the home within political philosophy is frequently bound to a strict understanding of the *Heim* (home) as the seat of the *Heimlich* (homely, canny), where the home promises an order that parallels that of the (imaginary) nation. The paradox of security/insecurity articulated within the nation as a result of its fear of the *Unheimlich* is mirrored in this conception of the home. The tradition of obfuscation—where the *Unheimlich* is repressed at all costs—informs the trajectory of political philosophy and, by extension, the representation of the home. This positioning of the home within the narrative of the nation-state remains largely uncontested despite the evidence that no home, or nation, is completely safe, since every home carries within its etymology the potential haunting of its unfamiliarity.

A critical engagement with the figure of home takes place through the discourse of security, since security remains at the heart of our vocabulary of both the nation and the home. Any reconceptualization of the political—be it at the level of state sovereignty, national identity, or the politics of the home—requires us to explore the paradoxes of the *Heimlich* and the *Unheimlich*. As long as security is understood as the ground of the political, security will work to conceal the transgressions within its own shifting etymology. By focusing on the infiltration of the discourse of the *Unheimlich* into the *Heimlich*, we begin to subvert security's hegemonic presence within the discourse of the home, thus becoming attentive to the ways in which the political—and, by extension, the home and the nation—is trapped within a framework of metaphysics[2] that controls the dissemination of its representations.

An underlying motif of the metaphysical tradition, security is the ground on which the political discourses of modernity are constructed, informing and constituting the practices of the state as well as those of modern (inter)national politics. As Michael Dillon writes, "If one has to account for security's entry into discourse at all, one has to address the very terms in which the political has been thought within the tradition of the 'West'" (1996: 19). Metaphysics, as a tradition that spans from Plato to Hegel, through Heidegger and beyond, can be articulated as a tradition that identifies the ground as supporting presence, where the discourse of the ground is always complicit in the securing of that which emanates from it. Within such a thinking of the ground, spatial metaphors abound. This suggests that it is only through an identification with bounded space—or grounded space, as it were—that the political can be thought. Laying the ground as the projection of the inner possibility of metaphysics is therefore a matter of letting the supportive power of the already-laid ground become operative.

It could be argued that modern philosophy is the construction of propositions that erect and ground, where the ability to erect is determined by the condition of the ground, resulting in a nostalgia for the home as the ultimate grounded structure. Philosophy is also the question of what the ground will withstand: in philosophy, the ground is constructed as a response to the prevailing homesickness that threatens to dislocate us from the ground. Interrogating the ground defines certain architectonic limits and structural constraints within which the philosopher must work as a designer: the metaphysical philosopher is first and foremost an architect, endlessly attempting to produce a grounded structure. The metaphysical notion of the home that continues to hold currency today thus implies an engagement with the ground and with the securing of space as tradition. To think critically about the home, the ground must be deconstructed in the Derridean sense, reinforcing its potential for displacing and unsettling philosophical categories that carry within themselves the weight of political and ethical positions.

To turn metaphysics against itself—to deconstruct the ground, as it were, demolishing the home from the ground up—necessitates, among other things, a rethinking of space as the articulation of *espacement*.[3] As Derrida suggests, metaphysics is no more than a mastery of space. A renewed engagement with architecture is called for, whereby spacing (*espacement*) becomes operative, rearticulating the conditions of the ground. Space becomes writing, both in the sense of creating a fissure in an established structure or landscape, dividing or complicating its limits, as well as in the sense of replying to and subverting a tradition. Such a transgression not only complicates the dichotomy between inside and outside, ground and structure, it also refuses to dissociate the concepts of spacing and alterity, resulting in a reconceptualization of loci of inclusion and exclusion such as the home and, by extension, the nation.

Chronotopic Encounters: Anne Michaels's *Fugitive Pieces*

Anne Michaels's *Fugitive Pieces* is a novel that explores critically the discourse of the security of national and domestic spaces in the wake of World War II. The story is narrated by Jacob and Ben, two Jews whose lives are inextricably marked by the violence of WWII, which, for them, results in the impossibility of "being at home," if "home" is understood as a locus of safety and protection. *Fugitive Pieces* highlights the manner in which the relationship to the home always refers to a violent dream of national unity and coherence.

This tenuous relationship to the home is expressed first through the words of Jacob, who, having successfully escaped as a child after watching the Gestapo destroy his home in Poland and kill his family, writes to come to terms with what he perceives as the impossibility of returning "home." Jacob does not recover his sense of "home," despite the fact that he is taken care of generously and warmly by Athos, a Greek geographer, who hides him in his house on Zakynthos—a house later destroyed by the same regime—and with whom, after the war, he emigrates to Toronto. Ben, the second narrator, also experiences the home as the repository of insecurity, though in his case it is the ghostly presence of a past that complicates his experience of the home in the present.

Unlike Jacob, Ben does not experience the war firsthand. Ben is the child of parents who were imprisoned in a concentration camp during WWII where their other children were killed. In their differing ways, both Jacob and Ben suffer the pain of disconnection. For both of them, the home becomes a central trope that mediates space and time, juxtaposed between geography's gradual evolution of the landscape and history's violent dominion over space. The home thus becomes the chronotope of *Fugitive Pieces*, the timed-space that reveals the traces of genealogies composed of accidents, impossibilities, and incoherences. Through the chronotope of the home, *Fugitive Pieces* questions the politics inherent in

the discourse of the home, foregrounding the home as the lived metaphor of the nation, where it is homelessness as a political gesture that
eventually enables Jacob and Ben to rewrite their narratives of the violence of containment.

To appreciate the ways in which a critical engagement with the chronotope of the home makes possible a certain rewriting of the political, we
must recall that the political is always an encounter between two heterogeneous processes, where the first is that of governance and the second
that of emancipation. As Rancière suggests, contrasting the political with
policy, politics has no *arche*, it "is not the enactment of a principle, the
law or the self of a community" (1992: 59). Rather, the political is always
the power of the *one more*, not the policing of the *self* of a community.
The political is always involved in the process of subjectivization, where
the self is not formed separately from its relation to the other. To function as a process rather than a law, the political must refuse reduction
to any modus of containment. The political is unplaced, unbounded, its
subjectivity always an interval or a gap. One could argue, then, that any
sustained desire to constrain the political within a structure effects a depoliticization, or a politics without ethics.

A rearticulation of the political through a different organization of
habitable spaces involves an encounter with alterity. In *Fugitive Pieces,*
homelessness as a political gesture calls for such a rewriting of the political to the extent that the political is reframed through a heterological
encounter with the other. One of the ways in which this occurs is through
a subversion of modernity's account of the discourse of time and space.
There is, within *Fugitive Pieces,* a questioning of the grounds according
to which accounts of political community have become reified within a
historically specific understanding of space-time relations. This re-vision
of the bounds of the political takes place through an exploration of the
geography of the landscape: the borders of the home are challenged by
a narrative that rearticulates the limits of inclusion and exclusion, space
and time.

An alternative theorization of accommodation through the figure of
the landscape is foregrounded in Jacob's description of his Sunday afternoons with Athos:

> Late Sunday afternoons, we climbed from the lake bottom, covered with
> prehistoric ooze, to surface under a billboard on St. Clair Avenue; the
> tram tracks shining dully under the weak winter sun, or stopped bright
> under the streetlights, the evening sky purple with cold or cyanotype

summer blue, the darkening shapes of the houses against the dissolving bromide of twilight. Muddy, clinging with burrs of enchanter's nightshade (stowaways on trouser legs and sleeves), we headed home for a hot dinner. These weekly explorations into the ravines were escapes to ideal landscapes; lakes and primeval forests so long gone they could never be taken away from us. . . . On these walks I could temporarily shrug off my strangeness because, the way Athos saw the world, every human was a newcomer. (1996: 102–3)

In this passage, being-at-home reveals not a bounded structure but an ephemeral space of encounter. Jacob and Athos are not *beyond accommodation,* yet neither are they housed within the tradition of political philosophy and metaphysics that gives platform to the violent practices of exclusion they experience in the aftermath of WWII. The strangeness that is temporarily alleviated by the geography of the ravine draws a fissure between the landscape as accommodation, where the landscape invites difference, and the home as a secured enclosure that reinforces modern practices of being-in-common. In the ravine on Sunday afternoons, the *Heimlich* becomes *unheimlich* as the *Unheimlich* becomes *heimlich.* Briefly, home-based practices of exclusion are lifted, the strangeness embodied by the other no longer a threat. This results in a momentary reconceptualization of the political: the political can now be enunciated as that which operates separately from discourses of containment and enclosure. Within this transitional geographical imaginary, gradual geographies become biographies of *espacement* as the interval that calls for the securing of the *(Un)Heimlich* is momentarily deferred.

Home as the repository for containment in *Fugitive Pieces* is written as the discourse of insecurity. Our first encounter with the home is one of destruction: "The burst door. Wood ripped from hinges, cracking like ice under the shouts" (Michaels 1996: 7). In the immediate aftermath of the invasion and devastation of Jacob's family home, Jacob escapes Poland and flees to Biskupin, where Athos finds him and offers him the protection of his home on Zakynthos for the duration of the war. For Jacob, however, whose first encounter with the home as a policed enclosure is one of terror, the home continues to mark a certain violence, even years after the war. On Zakynthos, for example, while Athos's home provides shelter, it also continues to be the potential site of invasion, as Jacob hides upstairs, year after year. Later, in Toronto, the home provides little more than shelter as Jacob's world continues to be plagued by the terror of memory and the guilt of being the sole survivor of the brutality inflicted on his family. The discourse of security is strangely enmeshed with that of insecurity as the enclosure carries both the promise of protection and the articulation of violence.

The incestuous relationship between security and insecurity fore-grounded in *Fugitive Pieces* not only alerts us to the confounding relation-ship between security and violence within the specter of the home, it also draws our attention to the manner in which the discourse of security em-bodies the promise of metaphysics, where metaphysics can be understood as the foundation of a narrative of containment that establishes a differ-ential hierarchy between self and other. As Der Derian argues, "[W]ithin the concept of security lurks the entire history of western metaphysics . . . as a series of substitutions of center to center in a perpetual search for the transcendental signified" (1993: 95). This return to the metaphysical dis-course of the center at the heart of the notion of security locates us once more within the philosophical concept of the grounded structure, where the discourse of the home assists in the cementing of the exclusionary borders of metaphysical political philosophy.

If we agree that "just as philosophical thought has its inception in metaphysics, so metaphysics has its inception in the *polis*" (Dillon 1996: 19), to secure security must always also mean to secure the political, where politics becomes preoccupied with realizing the securing of security. This preoccupation with security becomes the ground of metaphysics, since within metaphysical discourse the foundation of everyday life is secured on the basis of a will to mastery and certainty. Such a will to security re-sults in a prime incitement to violence in the western tradition of thought: danger is endangered in response to its own discursive dynamic. As the dissociation between freedom and politics becomes more pronounced and security is embraced as the foundational text of politics, security be-comes our only way of knowing freedom, often releasing us from the very burden of freedom itself.

Giorgio Agamben offers important insight into this paradox of se-curity. Critically assessing the violence inherent in the sovereign desire to secure the national, Agamben alters the topology of sovereignty by drawing our attention to the biopolitical and juridical containment and production of bodies within the regime of the sovereign. Agamben ar-gues that the sovereign is the one who operates both inside and outside the law due to the notion of the state of exception, which gives the sov-ereign the legal power to suspend the validity of the law and legally place himself or herself outside the law. Within this matrix of governance, the sovereign becomes the point of indistinction between violence and the law. He or she marks the threshold that sustains the passage of law into violence and of violence into law. The state of exception has implications in the discourse of the (in)security of the home insofar as the home becomes the site for the embodiment both of violence and the law. If we subscribe to Agamben's insights into the parameters of sovereign power, it becomes apparent that for a rethinking of the political to occur—if such a rethinking implies a reconfiguration of the spatial modalities of power and governance—accommodation must transgress and subvert the discourse of security (Agamben 1998).

The state of exception is both exemplified and discounted by the narrative of *Fugitive Pieces*. This situates *Fugitive Pieces* as a text that at once conforms to the laws of state sovereignty and seeks to exceed them. On the one hand, *Fugitive Pieces* reflects on the consequences of the state of exception, foregrounding the bitter wounds of war that complicate the relationship to the home for Jacob and Ben. On the other hand, the subtext of *Fugitive Pieces* comprises a sustained critical stance vis-à-vis the discourse of security and being-in-common. The challenge to the discourse of state sovereignty is exemplified most clearly in *Fugitive Pieces* through the questioning of the validity of the notion of the "politically qualified" household. The text opts not for the republican family model brought forward by Rousseau, which attempts to forge a continuity in time and space between the discourse of the state and that of the home,[4] but rather experiments with something akin to the Deleuzo-Guattarian notion of nomadism.

Fugitive Pieces challenges the discourse of sovereignty in two explicit ways. First, the narrative opts for nomadism rather than a republican family model. Second, *Fugitive Pieces* uses writing as a tool for the invention of an errant politics. Within *Fugitive Pieces,* writing is offered as a tool for the reconceptualization of the relation between actuality and potentiality. Writing demonstrates the manner in which sovereign power places itself at the intersection between constituting and constituted power, maintaining itself in relation to both. *Fugitive Pieces* responds to the claims of naturalized complicity between the political and the secure, reassessing the ways in which the discourse of security disallows a rearticulation of the political. *Fugitive Pieces* thus follows Agamben's wise suggestion that it is only when we begin to think the relation between actuality and potentiality differently—and even think beyond this relation—that we will be able to think a constituting power wholly released from the sovereign state of exception.

Through a writing practice that is nomadic, *Fugitive Pieces* attempts to subvert the myth of belonging that sustains the modern philosophical tradition. This is carried out through the words of the three main characters: Athos, Jacob, and Ben. Athos does so through rewriting of the past in his historical text about the archaeological site at Biskupin.[5] Jacob contends with the myth of belonging through poetry, which for him is a renunciation of the state of exception. Both Athos and Jacob understand that the renunciation of the state of exception can be achieved only through a rearticulation of the political that is always also a reworking of any discourse that celebrates being-in-common, be they those of political philosophy or, more generally, those of the metaphysical tradition.

How is writing a political gesture? To locate writing as a political gesture, it is necessary to attend to the history of writing within the metaphysical tradition, where the origin of truth is assigned to the logos, an event that results in the debasement of writing and its repression outside of "full" speech. This crisis of language is the symptom that indicates that a historico-metaphysical epoch must finally determine as language the totality of its problematic horizon. Within metaphysics, writing works as the translator of a full speech that is present to itself, shielded from interpretation as the ventriloquist of an originary speech. To transport language beyond the realm of metaphysics, and to affirm that the concept of writing exceeds and comprehends that of language, presupposes a rethinking (a thinking outside metaphysics) of both language and writing.

Derrida understands writing to be everything that gives rise to inscription. "That which governs a writing thus enlarged and radicalized," writes Derrida, "no longer issues from a logos, rather it inaugurates the destruction, not the demolition but the de-sedimentation, the deconstruction, of all the significations that have their source in that of the logos" (1974: 10). Writing—as that which resists and deconstructs the *logos*—is understood as that which not only undermines the hierarchy of presence and absence, but as the possibility of the renunciation and subversion of metaphysics and, by extension, of the modern philosophical tradition. Conceptualized in this vein, Athos's, Jacob's, and Ben's writing can be understood as a political gesture that attempts to rewrite a metaphysical and modern tradition that requires and condones violence in the name of sovereign practices of security. Hence, the violence Ben, Jacob, and Athos narrate is as much the acknowledgment of the end of metaphysics as it is the beginning of writing, where writing is associated with the violence of inscription, a violence that marks homelessness as a point of departure for a rethinking of time and space.

Writing, as that which potentially undermines the power of the sovereign, is evoked throughout *Fugitive Pieces* not only through the act of inscription; writing can also be located as the instantiation of textual linkages between language and the home. The connection between language and the home is brought to the fore upon Jacob's arrival in Greece. Here, language and the home are immediately intertwined, both uncanny, both subject to the necessity of rearticulation. "Then Athos said we were home, in Greece," writes Jacob. "When we got closer I saw the words were strange; I'd never seen Greek letters before" (Michaels 1996: 14). Jacob's encounter with the home in Greece serves as a reminder that we construct ourselves and the spaces we inhabit through language, even if the language is foreign and strange. Throughout *Fugitive Pieces,* the narrative often returns to this notion of the *Unheimlich,* suggesting that the home can never be a place of certainty; the home is always subject to bombardment and upheaval. Jacob spends a lifetime writing about this relationship between language and the home, eventually realizing through his poetry that while no home will ever protect him from his violent memories of destruction, language may provide a vehicle for a departure from the metaphysical assumptions of grounding and security.

Through language, Jacob exposes the violence of security as the moment where the ethic of the other is not respected because the other is not "housed" and therefore not "present" within the visible parameters of sovereign governance. For Jacob, writing becomes a way of exploring the chronotope that history denies and obscures in its narratives of war and peace. In an effort to remain vigilantly attentive to the paradoxical discourse of (in)security, Jacob invents, through poetry, a language in which the writing of history becomes a genealogical enterprise rather than a linear recounting of the origin. Jacob attempts to create a language that will allow him to begin to explore the possibility of thinking outside the historical trinity of event, witness, and perpetrator, shifting instead to a discourse that frees itself from the metaphysics of security and allows him to think the synchronicity of encounters without resorting to the language of enclosure and dominion.

Jacob's homelessness becomes his mark on the space/time continuum of the world, offering him a vocabulary with which to reinvent himself. This vocabulary allows him, eventually, to renounce the constraining and traumatic notion of home that haunts both his life and his writing. This shift takes place after years of writing poetry, upon Jacob's return to Greece at the end of his life. In Greece, Jacob comes to terms with his homelessness, realizing that it is precisely his strangeness that allows him to encounter the world differently:

From the first, I felt at home in these hills, with broken icons hovering
over every abyss, every valley, the spirit looking back upon the body [. . .].
But I also knew I would always be a stranger in Greece, no matter how
long I lived here. (Michaels 1996: 164)

In the end, Jacob understands the impossibility of home as the potential
to rearticulate the political, which, in turn, allows him to be accommodated differently. His homelessness thus becomes an ethical engagement
that allows him to rewrite the political as that which interrogates the
"lawful" violence of state sovereignty.

In a refusal to become complacent, Jacob explores, through writing,
the ethics of the enclosure. Through his poetry, Jacob complicates what
it means to "be at home" while at the same time enjoying the comforts of
transitory accommodation. Jacob understands that he is accommodated
only insofar as he remains homeless—that is, housed outside the realm
of the violent discourse of state sovereignty. Not being beyond accommodation suggests, in Jacob's case, that he be able to enjoy the possibility
of togetherness often associated with the discourse of the home while
remaining critically skeptical of the violence of the home, and, by extension, of the sovereign. Jacob's writing demonstrates—in a nuanced narrative where the longing for accommodation is not negated—the ways in
which history writes geography as geography writes history. His writing
thus enables a renewed engagement with the biopolitical, where the body
becomes the site not only of governance, but also of recalcitrance.

What Jacob seeks is an ethics of responsibility. For Jacob, this involves
a refutation of the face as the emblem of the ethical.[6] Jacob opts instead
for the figure of the hand: "For a long time I believed one learns nothing
from a man's face," Jacob writes. "When Athos held me by the shoulders,
when he said 'Look at me, look at me,' to convince me of his goodness, he
couldn't know how he terrified me, how meaningless the words. *If truth
is not in the face, then where is it? In the hands! In the hands!*" (Michaels
1996: 93, emphasis mine). For Jacob, the political, understood as the basis
for the ethical, shifts from an ethics of the face to an ethics of *espacement*,
of space as writing, with the hand as the symbol—or the trace—of alterity and difference. Ethical responsibility thus becomes an encounter with
the other through writing, where "spacing *(espacement)* is the impossibility for an identity to be closed in on itself, on the inside of its proper
interiority, or on its coincidence with itself. The irreducibility of spacing
is the irreducibility of the other" (Derrida 1981a: 94).

This ethics of *espacement* allows Jacob to occupy space in the world without feeling he is adhering to the violent discourse of the home. Jacob chooses instead a narrative of homelessness as *espacement,* which he understands as the renunciation of a stable ethics of self and other, homed and homeless. This reconfiguration of the ethical—and, by extension, of the political—is what ultimately allows Jacob to forgive himself for not having faced the Gestapo when they destroyed his family. By renouncing the ethics of the face and opting instead for an ethics of *espacement,* Jacob finally relieves himself of the burden of his effacement from a narrative of sovereignty that neither protected nor defended him. Jacob now understands that the Gestapo would not have been interested in his face. Free at last, Jacob can initiate a writing of accommodation that allows him, for the first time, to feel "at home." "I'm a thief who has climbed in through a window only to find himself struck frozen by a feeling of homecoming," he writes. "The impossibility of it; the luck" (Michaels 1996: 178).

Ben's narrative diverges from Jacob's mainly because Ben did not experience firsthand the violence of the Holocaust. Ben's parents' narrative is traumatic. Although he does not know the experience of the Holocaust as they do, Ben interiorizes their pain; consequently, he feels extreme guilt at the thought of leaving them behind and creating a world of his own. Leaving home is akin to relinquishing the link to his family, since, for his family, the home is the necessary repository for the pain of their experience. So extreme is Ben's parents' fear of losing their home that Ben recounts a story of their refusing to escape during a hurricane, even after warnings from the neighbors. For Ben, the home (of his parents) becomes the locus of captivity that is masked as the space of freedom, where the violence is kept inside to fester, unspoken.

Despite Ben's parents' attempts to hold him captive, his longing to escape the stranglehold of his home eventually leads him away from his parents into Jacob's life, though Ben continues to suffer terribly at the thought of abandoning his family and their fortress. As a way of countering the oppressive containment he continues to carry around with him, Ben is drawn into the compelling drama of weather patterns, through which he experiences the possibility of change and unpredictability. Ben's university pursuits—the study of weather within literary texts—reveals his deep desire to create an alternative narrative that mediates history with the impulses of geography, thus freeing him from the bonds of captivity reinforced by his parents' adoption of the discourse of the state of exception, a discourse in which they are ultimately not only victims but also perpetrators.

Ben's imprisonment within a narrative of violent containment—where he is the pawn of a history that writes him as its sacrificial victim—links his story to the work of Agamben, who elucidates the relationship between violence and the law in his reading of the biopolitic, advancing the figure of *homo sacer* as the originary form of life taken into the sovereign ban. Agamben offers the notion of ban or abandonment as that which characterizes the state of exception, and argues that it is only when we begin to think the Being of abandonment beyond every idea of the law will we have moved beyond the paradox of sovereignty toward a politics freed from every ban.

Returning to early Roman texts of the law, Agamben identifies the *homo sacer*—he who is captured in the sovereign ban—as the man who could be killed without repercussions, yet whose body could not be sacrificed. The category of the *homo sacer* was employed to incarcerate those who otherwise might have been saved by a trial. It was, therefore, in a sense, a license to kill. Agamben's analysis suggests that the category of *homo sacer* is used within the state of exception to defend the killing of those who will be neither tried nor sacrificed. This applies, among other cases, to the Jews during the Holocaust. As Agamben writes, "The dimension in which the extermination [of the Jews] took place is neither religion nor law, but biopolitics" (1998: 114). Agamben defines biopolitics along Foucauldian lines, suggesting that biopolitics is the growing inclusion of human beings' natural life in the mechanisms and calculations of power. Following Foucault, Agamben argues that the radical transformation of politics into the realm of bare life legitimates and necessitates total domination, as is seen with respect to the Jews.

In this age of biopolitics, the sovereign's power lies in the selection of which life ceases to be politically relevant: "Life—which, with the declaration of rights, had as such been invested with the principle of sovereignty—now itself becomes the place of a sovereign decision" (1998: 142). Agamben brings forth the concentration camp as the paradigm of political space where politics becomes biopolitics and *homo sacer* is confused with citizen:

> The birth of the camp in our time appears as an event that decisively signals the political space of modernity itself. It is produced at the point at which the political system of the modern nation-state, which was founded on the functional nexus between a determinate localization (land) and a determinate order (the State) and mediated by axiomatic rules for the inscription of life (birth or the nation), enters into a lasting crisis, and the

State decides to assume directly the care of the nation's biological life as one of its proper tasks. (1998: 174–75)

The terrifying implications of Agamben's thesis bear direct relevance to the insurgent nationalisms of the late twentieth century. Not to take these instances of nationalism as potential re-inscriptions of the bio-politic through the sovereign's state of exception is to be blind to the history of both the nation-state and modernity. As Agamben argues, the growing dissociation between birth (bare life) and the practices of containment with which we secure our existences is the fact of politics of our day. What we call "camp" is the disjunction between the two, and where we situate camp—be it in its most extreme forms the concentration camps of World War II or, in their less extreme incarnations, the refugee holding tanks at airports, in cities, on borders—depends on whether we are speaking from the perspective of a bounded space or whether we are willing to engage in a dismantling of the very dichotomy of inclusion/exclusion that makes such a notion of camp possible.

The reverberations of the "camp" mentality are explored in *Fugitive Pieces* through Ben's narrative. For Ben, the home is the locus of ressentiment, the place that could-have-been for his family had the war not taken everything from them: "There was no energy of a narrative in my family, not even the fervor of an elegy. Instead, our words drifted away, as if our home were open to the elements and we were forever whispering into a strong wind" (Michaels 1996: 204). Cognizant of there having been a terrible shift in weather that paralyzed his parents within the prison they call home, Ben spends his life reconstructing the past in the present through the study of the relationship between biography and weather patterns, attempting to shield himself from the elements by learning to forecast the weather. Finally, ready to admit defeat in his endeavor to order the chronotope of the past, Ben turns to Jacob's poetry, through which he begins to develop a sense of a genealogy—a gradual geography—which offers him an adjacent narrative to his suffocating home, allowing him to escape from the confines of his "camp" mentality. Through poetry, Ben begins to see geography—in the guise of weather patterns—as a potential tool to be used against the dangerous fabrications of sovereign politics.

Jacob's poetry extends to Ben the gift of gradual geographies of writing as *espacement* through which Ben can begin to situate himself, discarding the shackles of the imprisoning narrative of containment that has plagued him throughout his life. Reading Jacob's poetry as an instance of a gradual geography of writing, Ben begins to appreciate that the landscape can be written as the ecstasy of *différance*. This lesson Jacob learned from Athos, who taught him to associate language and the home, and, by extension, writing and the landscape. Through Athos's association of poetry, paleontology, and geography, Athos impressed upon Jacob the importance of exploring the ways in which the drifting objects in the landscape can be seen as nomadic instances of an *unheimlich* accommodation that resists the discourse of security. As Athos seemed to suggest, if accommodation could be located elsewhere than in the exclusive and bounded figure of the home, there might be a way of subverting the bio-politics of bare life.

Without the secure enclosure as its point of departure, the value of life cannot easily be measured; consequently, the (bio)political finds that it has been re-inscribed alongside the contingencies of the weathered landscape, the memories of violence and subjugation imprinted on its already imperfect, protean, geohistorical surfaces. Storm warnings are in the forecast. Each memento to space and time—to home—becomes a moment in which life is interrupted. Subjectivity, as *asujetissement,* is mapped onto this interruption as it sorts through tangled landscapes. The landscape thus becomes a doubled gesture, a reading and writing, a knitting and unraveling of identities, subjectivities, subjections, histories, and spatialities.

The mirrors and tides deflect as they reflect the landscape, re-membering and distorting the gashes left by history. Space speaks time and allows time to speak, forging a fissure in space and time for the shrill screams of the dispossessed, demonstrating the fact that "geography is not an inert container, is not a box where cultural history 'happens,' but an active force, that pervades the literary field and shapes it in depth" (Moretti 1998: 3). Space becomes time and time becomes space at the intersection that calls for a location for the event, where what happens depends on where it happens. A shift in the modern chronotope ensues, its adjacent homesickness displaced by a narrative that no longer relies on modern politics of containment.

In response to a renewed configuration of the political, time and space react to create a geography of smells, of sounds and memory, collisions that force trenches into virgin land, into land that is always already colonized. "One can look deeply for meaning or one can invent it," Jacob writes (Michaels 1996: 136). As with the Catalan Atlas, where the most important contributions are those that are left out, the terra incognita becomes the collision that creates the spark that ignites the landscape. Writing produces new lines of flight, giving birth to the infants of catastrophe and juxtaposition. Maps of history, however, as Anne Michaels points out, have never been so honest: within history

> terra cognita and terra incognita inhabit exactly the same coordinates of time and space. The closest we come to knowing the location of what's unknown is when it melts through the map like a watermark, a stain transparent as a drop of rain. (Michaels 1996: 137)

The map of history refutes the unknown precisely because it is invested in the securing of its land, of its language, and of its ontology. However, as Michaels suggests, through a critical engagement with the discourse of security—an abandonment of the ban, as it were—the historical split second can become the geographical gradual instant, resulting in a shift from the haunting trinity (perpetrator, victim, witness) to the slow transformation of wood to stone, peat to coal, limestone to marble.

Gradual geographies are biographies of *espacement*, of intervals and differences, of openness to an outside that discredits any notion of an absolute inside. We must remain weary of absolutes. As Jacob warns, "Never trust biographies. Too many events in a man's life are invisible" (Michaels 1996: 141). Biographies of the landscape must continuously be rewritten to undermine a tradition that not only grounds a certain domestic space, but extends, sustains, and protects a metaphysical definition of the domestic. Within such a metaphysical definition, the home's ability to domesticate is also its capacity to define inside and outside, not simply because that which is located inside is domesticated, but because the "outside" continues to be organized by the logic of the enclosure. To be excluded is to be subjected to a certain domestic violence that is both organized and veiled by metaphysics. In *Fugitive Pieces*, the critical engagement with the specter of the home politicizes the parameters of sovereignty, questioning the discourses of power and stability.

To think of the home as a marker of identity and difference, of inclusion and exclusion, of the *Heimlich* and the *Unheimlich*, is to begin to explore the consequences of the state of exception, of safety and insecurity, of inhabiting or resisting strict enclosures. The critical renegotiation of the specter of the home in *Fugitive Pieces* demonstrates a critical engagement with the discourse of the political. *Fugitive Pieces* resists a conception of home that draws firm lines around the edifice, where a grounded continuity and a gnawing homesickness prevail in the name of metaphysics and sovereignty. *Fugitive Pieces* offers an alternative to ground as a basis for thinking, suggesting instead a certain necessity for movement that can be conceptualized as a shifting from poetry to palaeontology to geology.

Such a rewriting of the political through a critical engagement with the figure of the home acts as a reminder that the poetic does not merely inhabit the political, but makes way for it. However, as Dillon warns with respect to the conjunction between poetics and politics, "this is a fragile habitation, itself concerned with the fragile" (1996: 203). With the fragility of its politics in mind, the poetics of homelessness in *Fugitive Pieces* seeks to ensure, through a continual renewal of its vocabulary through writing, that any figure of accommodation remain an unstable signifier that resides between violence and memory, between destruction and creation. *Fugitive Pieces* directs our attention beyond the home to a thinking of accommodation that underscores this very fragility. This notion of fragility is also what is at stake in Atom Egoyan's *The Adjuster*, with which I engage in the following section. In *The Adjuster*, the home is that which must at all costs be protected, revered, and itemized. Ironically, however, the home also proves to be that which one cannot hold onto, no matter how tightly one insures and secures it. For the home is simply another instance of the political, which, as we are beginning to see, is the most fragile of habitations.

Securing the Insecure: Adjusting the Political

"Atom Egoyan makes bitterly disappointing films," writes Jonathan Romney in an article for *Sight and Sound;* "when they finally deliver what we're looking for, they invariably frustrate us—all we discover is that revelation can never be satisfactory" (1995: 15). The frustration that marks many viewers' experience of watching Atom Egoyan's films is due to the illusory impossibility of communication foregrounded in films such as *The Adjuster*, where meaning cannot, once and for all, be secured. In Egoyan's films, the image that is always both under suspicion and that acts as the vehicle for seduction is a nagging reminder of the impossibility of the referent. This is even more apparent when the image crosses the narration, disrupting all illusions of seamless progression. Each of these traits is visible in Egoyan's *The Adjuster*, which expands on Anne Michaels's theorization of the home by emphasizing the impossibility of the referent.

In *The Adjuster* the direct time-image[7] foregrounds in an extreme sense the displacement from movement to image, space to time. At the outset, the shift from movement to time through the direct time-image in *The Adjuster* would seem to contradict Michaels's narrative in *Fugitive Pieces*, which attempts to bring movement to the fore rather than focusing only on the temporality of history. This is not necessarily the case. Although *Fugitive Pieces* and *The Adjuster* differ greatly in their use of time and space, the representation of movement in *Fugitive Pieces* is in many ways analogous to Deleuze's time-image, which not only reveals the false continuity of history, but also exposes difference within the image. Deleuze argues that what is specific to the time-image is its concerted attempt "to make perceptible, to make visible, relationships of time which cannot be seen in the represented object and do not allow themselves to be reduced to the present" (1989: xii).

The transition from *Fugitive Pieces* to *The Adjuster* is complementary, despite that we are shifting from a literary to a cinematic genre. Egoyan's *The Adjuster* calls forth the modern relation of time and space through a cinematic exploration of the effects of resistance between image and narration. *The Adjuster* evokes a supplementarity within both the image and the narrative that is a complement to the manner in which *Fugitive Pieces* engages in a rewriting of the relationship between time and space. *The Adjuster*'s challenge to narrative continuity is expressed in the film's foregrounding of the impossibility of the referent, which emphasizes the discourse of (in)security at the levels both of the image and the text.

In a repudiation of the parameters of modern politics of security, the film plays with the notion of the insurance policy. The paradox of security/insecurity is brought to life through the figure of the adjuster. In the first scene of the film, we encounter Noah (the adjuster) standing by the window, as though expecting a disturbance. In this scene, the image and the narration are discontinuous, as though various strata of time were operating simultaneously. As viewers, we are encouraged to engage both with the narration and its demise as we reach beyond the movement image, which provides us with no more than a man standing by the window, waiting for a phone call, and a woman sleeping. When we leave the organic regime behind, what the time-image reveals is that juxtapositions are taking place: contradictory and superimposed levels of time are being explored, some of which correspond to the image at hand, some of which exist outside the narration.

This first scene alerts us to a discontinuity within the narrative before any "action" takes place. From the beginning, therefore, we are suspicious of the image, aware that the film operates in a variety of time-frames. Hence, when the phone does ring, we are poised for the disjunction that follows: Although Noah seems at first to prefer not to wake Hera, his wife, before leaving the house, he calls her from his car phone as soon as he is on his way to another incendiary destination. "What is it?" Hera asks, woken in the middle of the night by the phone. "Nothing . . .," Noah replies, "just began to think about our house . . . imagining things . . .

were you having a bad dream?" But Hera is no longer listening, the receiver lying on her chest, her face set in an exasperated grimace. Like many of the scenes that follow, this shot remains detached from what might be termed a "narrative whole," offering no sense of continuity in the (family) narrative.[8] The juxtaposition between the movement image (Noah's departure from the house toward the scene of the fire) and the time-image (the cutting back and forth between the outside and the inside of the house) is evident, revealing the discontinuity within the narrative of the home without ever referring to it specifically. Already, via the time-image, there is a sense that the home is not a locus of safety: the home is always already threatened both from the inside and the outside by the presence of the adjuster, whose job it is to wait for the home to self-destruct.

The family, as that which exists in a state of in-completion, (in)security, and (mis)communication in *The Adjuster,* is contrasted by Noah's "other family," the victims of loss for whom he adjusts insurance claims. This second family, which Noah houses in a small motel, offers him the sense of security and completion his first does not. Whereas his family at home is composed of people who do not communicate in a straightforward manner (Hera's sister and her son live with them, both of whom speak a language Noah does not understand), Noah *provides* the language for those who stay at the motel, instructing his clients on what to write in their claims. From his clients, Noah is sexually reimbursed and treated like a savior. As a result, Noah is continuously drawn to the site of the catastrophe, always waiting for the phone to ring in the middle of the night and then scurrying off to sort through the various junkyards of personal destruction. Out of the ruin, Noah seeks preservation. It is Noah's parasitical allegiance to other peoples' lives, through pictures and lists, that allows him to feel secure about his position in the world.

Hera's discordant narrative, on the other hand, unlike Noah's teleological desire for straight lines, tells a story of incomplete unspoken nightmares, of pirated tapes and censored porn films, of the violence of a destroyed neighborhood in another country, and of a sister and a child who refuse to speak English. Like Noah, Hera is a witness, a voyeur. But unlike Noah, Hera's gaze does not seem to require the precision of lists, of order, of security. Instead, Hera's gaze wanders, taking home to her sister the images she cuts. Since Hera does not desire security, she does not feel compelled to evoke a discourse of insecurity. Hera seems instead quite comfortable with the notion that there is no referent. Hera's job, after all, consists in cutting parts out of pornographic texts. She does not worry whether these texts will "make sense" without the "missing" images. Quite the contrary: Hera exists in a world of fragments. "Since I started taping she can see what we cut, what we don't allow other people to watch," Hera explains when she is caught by her boss taping the images for her sister. "When she watches the decisions I'm making, she's very proud." What is masked as a childlike innocence is in fact a stark realization on Hera's part of the impossibility of securing the image as originary in the absence of an organic narrative.

Another family in this strange tale is that of Babba and Mimi, who come upon Hera and Noah's house and decide they want to use it for the shooting of a film. The attraction to Noah and Hera's home seems strange at the outset. Noah and Hera's home is but one lonely house that was to be part of a settlement. Surrounded by an invisible community and held together by spineless books, Hera and Noah's house resists grounding in the narrative of the happy family home. Instead, alone in a colorless desert, the house presents itself as the miserable backdrop to a billboard that shows a solid home with a smiling white heterosexual couple and child, a perfect blue sky, and a lush landscape. In sharp juxtaposition to this subtext of suburban bliss is the image of the hard soil and the displaced characters in the middle of a vast nowhere. Nonetheless, or perhaps because of its alienation within the landscape of the suburb, Babba and Mimi choose to take over this "family home" for their taping of the film within the film.

The appearance of Babba and Mimi within *The Adjuster* exposes Noah's narrative for what it is. Noah's dependence on his position as the insurance adjuster becomes increasingly apparent as Babba and Mimi attempt to draw him into a web of insecurity by using his home as the birthplace of contingency. Playing with the (im)possibility of the security of the home as policed enclosure, reversing the roles of the characters within the household—giving Noah's sister's wife and child a role in the narration, for instance—Babba and Mimi undermine the stable dysfunction of Noah's home-based production. Consequently, Babba and Mimi's film within the film collapses Noah's deep longing to narrate a story of enclosed cohesion, rendering him insecure and challenging us, as viewers, to develop a critical awareness with respect to the seamless image.

This is a lesson Noah resists, as is dramatized in a scene in which Noah is at the motel making love with one of his clients, Arianne. Aroused by the idea of the claim, thinking of the list that can sort things out and recreate a lost life, Noah pleads with Arianne, telling her amid gasps and moans that she must make a thorough claim listing all her belongings and hand the list over to him as soon as possible. Arianne, however, has no need to claim that which she no longer owns and tries to explain to Noah that she has no desire to reclaim the past in an attempt to secure her present. Arianne knows that her present—like her past—is insecure and that her story cannot be organized within a coherent narrative. She prefers not to pretend otherwise. "Everything is destroyed," Arianne tells him. "That's not the point," Noah replies. "I don't see the point of itemizing what we already know," Arianne says. "It's not that simple," Noah responds as he explodes into orgasm. For Noah, the blank spaces are there to be reclaimed, to be listed in what one hopes is a secure insurance policy.

Repetitively, Noah explains to his clients that there is much he needs to know before he can submit a claim. Living vicariously through other people's lists, Noah holds his victims prisoner under one roof where he is intimate with them all, sharing his platitudes and his body, filing their claims and promising them security. In exchange, his victims provide him with the details of their incinerated lives, with pictures, and, ironically, with love, trust, and respect. For them, Noah is the angel who seeks the resurrection of lost belongings. And yet, despite the attention Noah grants his victims, sooner or later both he and his clients realize that even he has no control over the ultimate reception of the claims he sends, that not even he can secure their lives. "You know, it doesn't always work out this way," he tells Tim and Lorraine,

> that the claim comes through—especially in a situation as complicated as yours . . . sometimes people are surprised by their policies—they're not covered for what they thought. . . . I'm stuck in the middle. . . . I didn't sell them their insurance—I'm just there when they need it—to make the claim . . . sometimes I feel like I'm the bad guy. . . . I'm just there to clean up the mess.

Despite his impotence in the face of their claims, Noah continues to dictate the criteria for his victims' return to the world, keeping everyone under one roof where he can observe and guide them, deciding in advance how their claims will be read. As Noah tells Arianne: "It helps also if you have a plan—it makes things a lot clearer." However, the plan Noah outlines for his clients is *his* plan, it is the story *he* yearns to conclude. It is imperative for Noah that he be in charge of the order that displaces the catastrophe. Placing himself at the mouth of chaos and itemizing the destruction, holding people captive, Noah feels in control of people's lives and of their insured textual narrations, and, by extension, in control of the chaos that reigns in the absent text he calls home.

This is even extended to his own home. When Noah and Hera's home is threatened and ultimately destroyed by Babba and Mimi's violent narrative, Noah's position as an adjuster falters. Suddenly, he is faced with the realization that it is insecurity he adjusts, not security. With his hand held out to the fire, in shock, Noah simply watches as his home burns to the ground, faced with the realization that the ground no longer carries the illusion of safety and coherence. Charred, the ground is exposed as the misplaced emblem of a modern homesick tradition that gapes in horror at the prospect that the philosopher—or, in this case, the adjuster—will not be able to protect the elusive discourse of the home as the basis for thinking about exclusionary space-time relations. Egoyan's film thus counters the notion that the home can be rendered safe through a tightening of practices that secure its foundations, reminding us that it is only when the home is in-secured, rendered transient and transitory, that it escapes the metaphysics of security. As in *Fugitive Pieces,* we are warned by the fire that any notion of habitation is fragile.

Securing the Public: Un-Homely Bodies

The ruins of the home bring to the fore not only a different reading of the political, but also a recalcitrant body that resists the narrative of the enclosure. The recalcitrant body is not a homogenous dweller. The recalcitrant body emerges in the interstices of the state, the home, and the nation, residing at its limits, calling forth the necessity to retheorize the political according to the bodies that remain outside the bounded limits of what is ordinarily thought of as "politics." Among these contestatory bodies, we have those who actively seek to rewrite their homelessness in the world, such as Jacob and Ben; those who do not seek coherence, such as Hera; and those who are never invited into the fold at all, such as the homeless who survive and live on the fringes in Bruce Beresford's *The Fringe Dwellers.* These are the bodies that rewrite the political by accommodating themselves outside the normative structures of containment, refusing to subscribe to the biopolitical imperatives of their time.

Such recalcitrant bodies provide us with an opportunity not only to theorize unhomed spaces and bodies, but also to engage critically with the discourse of security at the level of the body of the nation. The dichotomy of the homed and the homeless is one that not only sustains the coherence of the nation-state, but also one that perpetuates the violence against the other in the name of the discourse of the home.

Samira Kawash argues that "[p]erhaps it is the visibility of the violence of security through which the homeless body emerges, rather than

the visibility of the homeless as such, that holds the promise for interrupting the exclusionary imagination of the public" (1998: 336). Kawash's
argument is centered on the juxtaposition between secured public space
and the insecure figure of the homeless who must be removed from the
city in order to resecure public space. The public, she claims, is always
defined "as against the visible, street-dwelling homeless," where "homelessness is not a problem that occurs within the public but a threat that
appears from elsewhere" (320). Consequently, the homeless body cannot
be properly identified. Rather, it is an "emergent and contingent condition that traverses and occludes identity" (324). The homeless is thus
recognized not in relation to homeless practices as such, but through the
public struggle to define and secure itself as distinct and whole.

If homelessness is articulated as the site of antagonism (the filthy
body as an embodiment of *homo sacer,* a body that can be killed but
not sacrificed) or as the failure of society to achieve closure, it must also
be acknowledged that the mechanisms that achieve this dichotomy of
the homed and the homeless are inexorably violent. Within the "war on
the homeless," it is therefore not surprising that the homeless body must
be eliminated at all costs, a response that we must learn to view as an
everyday practice in which the state of exception is evoked and the public
is restored: homelessness reveals politics as the exception.

The paradox is that the homeless continue to populate our streets, despite our efforts to displace them, both physically and conceptually, as a result of which the concept of public security itself is infiltrated with the discourse of homelessness. The public counters this state of contingency with
violence: the public is maintained by a level of security that is itself always
haunted by its insecure, and therefore violent, condition. Kawash writes:

> If the homeless appear to threaten public security, it is because public
> security is itself a threat—to the homeless and to others constitutively
> excluded from the public, who emerge as the casualties of the attempt to
> maintain an impossibly homogeneous and coherent image of the public.
> But public security is also a threat to itself, a perpetual state of violence in
> which the very acts of security contain their own undoing. (336)

It is not simply the home, then, that is at stake in the discourse of (in)security,
it is the very possibility of the public, where the public is constructed by
the sovereign who attempts to impose a national coherence in the hope
of eliminating those whose insurance claims cannot be filled.

Beresford's *The Fringe Dwellers* evokes this paradox in a haunting and
powerful manner. In his film, we alternate between the chaotic, often

muddy life of the "homeless" aborigines who live in shacks in a shanty-town at the edge of the city and the sanitized, quiet, and coherent world of the white "homed" citizens. In the white neighborhood, the sounds, images, and populations are controlled, true to the image of the public as that which is secured. In the shantytown, on the other hand, the bound-ary between the space of the self and the other is far less clear: shacks are missing doors, and families and friends cohabit space in an appar-ent refusal to adhere to any notion of the bounded family enclosure. Paradoxically, however, the discourse of homelessness does not seem to exist within the muddy river dwellings. It emerges, rather, from within the white public sphere, which decries the aboriginal other as the fester-ing wound on its otherwise pristine landscape. *The Fringe Dwellers* cap-tures this dichotomy between the public sphere (the white Australians) and the homeless (the aborigines) in a compelling manner in one scene where Trilby, an aboriginal daughter who is quickly learning the lan-guage of the white man, stands before the principal of the school in obei-sance after having slapped a white girl. When the principal refers to "her people," Trilby responds, "My people? Aren't we all Australians?"

The world of the white man is foregrounded through the figure of the home, and it is the possibility of entering this enclosed, apparently secure structure, that becomes Trilby's dream of emancipation from the homelessness she perceives around her. It is clear, however, through vari-ous camera shots that display the comfort of the aborigines within their chaotic surroundings, versus the often repressed and morally bankrupt images of the racist white public sphere, that Trilby's attempt to mark a passage from homelessness into the public sphere is invested with the normative features of the white man's language. Trilby's dream of the home "without relations, with a garden and new furniture" can be real-ized only by renouncing the rhizomatic quality of her family life, adher-ing instead to a coded and stratified language of inclusion and exclusion taught by the white man.

Trilby's dream will never be the dream of her people, especially not that of the older generation for whom the company of strangers and friends is what constitutes the possibility of accommodation. The camera demonstrates this beautifully in a lonely shot of Trilby, framed against a vast landscape with an immense sky, looking yearningly at a subur-ban house. The house is portrayed in a set of time-images, juxtaposing Trilby's face in the one shot and the deserted house in the following shot, resisting a complete adherence between Trilby and the house. This camera work foregrounds the situation within the home that takes place later in the film, when Trilby finally manages to move her family from the river to the suburbs. Although she briefly succeeds in displacing them, the contained suburban house never becomes their home in the sense Trilby desires it to be, for no matter where they live, theirs isn't the discourse of the homed.

In Beresford's film, to be homed implies living within a policed enclosure, as is evident when the police pay a visit to Trilby's family for disturbing the peace. Irrespective of the fact that they successfully escape from the shantytown along the river to rent a suburban house where they attempt to comply with the white man's spatial rituals, the aboriginal relationship to space cannot be subsumed into the white man's desire for order and maintenance of the uncontaminated public sphere. The aboriginal—according to the white law-enforcement officer and the meddling white neighbor—remains unruly, loud, different. Yet this difference is also what allows the aboriginal people to develop an ethic of encounter that is based on more than a territorially bounded enclosure. Trilby's dream of national coherence, her desire for a policed enclosure, is juxtaposed not first and foremost with the white man's apparently secure, fenced-in home, but with the vital closeness of a family that does not feel debased by what others perceive to be their homelessness. As Trilby's mother tells her when Trilby kills the baby she felt would have imprisoned her within the discourse of the homeless, "When I was a child, sometimes we had a house . . . plenty of times we just slept under the stars." A sense of worth is derived not from the bounded enclosure, but from the promise of love and acceptance.

Although Beresford's scenario is simplified and therefore negates the nuances of the white community, what his film implies is that often there is more music and closeness in the haphazard constructions that set the aborigines apart from the white people than in the ordered white public sphere. As Beresford aptly demonstrates, the violence often comes not from within "homeless" existence, but from the endangered public sphere who sense a trembling in their apparently secure edifices. In the following chapter, this dichotomy between the homed and the homeless is sustained, this time with a focus on the manner in which liberal policies such as multiculturalism and pluralism dictate the terms of belonging within the politics and policies of the nation-state. Through the films of Clement Virgo and Charles Binamé, I question the preordaining of the categories of acceptance into the public sphere, exploring the manner in which cultural enunciation can expose the public to violent practices of sequestering the racial and homeless other outside the domain of the political.

3. Where the Zulu Meets the Mohawk

National narratives in Canada are written to support the elusive notion of "Canadian identity." At the basis of the concept of "national identity" lies the idea that Canada (as long as we occlude the native presence) is a "nation of immigrants" whose separateness can be mapped onto their places of origin. "Canadian identity" thus depends on a mortgaged investment in the specter of identity, where identity is conceptualized as the voice of a singular culture. The idea of a culture that belongs to "us" remains rooted in an essentialism about who "we" are, underscoring a desire to remain rooted even as we speak of transnational and global phenomena, of boundary crossings and social movements. Within such a frame, any discussion of culture is inextricably bound by the limits of identity politics.

One response to the essentialization of identity through culture is to seek a multiplication of identities, whereby that which is essentialized is diverted by a subversion of the notion of identity itself. The stumbling block here, however, as Judith Butler warns, is that if identity remains the fundamental term of the analysis—where the multiplication of identity becomes the way in which plurality is figured—then it is likely the case that identity has not successfully been displaced as the focus of political reflection (1995: 439). With "identity" as the necessary presupposition, the frame is simply set on its side; thus, for instance, a surface reading might suggest that the racialization of culture is no longer what is at stake, even while this very racialization continues to prevent a critical renegotiation of the subject-position within the discourse of the nation-state. What results is a depoliticization of the issue of identity, which prevents a critical engagement with urgent issues such as racism, cultural difference, and democracy.

Identity, as the basis for national unity, relies on a simplified notion of culture that ignores the disjunctions and contradictions within historical and social (trans)formations: even in the name of cultural difference, it seems that what we expect from the term identity is cultural specificity. This assumption is rendered even more complex by the fact that neither identity, subject formation, nor culture exists in an ahistorical political realm. Rather, each of these terms is continuously subject to transformation and renegotiation:

> Identity as effect, as site, as dynamic, as simultaneously formed and formative is not equivalent to the notion of identity as *subject* and *ground*. Reading identities as they are situated and formed in relation to one another means moving beyond the heuristic requirement of identity itself. (Butler 1995: 446)

If we seek to critically reposition ourselves within the discourse of identity, we must realize that any reading of identity is always also a rereading of the possibility of identity itself. Identity as a reconceptualization of the limits of the national imaginary must always be that which is under construction, refigured and disfigured by the other. For such a deconstruction of identity to take place, the other must no longer be the accessible and identifiable measure of difference negotiated by the powerful center. Encounters must be challenging, and, as such, they must subvert the boundary formations that seek to prevent a traversal and translation of texts.

The porousness of boundaries must be addressed, be they the borders of our selves or the political boundaries that dictate our sense of belonging within the home and/as the nation. Through a renegotiation of the naturalized aspects of our cultural and political identities, we become aware that we have been taught that to understand who we are, we must be capable of appropriating a past as our own. To appropriate that past, we have been taught to conceive of history as the mechanism that guarantees both our identity and our culture. History, understood in these terms, is theorized as the construct that forms the basis for the narration of the national imaginary, operating through a translation of the past into the present with an emphasis on a certain order of narration that prioritizes the events of the center. In a renegotiation of identity practices, it becomes necessary to problematize such a reading of history.

The writing of history—historiography—forms the ground for the narration of the national imaginary. Problematizing history's naturalizing practices involves critically envisaging the practice of writing the past into the present. In so doing, we begin to question the historical separation imposed and policed between current time from past time, or the living from the dead, since, by implication, this fissure in time and space suggests that there exists an "other" time wherein interpretation is legitimized. The problem is not with the notion of interpretation as such, but with the assertion that "truth" belies interpretation. It is often the case in historiographic accounts, for instance, that the present is legitimized through a "truthful" reading of the past that attempts to silence resistances to that narrative in the present. This labor of writing that purposefully does not reveal the power structures inherent in the documentation of identity politics is a condition of historiography, which depends on the ongoing narration of a past that has been sutured.

If we understand historiography to be a selection of the past reorganized for linear representation in the present, it can be surmised that intelligibility written through the armor of history is articulated through a hierarchized relation with the other that relies on a certain organization of time and space. History "progresses" by selecting and defining this "other," basing its mastery of expression upon what the other keeps silent, either because the other is not "there" to respond or because the other has not been given the tools to speak. Historiography thus uses the past to articulate a law that inscribes (national) identity and unity, discarding any narrative remains that counter the homogeneity of the nation as bounded community. Rather than describing the silent practices that construct it, historiography effects a new distribution of already semanticized practices.

Through its performativity, historiography fills the lacuna, using this locus to divert the anguish of forgetting and transform it into a lesson. Within historiographic practices, narrativity finds its support precisely in what it hides: the dead of which it speaks become the vocabulary of a task to be undertaken. It is here that the ambivalence of historiography reveals itself. Historiography is both the condition of a process and the denial of an absence, acting in turn both as the discourse of the law and as an alibi. As Michel de Certeau writes: "*One and the other*—the occupant and the ghost—are put into play *within the same* text; present theory meets the unassimilable element returning from the past as an exteriority placed within *one* text" (1988: 346).

This chapter challenges the writing of history by questioning nationalizing practices wherein identity is fixed at the point of departure to the notion of belonging. I draw attention to the fact that any articulation of the national—even an enunciation that is critical of nationalizing practices—undoubtedly upholds within its terminology the residue of a historical tradition that denies the very possibility of narrative transgression. This paradox comes to the fore through a reading of Clement Virgo's *Rude*, which, as a cinematic event, has a tendency to resort to the current discourse of race rather than to extend beyond it. As I argue with respect to Virgo's film, such a borrowing of terminology is inevitable. More important than policing this sharing of terms, it is necessary that we become aware of the ways in which we uphold vocabularies that counter our practices of political emancipation. This involves critically envisaging terms such as identity, community, race, and ethnicity. In this chapter, I shall turn to Clement Virgo's *Rude* and Charles Binamé's *Eldorado* to demonstrate a cinematic challenge to nationalizing identity politics. Foregrounding the complexities of race and migration, these films are attentive to the fact that within "identity politics" resides the forgotten story of difference's un-utterability.

Poetic Disturbances and Encounters of Difference

The legend of El Dorado is a beguiling story that caught the imagination of the conquistadores, luring hundreds into desperate expeditions. In El Dorado, so the legend runs, nature showered her gifts more lavishly than on any other region of the world. The results were stupendous: around the Caribbean were said to be rich mines, ancient civilizations of great wisdom, vast plantations under balmy skies, and an unopened Pandora's box of trade and commerce. Charles Binamé's film *Eldorado* (Canada 1995) reflects with an ironic twist the elusive quest for El Dorado by drawing our attention to the manner in which the history of territories is written. In the case of Canada, the writing of the nation involves conflating identity and territory in the production of the "perfect home"— an El Dorado of sorts—replete with natural resources, a strong economy, and a diversity of peoples. Binamé's reference to El Dorado thus links the deployment of space (the sublation of identity into territory) to time (the writing of the history of the nation).

By critically engaging with the exclusive politics of the nation and its narratives of identity, we depart from the claustrophobic agendas of cultural nationalism. *Eldorado* is a case in point. The foregrounding of the failed quest for El Dorado in Binamé's film emphasizes the fact that adorning the nation with the myth of perfection results in rendering the nation stagnant, thus depoliticizing the nation's cultural vocabularies of resistance. The pursuit of a perfect coherence can result only in the failure to trace new maps. As exemplified by *Eldorado*, "Canadian cinema" today represents a negation of utopic renderings of territory through a multilayered shifting of the cultural and political boundaries of the nation. In *Eldorado,* we witness a complex questioning of the conflation between territory and identity, as well as an attentiveness to the politics of language, religion, race, and ethnicity. *Eldorado* can be read as a counternarrative to the nation that openly negates all myths of cohesion, foregrounding instead a continual displacement between the presumed secure categories of self and other, white and black, homed and homeless, national citizen and immigrant.

This chapter focuses on the troubling effects of the discourse of El Dorado in Canadian cultural politics. I expose the ways in which Canadian cross-cultural cinema undermines and subverts a liberal pluralist discourse of El Dorado. To illustrate this shift within Canadian cinema, I undertake an unusual task: I place, side by side, Binamé's *Eldorado* and Virgo's *Rude* (Canada 1995), the first a Francophone film from Montreal, the second an Anglophone film from Toronto. While this may at first not seem out of the ordinary, what makes this reading potentially challenging, in a Canadian context, is its crossing of provincial and ideological borders. Very rarely in Canada are Quebec films discussed alongside films spawning from the rest of Canada, and such a joining is especially seldom undertaken in the case of "black" and "white" films.

If we are to conceptualize a shift in the nationalizing politics of Canadian cinema, I believe it necessary to break down culturally (and provincially) exclusive boundaries. Hence my rapprochement of the two films. Reading *Eldorado* and *Rude* together, I explore the effects of a politics of El Dorado on Canadian cinema in a marked refusal to become assimilated within the divisive cultural and provincial politics of the nation. This, in turn, provides access to an unusual way, within Canadian cultural politics, of engaging with and recasting important political issues such as racism, multiculturalism, and pluralism.[1]

Placing *Rude* and *Eldorado* side by side, I explore the facets within each film that set their images and stories apart from those of the dominant cultural narratives of the nation-state. I complicate the notion of narration by suggesting that official stories can be subverted by potentially divisive cultural enunciations. Official stories are articulated in relation to the rights and privileges of the national individual, where the status of the individual is determined according to the parameters of "belonging" within the political vocabulary of the nation-state. What interests me with respect to *Rude* and *Eldorado* are the ways in which the films subvert the dominant narratives of the nation, proposing strands of resistant articulation. Both films alert us to the fact that, since no narrative can ever be completely static or monolithic, even official narratives are subject to change in response to contending stories of the nation and of the individual. Both *Rude* and *Eldorado* demonstrate how storytelling can involve a process of rehistoricization that can be used as a critical tool for a retheorization of terms such as "identity" that give rise to the presumption of national unity.

Rude and *Eldorado* are eerily similar despite that there is little or no reason to believe they shared in the process of production, as there is, historically, little dialogue between "Quebec" and "Canadian" cinema. Not only do their narratives in many ways congeal—they are both films narrated by deejays that tell the story of the homeless and the disenfranchised— the films also correspond in their desire to create a dissonant narration through an emphasis on the Deleuzian time-image. In addition, both films offer a fragmented view of the inner city, *Eldorado* in Montreal and *Rude* in Toronto, with a strong emphasis on disjunctive camera work and the use of red, yellow, and blue to depict states of terror, belonging, and difference. My purpose here, however, is not to seek documented "proof" of their similarity, but to explore the consequences, both political and aesthetic, of a critical rapprochement of two films, one depicting the black inner city of Toronto, the other foregrounding the desperate homelessness of the Montreal night world.

The cultural, understood as an enunciation that potentially challenges the linear representation of time and space, can act as a harbinger of the demise of the normative codes of nationalist thought. As *Rude* and *Eldorado* demonstrate, cultural texts do not necessarily depend on the metaphysical groundwork of identity politics through which a certain narration of history is guaranteed. In *Rude* and *Eldorado*, cultural difference alerts us not to the stability of our predetermined cultural identities and the discourses that emanate from these nationalist swamplands. Rather, cultural difference is theorized as the possibility of an enunciation that refuses to celebrate the great continuities of the invented past, including seamless narratives of progress. *Rude* and *Eldorado* draw from a network of genealogies, thereby intervening in the way discourses of modernity structure their objects of knowledge.

A critical emphasis on the role of historiography within the negotiations of cultural politics results in a renewed space of cultural translation where culture can be envisaged both as the enunciation of the social imaginary and as that which "[grafts] the voices of the indentured, the displaced, the nameless, onto an agency of utterance" (Bhabha 1995: 52). In these cases, culture decentralizes historiographic narrations, alerting us to the exclusionary manner in which identities are constituted. This occurs in both *Rude* and *Eldorado,* where we witness a resistance to the dominant codes of cultural belonging. In both films, identity emerges as the historicization of the subject-in-progress, where history bears the contingency of a Foucauldian genealogy, understood not as a stable ground but as a parchment on which the accidents, horrors, delights, and chance encounters of life are imprinted.

Black Canada

Clement Virgo's *Rude* takes us on a journey through black Canada. This is not a simple proposition. In Canada, blackness functions as the signifier of disappearance—that which is always out of sight, out of history, and out of circulation. By placing blackness "elsewhere," Canadian history has and continues to obfuscate the black presence in Canada, which dates as far back as the sixteenth century, with the arrival of Jacques Cartier. The popular myth that all blacks in Canada are part of a recent migration not only reinforces the well-established French-English duality inherent in the narrative of the "founding fathers" of Canada, but also serves as a reminder of the ways in which history functions as a revisionist practice that reinforces the power of the hegemony. For the history of blacks in Canada is not only a long one, but one fraught with pain and subjugation. According to official histories, it must therefore be forgotten, since, if rendered central to the narratives of "Canadian history," blackness in Canada would divert attention from the white narrative of the "founding fathers." This would alert us to the fact that Canada's legacy was never purely bicultural.

Part of the forgotten history of blackness in Canada is the story of slavery, which was sanctioned roughly between 1680 and 1820, during which period thousands of slaves were held in the urban centers of Halifax and Montreal. As Dorothy Williams attests:

> In legislation passed to encourage immigration to British North America, one article specifically allowed the importation of "negroes," household furniture, utensils of husbandry or clothing. The same law discouraged the immigration of free Blacks. (1992: 127)

In addition, contrary to popular belief, the first underground railroad between the United States and Canada existed not for the emancipation of African-American slaves, but to free slaves held on Canadian territory: between 1788 and 1792, slaves fled from the Canadian provinces to the free northern American states.

A brief foregrounding of this lapsed history is necessary, not to dwell on slavery in Canada as such, but to highlight the ways in which histories are written. The obfuscation of slavery in Canada alerts us to the ways in which blackness in Canada as a historical presence is a threatening invasion into the national imagination. The national imagination would prefer to recognize blackness as a liberal instance of multicultural diversity rather than integrate blackness within the nation's problematic foundation(s). As Rinaldo Walcott writes:

> In a Canadian context, writing blackness is a scary scenario: we are an absented presence always under erasure. Located between the US and the Caribbean, Canadian blackness is a bubbling brew of desires from elsewhere, disappointments in the nation and the pleasures of exile—even for those who have resided here for many generations. (1997: xiii)

In Canada, this is complicated by a stubborn insistence on the elusive (white) national identity, which is based on the dualistic French-English model. This version of Canadian history emphasizes the narrative of Canada as a generous land open to immigrants (where the other is welcome on *our* soil).

The study of blackness in Canada—where blackness as a signifier exceeds the categories of both the biological and the ethnic—is imperative as part of an exploration of the effects of white supremacy[2] on blacks in the diaspora. It can also be the starting point for a necessary dialogue concerning national policies in Canada such as multiculturalism, which "support identity politics and limit political imaginations and possibilities" (Walcott 1997: 23). For while black experiences necessarily involve a diasporic element, all theorizations of diaspora must also be attentive to national and other forms of institutionalized power. Whether it be to foreground the obfuscation of First Nations and blackness from Canadian history books or to highlight current efforts to depoliticize issues such as multiculturalism, we must attend to the mechanisms that sanctify the disenfranchisement of large groups of people in Canada.[3]

Virgo's *Rude* is a complex film from which to begin such a discussion, not least because of Walcott's disparaging comments concerning the film. Narrated by a sultry Jamaican-accented voice that speaks over three fragmented black inner-city Toronto narratives (one of a woman coming to terms with an abortion, one of a black man facing his homosexuality, and one of a drug dealer recently out of jail), *Rude* is an important introduction to blackness in Canada.[4] Due to the underrepresentation of blackness in Canada, however, *Rude* has a lot of ground to cover, and, according to Walcott, comes up terribly short. I turn first to Walcott's reading of *Rude* to set the stage for a subsequent reading of *Rude* from a perspective that, although always in dialogue with Walcott's observations, perhaps demands less from the film and, as a result, sees, within the film's narrative, the possibilities of a rich and visually stimulating postnational geography of race.

Walcott places *Rude* in the tradition of the depoliticized American hood film. He argues that the politics of place are not adequately addressed in *Rude,* and thus the politics of blackness in Canada are not theorized. One consequence of such a depoliticized rendition of place, according to Walcott, is that Rude, the deejay in the film, is prevented from embodying her political persona, since her metaphoric and literal immobility contain her within the apolitical realm of blackness in Canada. A moralizing conservative politic is the result of this predictable rendition of the black body, since, "when [folks] encounter Virgo's cinematic representations they're not incited to trouble the body" (1997: 69).

Another of the important issues avoided by *Rude,* according to Walcott, is the negotiation of blacks *in* Canada, where there continues to be a silencing of the ways in which the immigration of nonwhites disrupts the imaginary of the homogeneous nation-state. Walcott would like to see represented in *Rude* the manner in which immigrants render visible the denial of otherness within a national imaginary that seeks to produce and naturalize racial singularity at its foundation. Walcott thus locates *Rude* as a cultural event that upholds the official multicultural policy in Canada, which claims that, even as they become Canadian citizens, all others can and must be identified by their attachments to *another* nation-state:

> Because community is understood as the public qualities of language, "culture," and ethnicity, official multicultural policies at both the federal and provincial level support this idea through a discourse of heritage—in Canada "heritage" always means *having hailed from somewhere else.* (1997: 78)

According to Walcott, the film perpetuates the notion that the colonizing French and English must remain textually intact as "real" Canadians, while legislation is needed to imagine other folks as Canadian; consequently, blackness remains an absented presence (a visible invisibility) in the imagined community and landscape of Canada.

Because *Rude* fails to address these important issues, Walcott holds *Rude* responsible for perpetuating a depoliticization of black images that inevitably reinforces and reinscribes white supremacy. A more generous reading might provisionally forgive Virgo for this political lapse since

"Canada" has collectively made few, if any, revolutionary interventions in the area of race and representation. Virgo has little to work with in the construction of alternative images of blackness in Canada, where the dominance over the image has and continues to be the tool of a white supremacy that recognizes that control over images is central to the maintenance of any system of racial domination. Hence, it is hardly surprising that Virgo resorts to images of blackness created by the dominant cultural narratives of the nation-state. On the other hand, Walcott's position is also extremely important: if we are to reenvision blackness, we must do so through the proliferation of images of blackness that contest those perpetuated by white-supremacist culture.

Walcott calls for the transformation of the *image* of blackness, whereby "black Canadian," as both name and metaphor, would disrupt the ethnic claim to blackness as a sign of otherness and disappearance, recasting blackness not only as visible but as performative. *Rude* is a black-Canadian film, where "black Canadian" continues to be a largely unchallenged concept. In my reading of *Rude,* I suggest that what is not represented in the image and text of *Rude* is the impossibility for blackness to "be at home" in Canada. What I attempt to unveil in my reading of *Rude* are the subtle ways in which blackness in Canada is both represented and transformed. In this regard, my reading is more generous than Walcott's, since what I seek are the small steps made by visual culture toward the transformation of images of blackness, of black people, of our ways of looking and our ways of being seen.

The paradox of Canadian multicultural policy and "national identity" is symbolized in the desire to make contact with the Other, even as we wish the boundaries of self and other to remain intact. This commodification of difference, observed through "the West's fascination with the primitive [that] has to do with its own crisis of identity, with its own need to clearly demarcate subject and object even while flirting with other ways of experiencing the universe" (Torgovnick in hooks 1992: 22), promotes paradigms of consumption, wherein whatever difference the other inhabits is eradicated. Such consumer cannibalism not only displaces the other but denies the significance of that other's history through a process of decontextualization. Hence, "[w]hite racism, imperialism, and sexist domination prevail by courageous consumption. It is by eating the Other . . . that one asserts power and knowledge" (hooks 1992: 36).

The contradictory longing both to possess and excrete the other without digesting the problematic effects of such a consumption reinforces a negation of the other as a historical subject-in-process, rendering the other a victim of imitation, a two-dimensional object in a sea of whiteness. This absence of recognition of the other as a reflection of horrific white practices renders the other faceless among face-to-face encounters of sameness. White supremacy is another name for the horror of the cannibalistic gaze:

[A]ll blacks in the West stand between (at least) two great cultural assemblages, both of which have mutated through the course of the modern world that formed them and assumed new configurations. At present, they remain locked symbiotically in an antagonistic relationship marked out by the symbolism of colours which adds to the conspicuous cultural power of their central Manichean dynamic—black and white. These colours support a special rhetoric that has grown to be associated with a language of nationality and national belonging as well as the languages of "race" and ethnic identity. (Gilroy 1993: 1–2)

The reductive understanding of culture that results from such a commodification of blackness in the name of racial (in)visibility forms the substance of the kind of racial politics Walcott addresses in his reading of *Rude,* a politics entangled in the history of the idea of culture in the modern West. What Walcott demands first and foremost of black Canadian cinema is not a textual depiction of place so much as a renunciation of modernity's assertion that there is no place for blackness in the modern world. For as Paul Gilroy points out, modernity's trajectory is anything but white and linear: modernity exposes at various junctures the performance of resistant black narratives.

Within a politics of the transfiguration of modernity through black poetics, race functions not as a transhistorical discourse grounded in biology, but as a discursive logic through which the binary coding of race is dependent on the meanings it grants relationships of power and representation. Culture—whether in the form of poetry, music, cinema, literature, visual art, or dance—no longer simply constitutes the terrain for producing (racial) identity and coded subjects. Rather, culture functions as the vehicle for a different kind of speech that critically reenvisages the past while it reclaims the present. Identifications, not identities, are central to the process of transfiguration: identification calls for a political struggle that is always in process, imagining the end of the essentialized black subject, and with it the end of an essentialist conception of the black experience.

A politics of transfiguration amounts to a reworking of modernity's master narratives. The modern itself becomes the locus of a complicated and differentiated line of struggle between those who have been and continue to be identified as the "racialized Other" on the one hand, and those who take part in the cultural nationalist racism that is the backlash against this repudiation of history as a linear discourse of exclusion. As Patricia Williams warns,

> [I]f you open yourself to the politics of cultural difference, there is no safety in terminology.... After all, it is because their history and ours is so deeply and profoundly and inextricably intertwined that racism exists. For, otherwise, how could they keep us apart? (1998: 299)

Stranger Than the State

Race as a construct is never peripheral to the discourse of the nation. Race renders the exclusionary discourse of the nation possible, solidifying and edifying the borders of the nation-state through the delineation between who is "at home" and who comes from elsewhere. Often, race signifies the "elsewhere." This "elsewhere" is defined and coveted by the white supremacy either covertly in the name of such pluralist liberal discourses as multiculturalism or overtly in the blatantly racist discourses that form the vocabulary of nationalism. A critical exploration of the effects of race must therefore involve an encounter with the politics of white supremacy. One of the ways of confronting the nationalizing politics of white supremacy is by exploring the position of the stranger within the discourse of the nation-state.

Within the vocabulary of the nation, the figure of the stranger is often contrasted with the bounded (white) self, bounded, as it were, within the nation-state as "home" and within the self's own cohesive imaginary. To explicate this correlation between race and nationalism, I draw an analogy between the stranger as racial other and the bounded self. I do this through an exploration of the politics of migration. Within the politics of migration, the immigrant has no choice but to remain on the limits of the nation, from whence he or she is included only as a cannibalized other. While there is certainly an abyss between the notion of the stranger as the other and the migrant or refugee who is forced to secede his or her sense of home due to political, racial, or economic conditions, I argue that each of us, at one time or another, must come face-to-face with our own difference, a difference that prevents us—however provisionally—from comfortably partaking in the national imaginary that condemns, segregates, and ultimately excludes all strangeness from the state.

The stranger, as other to the concept of bounded space and national subjectivity, stands at the border between inclusion and exclusion. This border, at the cusp of which the stranger either accedes to or contests the nation, is continuously guarded, reinforced, destroyed, claimed, and reclaimed. The border encourages a dynamic relationship whereby the stranger is both encouraged to remain a subject-in-process and reminded that he or she must endure the pain of being neither here nor there. At some level, the border symbolizes the impossibility of integration and assimilation while holding captive the dream of territorial integrity, reminding us that, as strangers, we find ourselves in transition, incapable of delineating clearly the line between here and there, self and other.

The border both ensures the coherence of the center and disrupts it. As a space of rupture, the border can be conceptualized as an emergent space for radical multiculturalism, but only if the border is understood as a "space where one can find an overlay of codes, a multiplicity of culturally inscribed subject positions, a displacement of normative reference codes, and a polyvalent assemblage of new cultural meanings" (MacLaren 1994: 65). However, a radical politics of polyvocality will emerge from such border identities only as long as we refrain from subsuming border identities within either analytical or dialectic logic, locating the border instead as a deterritorialization of signification in a postnationalist cultural space. For borders are also demarcations that strictly police self and other, citizen and noncitizen. Borders are linguistic, spatial, ideological, and geographical sites that stipulate the manner in which otherness is maintained and reproduced.

For border identities to reflect a radical multiculturalism, the stranger or racial other must be capable of turning the border inside out by reworking the official narratives that render the border the policed and heavily guarded marker between the nation and its outside. When the homeless, exiled stranger attempts to move beyond the nationalizing discourse of the border, he or she must create his or her precarious and fragile space of habitation outside the parameters of the fissure that presides between inside and outside. The stranger achieves such a rearticulation of border practices through a reconceptualizing of what it means to "belong," thereby creating a discourse through which he or she can begin to house him- or herself that diverges from the nation's official narratives of inclusion and exclusion. Such a resituating of the politics of belonging can be articulated through storytelling. Narration in such cases becomes the nomadic home, a tenuous place of homelessness where *l'étrangeté*— interpreted as strangeness, estrangement, alienation, foreignness, and the uncanny—takes up residence.

Because the stranger is linked to homelessness, he or she cannot partake in the nation's narrative of the home. As a result, the stranger must compose a story of belonging that escapes the vocabulary of confinement that ensures that the homed be immediately distinguishable from the homeless. This results in a tenuous relationship to "home." Alienation from the "security" of the territorial imaginary that undergirds the discourse of the nation-state ensues. Such a sense of alienation is not always welcome, even among those who would seek a departure from the racist exclusions perpetuated by the discourse of home within the nation-state. "Would life in this renovated house mean eternal homelessness?" Toni Morrison asks (1998: 4). In response to Morrison, one might suggest that the homelessness the stranger's presence reveals need not mean the impossibility of "being at home" altogether. Rather than signifying a placelessness in the world, this state of homelessness might act instead as a political marker, as it does for Jacob in *Fugitive Pieces*. Homelessness, understood as a renunciation of the discourse of the nation-state, would not necessarily prevent us from feeling "situated" or "accommodated."

The stranger's language of nonadherence displaces not the notion of home as such. It alerts us, rather, to the fact that the home exists as a stable entity only for the "citizen,"[5] who, without questioning his or her eligibility, lodges him- or herself within the mortgaged enclosure of the home, confident of his or her position within the exclusive citizen/nation/state triad. As a beacon who stands in opposition to the figure of the homed citizen, the stranger seeks not to render all peoples outside the nation homeless, but to displace the notion of "the same" *(le même)* that is central to the concept of national identity so dear to the nation-state's organization and dominion of space.

Abdul JanMohamed argues that

> if the border is the site of infinite regression and if the border subject is the site on which the group defines its identity, then the ruptured body of that subject becomes the text on which the structure of the group's identity is written in inverted form—the information of the group is inscribed on the body of the border subject. (1992: 115)

The center requires the border subject to ensure its coherence. The nation-state creates the fiction of the border to strengthen its official narratives of inclusion and exclusion. Focusing on the ways in which borders are at once policed by the state, internal functions of the state, and sites of resistance to the state, the task of the racial other as stranger is to illuminate the ontological determinism of international state-centered politics. Considered at heart to be neither a co-national nor a national, the stranger as racial other, migrant, or refugee is distinguished from the citizen insofar as he or she inhabits the placelessness of estrangement located between nations.

The citizen empowers and is empowered by the state. It is under these conditions that the citizen claims allegiance to the nation-state and in return is protected by the state within the clearly demarcated sovereign national territory. Within this citizen/nation/state triad, the stranger has no protection, neither in terms of the state's powerful security machine nor with respect to the racism at the core of the state's sustaining concept of sovereignty. Cast outside the citizen/nation/state triad, the stranger is forgotten as the other for whom the vocabulary of the nation-state remains lacking. The stranger is the one for whom the state has no meaning—as well as the one who means nothing to the state—since he or she lacks affinity with (and is excluded from) the national community as the other the nation must deny in order to identify itself as coherent.

In an imagined community that is composed of mutually exclusive, territorially bounded spaces and subjects, the stranger is conceptualized as an aberration of the proper citizen, belonging nowhere. From this standpoint, the stranger has a number of options, one of which is to

> inscribe, stabilize and render effective a certain figure of the citizen that the modern state would represent and on the basis of which the modern state would claim to effect its sovereignty, its powers, and indeed its right to rule over a territorial inside. (Soguk 1999: 14)

However, assuming such a subject-position is difficult for the stranger as long as the nation-state continues to assert itself in the name of a liberal pluralist white supremacy. Even if it could be achieved, it would place the stranger in a relation of acquiescence with respect to the racist discourse of territorial sovereignty. In addition, even in this scenario, the stranger or racial other's subjectivity would continue to be inscribed negatively as lack or aberrance. A more radical but more appropriate choice is to envisage the presence of the stranger—as stranger than the state—as a necessary disruption to the political project of the nation-state.

As a disruption to the discourse of the state's exclusivity, the stranger as stranger than the state incites us to retheorize both the discourse of the other as stranger, refugee, or migrant and the discourse of state sovereignty. In so doing, we become aware of the ways in which the stranger is instrumental to the enabling of a certain version of citizenry based on the bounded subjectivities, relations, and institutions of the modern territorial state. As a mechanism of resistance to the nation-state, the stranger as racial other perpetuates a crisis of representation: the stranger exposes the technologies of governance of the nation-state. The stranger thus alerts us to the fact that the ontology of the nation-state depends on the other to fulfill itself as the promise of a whole and essential entity.

Ultimately, the stranger betrays the racism that is at the heart of the vocabulary of the nation. The stranger is a radical agent for the inception of a polyvocality that transgresses the exclusionary discourse of the nation-state. Because it is vocabulary that is at stake, language can become the instrument of political negotiation for the stranger. In such cases, language becomes a migrating home that renews itself endlessly. Through the stranger's rearticulation of what it means to be at home and to exist on the border, the stranger is capable of initiating a fissure in the imaginary of the nation from which he or she is excluded. One of the ways in which such a counterwriting is undertaken is through cultural representations. It is with such a re-vision of the language of the national imaginary in mind that I now turn to the films of Clement Virgo and Charles Binamé.

Rude and Eldorado

Charles Binamé's Eldorado and Clement Virgo's Rude reflect the nationalist and racist violence inherent in the pursuit of the kind of utopia evoked in the myth of El Dorado and pursued in the guise of "Canadian identity." Despite that they hail from two distinct parts of Canada (Montreal and Toronto), and foreground complex and divergent cultures, races, and ethnicities (mainly French Canadian in Eldorado and black Canadian in Rude), both films explore in an eerily complementary manner the complexity of multiethnic inner-city cultures through an emphasis on the often painful and difficult practice of everyday life in a racist, classist, nationalist world. Narrated by deejays whose voices leave gashes in the night, whose words mark the lives of those who listen to them, linking these listeners to one another through their pain and ecstasy, neither Eldorado nor Rude is a heroic journey toward magic, golden cities. Rather, Eldorado and Rude are stories that transgress the nation's pretense of homogeneity by exploring the underground and often forgotten world of longing in Canadian cities, crossing a territory that stretches "from the land of the Zulu Zulu all the way to the land of the Mohawk" where "for the next two nights we steal Babylon's airwaves and reevaluate their immigration policy."[6]

A dialogic reading of the two films might be considered problematic due to the divergent qualities of the films, including their locations and racial agendas. It is rare, as I mentioned earlier, in Canada that a Quebec film stands beside one made in Toronto, and even more uncommon for a white film to be discussed in light of a black one. I set the two films side by side partly to begin to break down such essentializing borders—where the border as an instantiation of dominant cultural politics attempts to naturalize all notions of culture, race, and ethnicity by creating and per- petrating the assumption that what these films stand for is uniquely their "blackness," "whiteness," "Frenchness," etc.—and partly because such a juxtaposition allows us to begin to conceptualize the ways in which I believe the films point to an altered understanding of the multicultural through a critical renegotiation of immigration policies in Canada. To clarify this position, I draw from Deleuze's theory of the direct time- image. Through the time-image, I focus on the ways in which the images in both films offer a disjunctive sense of time and narration that disrupts the linear trajectory of the imaginary of the nation.

"Nowadays," writes Nevzat Soguk, "to study immigration or refugee- ism is inescapably to study issues of democracy, citizenship and nationali- ty" (1999: 208). Immigrant subjectivities are paradoxical: they alert us to the possibility of radical changes in various sites of territorial governance while revealing themselves as vulnerable, both literally and metaphori- cally, to the vocabularies of race, ethnicity, religion, and culture. Any activity centered on the construction of the noncitizen, the stranger, the migrant, or the refugee is always also implicated in the construction of a citizen who is organized into a community with its peculiar strategies, hierarchies, and bounded territories. On the one hand, then, the pres- ence of the racialized other testifies to the imagined completeness of the category of citizen. On the other hand, the stranger's presence reveals an aberrance within the subject-position of the citizen. Consequently, as the immigrant or racialized other attempts to move into the position of the citizen, he or she is potentially cast as the one who seeks to truncate the "inside" of the nation, thus standing in the way of the maintenance of a viable community based on the notion of cooperation and solidarity in the democratic organization of the polity. These effects breed a renewal of normative identity practices that recognize as rational, moral, and universal the hegemony firmly implanted in the institutions of the "liber- ating" territorial democracy practiced in the name of the nation-state.

In contrast to such a "liberating" democratic concept of immigration based on a white-supremacist understanding of multiculturalism, the immigration policy designed by Rude ("for the next two nights we steal

Babylon's airwaves and reevaluate their immigration policy") and explored throughout both *Rude* and *Eldorado* is disjunctive and complex, reflecting the forgotten histories of the unrepresented and the voiceless gasps of the disenfranchised. This counternational immigration policy emanates from the loud and pulsating music, can be heard in the moans of sexual intercourse, is pumped into the blood of heroin addicts. It challenges the limits of identity politics, questioning the power structures that open and close doors, that bend boundaries and expand walls. This immigration policy is not based on a normative sense of identity, on clear lines that differentiate between white and black, between straight and gay, between young and old, Francophone and Anglophone.

This immigration policy is spectral, revealing a politics that is always, in Derrida's words, "a politics of memory, of inheritance, and of generations" (1994: 4). It troubles sovereignty's claim on the other as "non-citizen," introducing the possibility of an other whose allegiance is bound not to the nation's strictures, an other whose writing exceeds the nation. *Rude* and *Eldorado* confront liberal pluralist immigration policies that mirror and sustain the often troubling discourse of multiculturalism, suggesting that these policies are symptoms of the silencing discourse of historiography. Of course, the liberal pluralist immigration policies about which *Rude* and *Eldorado* are critical are neither all-exclusive nor all-inclusive. In fact, these liberal pluralist policies often even encourage the other to speak and be heard. But they do so through a narrative of pluralism that is celebrated and sustained by the discourse of the nation-state, rather than one of pluralization, which exceeds the imaginary of the nation, a distinction that is elaborated below.

Both *Eldorado* and *Rude* open onto darkly lit city nights. The deejays' voices punctuate the darkness:

> The young man gets into his car, the young woman leaves her place, five girls enter a bar, the bus takes off, the bouncer frowns, *the beat is on,* the light screeches, the young man weeps, the old lady dies, the man hits, his lover falls, the neighbor calls, the cop fires, the window breaks, and then she kisses him, she licks him, and he smiles—good evening, I'm Gaspard—and welcome to *Exterior Night,*

drawls Gaspard/Lloyd's voice in *Eldorado,* setting the stage for the nights to follow. Rude does not introduce herself. Not yet. Inviting callers to engage in verbal intercourse with her over the Easter weekend, Rude summons the lion of Judea and sets him loose on the streets of Toronto's inner city, speaking to those who have the courage to listen: "It's Easter

weekend, and like every year this time I come to you via the last neighborhood in the world—Pirate Radio."

Summoning their listeners, *Eldorado*'s and *Rude*'s narratives are propelled via sound waves that echo with murmurs of death and resurrection, sex and destruction, ghosts past and present. *Eldorado* and *Rude* tell
contradictory stories of wrath and crime, of voices that should, according to the policing of the other, be silenced and banned. "If you have a
tale to tell in this scene of death, resurrection, and rebirth, I'm all ears,"
taunts Rude. The voices that spear *Eldorado* and *Rude* resonate to the
mayhem which is the inner city, creating a rhythm that calms and infuri-
ates, that speaks to the disenfranchised: "And then we see a redhead walk
by, a blond woman, a black woman, a junkie, a pierced woman, a broken
woman, a cripple, a normal woman, a lesbian," Gaspard's voice drones,
"the specimens of fifty-five countries of refugees who have come to our
city tonight to celebrate with the lost souls who take their solitude to be
their freedom." The deejays' voices do not draw a separation between inclusion and exclusion. Rather, through a violent dissonance that cannot
be silenced, they speak the troubling noise of recurrence, of intimacy, of
degeneration and experience.

Filmed from rooftops, *Eldorado* exposes a Montreal that is enveloped
in an uncertain vertigo. *Rude*'s Toronto is shown fleetingly, chaotically,
with Luke's painted wall[7] as the compass of the inner city: the locus of
creation and destruction. The cities are filmed mostly at night, the shots
moving quickly, disorienting the viewer even while leading the viewer
to the scene of the crime, to the voice, to the image. The crime is never
clearly enunciated. It remains the story of the other who does not and
cannot belong, the other who seeks an immigration policy that would
recruit him or her into the world of the living. Homeless characters
people the streets, shooting up, waiting for food, begging for alcohol and
sex. Even those who have homes are isolated, confused by the homelessness they feel despite the pretense of citizenship within which they live.
"All I want to do is go home. . . . All I want to do is come home," Luke
tells Jessica in *Rude*. After a year in jail, home for Luke is a return to his
wife and child. Yet at the same time, Luke's return "home" also implies a
return to the streets, to the only life he knows in a nation where the black
man still remains a "nigger."

In *Eldorado* and *Rude,* the attempt to negotiate the complexities of the
Unheimlich is in accordance with the exclusionary nature of the current
immigration policies in Canada. In *Eldorado,* this is apparent in the case
of Rita, who never feels "at home," not even when she is rescued from

the streets by Roxan, who believes that by housing Rita she will not only purge herself of her upper-class guilt, but will also be able to offer Rita— and, by extension, herself—the sense of belonging she lacks. If we locate Roxan's attempt to domesticate Rita as a version of a state-centered immigration policy, where the home is understood as a stand-in for the nation, we can better appreciate the ways in which all immigration policies remain exclusive, since they are, by implication, written in the vocabulary of the nation.

In *Eldorado*, Rita cannot abide by Roxan's house rules since she prefers to remain outside the discourse of the homed perpetuated by the discourse of the nation-state. Roxan, on the other hand, cannot envisage the possibility that homelessness might be the political voice she seeks and therefore cannot identify Rita's needs. Despite her generosity, Roxan solidifies the distinction between the stranger and the citizen by assuming that, as the citizen, she can prescribe to Rita what she needs to "belong." In so doing, Roxan continues to treat Rita as the other. Rita and Roxan therefore operate at cross-purposes: Roxan's attempt to house Rita has more to do with her desire to efface the specter of homelessness that haunts her otherwise secure edifice, while Rita's need is not to be homed, but to find accommodation within her homelessness.

In an attempt to undermine the preordained link between the state and the citizen, both films call into question the constructs that naturalize the citizen/nation/state triad that is the grounding feature of the nation-state's immigration policy. Developing such a language of resistance is a complex task, however, as demonstrated by the very real and troubling sense of dissociation and terror experienced by the characters in both films. Homelessness is visualized in *Rude* and *Eldorado* as the instantiation of a tenuous subjectivity-in-process, where what is sought is not coherence but the willingness to articulate the political in a manner adjacent to the politics of the nation. Homelessness is not a story with a beginning and an end, but an attempt to begin a dialogue that speaks of a different way of encountering time as incoherence and space as disjunction that would inaugurate a rewriting of the narratives of racism and national inclusion that trouble the home/land.

The injunction to deconstruct existing policies of immigration to enunciate what it means to be at home in the nation is expressed in both films through a variety of techniques that involve the manner in which the image renders the narrative unstable. Deleuze's concept of the direct time-image is a useful way of encountering the manner in which Virgo and Binamé use the image in their films. The time-image refers to a rearticulation of the political through an envisioning of the dimensions of time as expressed through the image. With an emphasis on the direct time-image, *Eldorado* and *Rude* haunt the nation with characters that defy comprehension, inciting the boundaries of texts—be they historical, critical, literary, or filmic—to move beyond the parasitic frame of the nation.

To appreciate the ways in which the time-image in these films calls forth an alternative to the nation's institutions of immigration and multiculturalism, it is necessary to understand in more detail the manner in which the direct time-image functions. The Deleuzian time-image relies on the reversal of the subordination of time to movement. When time ceases to be derived from movement, time gives rise to "false movements." A "false continuity" results. When the image begins to tamper with time's linearity in a narrative that challenges dominant state-centered discourses, an unraveling of the nation's hierarchical systems of governance invariably follows, for the state apparatus relies on a linear historiography that depends on the continuity of both time and space.

What is specific to the time-image is the injunction "to make perceptible, to make visible, relationships of time which cannot be seen in the represented object and do not allow themselves to be reduced to the present" (Deleuze 1989: xii). Deleuze's concept of the time-image foregrounds the manner in which the image plunges into time rather than crossing space. This temporal structure that Deleuze calls the direct time-image moves beyond the accepted empirical succession of time we have come to know as past-present-future. Instead, the time-image coexists amid various distinct durations or levels of duration. Thus, a single event can belong to several levels of time. The sheets of time resist chronological order, inviting us to reconceptualize the Western obsession with rewriting the past in the image of the hegemonic present. Through the time-image, the past can no longer be thought simply as an invisible vehicle on which the present is written. This potentially destabilizes not only the historian's rendition of the past, but also the nation's narratives of identity in the present. Contrary to the movement-image, which is "the modulation of the object itself," and to the negotiation of a time-line that is linear and whole, where the narration derives directly from the organic composition of the image and its relationship to the text, the time-image offers an indirect representation that subverts narrative cohesion.

The difference between an organic regime (the movement-image) and a crystalline regime (the time-image) is that, in an organic description, the real that is assumed is assured by its continuity—even if it is interrupted—by the continuity shots which establish it and by the laws which determine successions, simultaneities and permanences: it is a regime of localizable relations, actual linkages, legal, causal and logical connections, (Deleuze 1989: 126)

whereas in a crystalline regime, the actual is severed from its motor linkages and the virtual, detached from its actualizations, becomes valid for itself. However, the time-image does not imply the absence of movement (even though it often foregrounds its increased scarcity), nor does it negate the possibility of the movement-image and the time-image operating together.

When the interval is opened by time as a force of the outside, space gives way to a series of irrational points and nonchronological relationships. Framing no longer simply serves to contain images, but gives way to a series of deframings, where time interrupts space: "The spectator is no longer included in the image as part of this expanding whole; there is no ideal or transcendent perspective from which the image must be judged in opposition to life" (Rodowick 1997: 144). The irrational interval created by the direct time-image offers us new ways of seeing, based not on totality and identity, but on the indiscernible, the inexplicable, and the undecidable. As D. N. Rodowick argues:

> The interval no longer serves as the frontier between the before and after, separating them into successive moments that are distinct and identical to themselves. Instead there is a passage of one into the other: the past becomes present as the present passes, the future emerges in the present as a new potentiality recognized in the present's relation to the past. (1997: 144)

Through the time-image, the spectator is no longer included in an expanding totality constructed through the narration.

It is via the time-image that *Rude* and *Eldorado* rearticulate the political. A rearticulation of the political takes place through the negotiation of a time-line that does not correspond to the organic narrative of the movement-image, whose location and dissemination would lead us back to the dominant discourses of containment. What the time-image anticipates is a fragmentation of narratives of continuity, as a result of which new images and narrations can be crystallized and reframed. In *Rude*, such a differentiation of time and narrative occurs both in the repetition of scenes and in the association of color with various time-lines.[8] A disjunction takes place in *Rude* between the voice and the text, between the black body and the narration, between the presumed outcome and the possibility of competing narratives that transgress the need for closure.

I envision *Rude* as a film that plays on the dissociation between movement and the time-image: the narration as movement-image follows the trajectory of the racist parameters of the nation's imaginary, which can only conceptualize one story—the story of oppression, male violence, and self-destruction—while the direct time-image repeats these scenes of containment, foregrounding both the contingency of the narration and the possibility of an alternative to these racially binding images and scenarios. In *Eldorado,* the direct time-image is more dominant throughout, particularly palpable in the continual return to the dissonance of the cello player's music, which is associated with the figure of the train. The cello music challenges the dichotomy between the homed and the homeless by underlining the ways in which each character is caught in a web of discontinuity and contradiction, even those who presume themselves secure within the citizen/nation/state triad.[9]

A critique of the all-encompassing narratives of the nation-state, such as multiculturalism and immigration, ensues through the emphasis on the time-image. This critique is expressed with resonance through the voice of Rude, who invites those who are willing to take seriously time's incommensurability to rewrite their narratives of the past and the present. "This trip is about you bringing the verbal intercourse and I'll bring the noise," Rude challenges as the camera spins around her, creating a dizzying effect, "so code the hammer, sharpen your spears, the coup d'état has begun." *Rude* offers the black voice as the harbinger of potential emancipation, where the word and the act become one to disrupt "Babylon's airwaves and reevaluate their immigration policy." This initiation of the voice into the image prevails throughout *Rude* as the shot returns again and again to Rude's voice, refraining from offering her as a black body until the end of the film.[10]

Rude emphasizes that for an alternative to the current immigration policy to be envisioned, we must first suspend the black body as representation. In doing so, we refrain from composing the body in the image of the nation's comprehension of blackness, listening to it instead. In this manner, the body becomes the image without becoming organic and vice versa. In other words, the image must work, through the voice, to disrupt the containment of the black body and its positionality within the racist white-supremacist narratives of national identity. Throughout *Rude,* the black body is therefore conceptualized as a voice that cuts through the narrative of the nation. Despite Walcott's reservations concerning the black body's position within *Rude*, I would therefore suggest that the black body is indeed called into question—be it in the form of the gay man, the black unborn child, the father, or the drug addict—creating pause within the image's repetition for the unraveling of the narratives that contest the positionality of the black body in time and space.

In *Eldorado*, what is at stake is a similarly disenfranchised body, envisaged through the figure of the homeless who draws our attention not only to the abject poverty on the streets but also to the emotional disparagement within the lives of those who do not think of themselves as homeless, yet still do not belong. What *Eldorado* emphasizes through the figure of the homeless is the necessity to refrain from believing in a universalizing notion of the inside and the outside, where certain people are immune to the political homelessness that afflicts those who refuse to adapt to the depoliticized mortgaging of ideas that functions as the hegemonizing basis of the territorial nation-state. *Eldorado* thus calls into question imposed divisions between citizens and noncitizens, migrants and natives, multiculturals and monoculturals, asking us to reenvision our relationship to universal narratives of containment.

Rude and *Eldorado* draw our attention to the ways in which racism and cultural exclusion inform our current notions of universality. The films do not stop there, however. Both films foreground people who have been excluded from enfranchisement by existing conventions governing the exclusionary definition of the universal. In so doing, *Rude* and *Eldorado* set into motion a "performative contradiction" that allows for a rethinking of the constraints of the discourse of the universal. This "performative contradiction" exposes the contradictory character of previous conventional invocations of the universal, constituting "a challenge to those existing standards to revise themselves in more expansive and inclusive ways" (Butler 1996: 48). Such a revision is not only crucial to the crossing of cultural and racial boundaries (from Montreal to Toronto, from black to white, from gay to straight), but also to the elaboration and deconstruction of historical standards of universality perpetuated in the name of the nation-state. By reformulating through the time-image that which is speakable, these films foreground the constraints within the very enunciation of the universal, inaugurating a border of demarcation between the speakable and the unspeakable.

A reworking of the universal is apparent in the endings of both films. At the end of *Eldorado*, Rita's failed suicide attempt is invoked again through the haunting cello's dissonant musical tones, suggesting that, while there may be an alternative to the constraints of our everyday existences, it is by no means reached in a straightforward manner. Alternatives are not conceptualized as utopic promises of a better place, but as challenges toward the disruption of staid and stagnant narratives of identity. As Rita and Lloyd run along the railroad in the final scene of *Eldorado*, a sense of risk prevails similar to the violent uncertainty of the representation of the painful triad of mother, father, and son at the end of *Rude*. Although there is no imminent danger, both endings remind us of the contingency of the moment, whereby every choice affects not only one life, but all others. Rude's final words connote a similar haunting sense of responsibility in the face of the willingness to choose a new way of existing, and hence a new way of articulating the political and its narratives of racial containment and oppression. "It's Easter Sunday morning,[11] the sun is rising, the sun has risen, and the mother ship is leaving," Rude muses as her voice reveals her face for the first time. "Our majesty has forgiven us and our sins are washed away—we just heard trumpets disguised as gunshots signaling us home—so all aboard the mother ship for those who want a chance at a—rebirth."

Rude's final words signal a double reading: every image and every text is subject to interpretation, just as all notions of universality seek to deafen the unspeakable within the spoken. There is another voyage, Rude seems to say, a path that takes us toward a different understanding of home, migrancy, racial politics, and the nation. But this is not a straightforward or even necessarily a safe trajectory, for trumpets can easily be mistaken for gunshots. Every movement, every image, and every speech always risks performing in the name of the censor who governs the universal, its celebrated links to the nation, and its exclusionary practices of governance. The challenge, therefore, for those who seek the unspeakable in the name of alternative immigration policies, involves facing potential danger, acknowledging the risk inherent in any performative utterance that seeks access to the inside to undermine from within the terms of universality and difference.

When the utterance becomes a sign of conflict, we are faced with an interpretive dilemma. This interpretive dilemma can be understood as "the dynamic mark of an emerging democratic practice," whereby the "task that cultural difference sets for us is the articulation of universality through a difficult labor of translation" (Butler 1996: 51–52). Within the matrix of such an interpretive dilemma, the universal can be conceptualized and performed as that which is yet to be achieved and imagined, as well as that which, "in order to resist domestication, may never be fully or finally achievable" (Butler: 1996, 52). As instances of a deconstruction of the universal, *Rude* and *Eldorado* perform such a resistance to domestication that takes the form, in *Rude,* of Luke's refusal to conform to the parameters of the white man's expectations, and, in *Eldorado,* of Rita's will to deviate from the path of preordained self-destruction while remaining true to her distrust of the home and, by extension, of the nation's mortgaging of difference.

Through spirited attempts at rethinking the nature of immigration, racism, nationalism, and multiculturalism, *Rude* and *Eldorado* not only cross geographical borders, they also challenge conceptual boundaries by foregrounding that state sovereignty and national identity are neither wholly ephemeral nor permanent consequences of territorial governance. Rather, state sovereignty and national identity occupy a locus of effect from whence they propel into governance a set of practices that work "to affirm continuities and to shift disruptions and dangers to the margins" (Walker 1991: 48). Highlighting the rift between ephemerality and permanence within the narration of the nation, *Rude* and *Eldorado* focus on the complexity of the figure of the "other" for whom unifying immigration policies are written. By demonstrating the ways in which this other is relegated to the edges of the discourse of state sovereignty, even while state sovereignty depends on this figure of the other for its coherence, *Rude* and *Eldorado* alert us to the contingency within the citizen/nation/state triad. If the other can no longer be strictly relegated to the "outside," then neither can the citizen be securely located "inside."

What these films highlight is the fact that both the state and its practices of sovereignty are historical artifacts of governance organized within the parameters of statecraft at a particular historical juncture. As *Eldorado* emphasizes, that which is located outside the conceptual parameters of the nation-state within the dominant discourse of state sovereignty is a kind of speechlessness embodied in the figure of the homeless or disenfranchised human being. Within the vocabulary of the sovereign state, this homelessness represents a lack of agency, a facelessness within a history that continues to negate the presence of the other who exists both inside and outside the nation's walled enclosures. Located within this matrix of sovereignty, attempts at humanitarian intervention—Roxan's desire to feed and protect the homeless in *Eldorado*—reveal not simply the sorry state of those who have nowhere to go, but more important they alert us to the sovereign's need to categorize the other as the homeless victim.

Eldorado exposes the manner in which liberal pluralist policies such as humanitarianism and multiculturalism present themselves as discourses of inclusion while they perpetuate the shortsightedness of the nation's dominant discourses of exclusion. In the following section, I return to the discourse of multiculturalism to expose the ways in which multiculturalism follows the trajectory of the nation's white-supremacist agenda, positing whiteness as an invisible norm by which other ethnicities are judged and categorized. Using examples from both *Rude* and *Eldorado*, I emphasize the ways in which multiculturalism deploys terms such as "diversity" to conceal the ideologies of assimilation contained within its very terminology; consequently, ethnic groups are reduced to the status of supplementary[12] to the dominant culture. I argue, for instance, that the discourse of multiculturalism in Canada fails to interrogate the dominant regimes of the nation's discursivity; thus, the social and cultural practices of the nation continue to be inscribed through racist, classist, sexist, and nationalist agendas that falsely promise that every ethnic group can reap the economic, cultural, and national benefits of state sovereignty.

Multicultural Pluralization

Multiculturalism without a basis in an alternative practice of immigration is simply another accommodation to the social order that celebrates the affinity and interdependence of the citizen to the nation-state. As Peter MacLaren suggests, referring to multiculturalism's dependence on the narrative of the nation-state: "Often one is asked to show one's identity papers before one can begin" (1994: 52). A discourse entrenched within the vocabulary of the nation, multiculturalism is incapable of delving into the exclusionary practices of racism within a nationalizing regime. Multiculturalism, as a liberal pluralist policy that chooses "culture" over "race," diverts attention from the histories and social effects of racism rather than working as a challenge to politics of race and racial identity within the domain of the nation.

Replacing racial with cultural identity does not necessarily point to their union in racial ontology, however. Instead, what often results from such a displacement is the dehistoricization of culture that "wreaks havoc on descriptions of . . . racial relations and does so through a philosophy that, historically speaking, is white" (Gordon and Newfield 1995: 387). The move from racial to cultural identity is often celebrated within discourses of multiculturalism. This results not in the establishing of emancipatory polities, but in the denial of the ongoing struggle for power under conditions of inequality. As Avery Gordon and Christopher Newfield argue, "If we do not grant the presence of conflict and contestation, of politics and history, of context and determinations in the study of culture, we are not avoiding politicization, we are avoiding cultural knowledge itself" (1995: 400). In the name of alternative immigration policies, then, what we seek must delve beyond the parameters of liberal multiculturalism to an engagement with race relations. This requires supporting race consciousness to pierce the receptacle of the politico-cultural national community.

Multiculturalism presupposes a unified concept of identity, where identity is understood as "the referential sign of a fixed set of customs, practices and meanings, and enduring heritage, a readily identifiable sociological category, a set of shared traits and/or experience" (Scott 1995: 5). The narrative of "Canadian identity," which envisions multiculturalism as its center, presupposes and celebrates the ideal of a coherence. As a result, in Canada, multiculturalism refers to a domesticated plurality that is always already defined by the binary structure at the basis of its founding narrative. The conflict in Canada between the heteroglossia of the population and the control of difference within a narrative of multicultural "plurality" can be understood as the tension between pluralization and pluralism. This distinction is elaborated in the work of William Connolly, who asserts that a conventional pluralist "celebrates diversity within settled contexts of conflict and collective action" and "bound[s] diversity by the territorial state, the normal individual, and monotheistic or monosecular conceptions of morality" (1995: xiii). Pluralization, on the other hand, recognizes the "paradoxical relation between a dominant constellation of identities and the very differences through which the constellation is consolidated" (1995: xiv).[13]

The stronger the drive to create a unified nation, the stronger the emphasis on the conversion of difference into otherness, and the more likely the proliferation of violence in the name of difference. Any consolidated attempt to unify a people in the name of territory necessarily engenders a kind of terrorist politics whereby land is associated with violence. The etymology of territory is a keen reminder of this terror inscribed within the organization of the state, since *terrere* means to frighten or terrorize. It follows, then, that any narrative of inclusion involves threatening all others who are not welcomed within the prescribed territoriality. Even within the parameters of pluralism, territoriality is implicated in such practices of exclusion. The discourse of multiculturalism can be understood as an instance of such liberal pluralism, for it protects some at the expense of others.

Territoriality houses its own pluralism and thus its own violence, excluding those who refuse to conform to the terrorizing politics of the nation's exclusivity. This practice of exclusion is achieved not through blatant measures, but by asserting dominion over time and space through the vocabulary of a plural identity within a prescribed territoriality. In Canada, such a paradoxical dominion is perpetuated within a discourse of multiculturalism that defines difference on the basis of a deviation from a binary French-English culture, whereby all (non-Francophone or Anglophone) others are silently relegated to an "elsewhere" that prevents them from taking part in the consolidation of the imaginary that presides over the discourse of identity and territory. This is not to say that these others are not provisionally invited into the fold, but rather to suggest that multiculturalism in Canada offers inclusion within the territoriality of the nation-state only insofar as all others conform to the (terrorizing) nationalizing politics at work in the elusive search for "Canadian identity."

Pluralist discourses can be challenged, however. Pluralization is an example of a contestation of the territorial imaginary of the nation-state. Pluralization foregrounds the instances where multiple territorializations are indispensable within liberal pluralist discourses such as multiculturalism, exposing the ways in which a modification of the ethos of territorialization occurs. Such a pluralization of the modern territorial imagination results in the fostering of a reciprocal hospitality that complicates the notion of the home as bounded space, celebrating the possibility of a responsiveness between interdependent and juxtaposed identities. Within such a matrix, no single line of territorialization becomes overcoded. Pluralization leads the way to a rhizomatic situating of the polity, whereby difference breeds difference rather than succumbing to a rooted notion of governmentality. As Connolly writes, within pluralization "[a]n ethic of care for the diversity of being honors both the indispensability and the fragility of ethics" (1995: 40).

Whereas a pluralist democracy relies on consensus, a pluralizing democracy is based on the contestation of a unified cultural identity and ethic that might make such a consensus possible. A pluralizing democracy enacts a resistance to the contemporary enchantment with arborealism, where arborealism is governed by the wish to secure ethical and practical guarantees in a realm where they are not available. What results is a "site of tension and ambivalence between politics as general action to sustain the economic and cultural conditions of existing plurality and the dissonant politics of pluralization" (Connolly: 1995, 97). *Rude* and *Eldorado* are instances of such pluralizing resistances to dominant culture. Both films subvert the dogmatism of identity by enacting a cultural ethos of responsiveness through which new possibilities for cultural co-existence are negotiated. In so doing, *Rude* and *Eldorado* open up new trajectories for a politics of pluralization, altering the tone of contention and collaboration between constituencies such as black/white, homed/homeless, multicultural/polyvocal.[14]

Nonetheless, even while we witness such transformative politics, it is crucial that we recognize the ways in which a pluralizing politics of disturbance can backfire, thus feeding the famished fundamentalist mouths of the nation and its monologic narratives of restriction and containment. Walcott's critique of *Rude* must be located as a warning that offers an important starting point from whence we can observe the ways in which the discourse of the nation-state is continuously reenacted, infiltrating every cultural instance, even when a conscious attempt is made to subvert liberal pluralist policies of racial and cultural containment. The conundrum that is at work in *Rude*—where Virgo attempts to exceed the expectations of "blackness" in Canada, even while blackness reasserts itself within the parameters for blackness constructed by the nation-state's pluralist ethos—reveals the challenge at stake in the shift from pluralism to pluralization.

The pluralizing of the national imagination in Canada is the process through which elements are identified that exceed state territorialization and identification. Race and migration are two key elements in this struggle for pluralization, since both discourses are forced to cross national internal and external boundaries to achieve recognition within the citizen/nation/state triad. In so doing, they exert pressure upon the nation-state as a cohesive construct, challenging the nation-state's monopoly over the allegiances, identifications, and energies of its citizens. By contesting the cultural assumptions inherent in the citizen's commitment to democracy as defined by the nation-state, issues of race and migration foreground the necessity for a critical responsiveness in the name of the other that implies a denaturalization and a reconfiguration of the notions of identity and difference. Through a practice of cultural responsiveness, a web is created that involves a dialogue between culture and the political through a pluralization of the sites of culture and politics and their complex networks of interconnection.

No one can claim mastery regarding the foundation of society and the organization of its peoples. In *Rude*, the deterritorialization of state sovereignty is portrayed through the image of the contestatory voyage—the mother ship—that brings together the Zulu and the Mohawk, where what is sought is neither the absolute unification of the "others" (the Zulu and the Mohawk) nor the assertion of a grounding principle (a black nationalism). What is emphasized is a bridging of thought and action that acknowledges the radical impossibility of multiculturalism as a final achievement. The dissonant cultural practices of *Rude* and *Eldorado* call for a critical engagement with the political shortcomings of a discourse of multiculturalism that silences a genealogical rendition of history. *Rude* challenges the obfuscation of race and racial relations as expressed by the white-supremacist nation and its whitewashed past.

With a similar pursuit in mind, *Eldorado* foregrounds the fact that home, as the nation's stable signifier, does not exist for those trapped within the racist and gendered discourse of homelessness. *Eldorado* suggests that "[h]ome, as the voice of the nation, domesticates the racial project" (Morrison 1998: 3) and therefore seeks to redefine the notion of accommodation to include the potential of speaking out from a locus of enunciation that defies the stultifying confines that undergird the narrative of the nation-state. *Eldorado* demonstrates that even a renovated race-house often continues to hold within its walls the scaffolding of the nationalizing impulse to depoliticize homelessness. The challenge remains, therefore, to learn to articulate the question of the home beyond the vocabulary of the nation, asking ourselves not simply, "How can we convert a home that is racist and transform it into a race-specific yet not racist home?" but more important, "How can we accommodate ourselves without renouncing the very homelessness that incites us to rearticulate the political?"

Social relations are constructed through asymmetrical regimes of power. In this chapter, I've outlined how a rearticulation of the political depends on a willingness to become acquainted with the vocabulary at the heart of the discourse of "Canadian identity" to understand the structures of power and dominance that continue to underwrite race and culture. The potential for the inauguration of an inoperative community that openly challenges discourses that celebrate being-in-common is the topic of the following chapter, where I turn to Srinivas Krishna's film *Lulu* (Canada 1996). In *Lulu*, we are presented with a character who, despite racial and cultural segregation, attempts to render herself visible within the pluralist agenda of middle-class white politics. Using this scenario as a point of departure, I explore the manner in which alterity is figured in political philosophy through a focus on the face of the other. I suggest that, if we seek politically viable forms of accommodation that defy the exclusive strictures of the home/land, our only recourse is to face the racism inherent in our horror of the face of the other.

4. Face-to-Face with the Incommensurable: Srinivas Krishna's *Lulu*

Postdemocratic objectification of the immigration "problem" goes hand in hand with fixation on a radical otherness, an object of absolute, prepolitical hate.

—Jacques Rancière, *Disagreements*

We are at a peculiar moment. Suddenly and without proper council, this erstwhile thing called "political philosophy" turns strange.

—Sue Golding

Beyond its contemporary currency in political philosophy and film theory, the emphasis on the face and its legacy on modern political thought can be traced through the history of visuality in art history. In art history, the face is evoked as a disquieting continuum between the somatic and the social. This organization of the face can be traced to the late nineteenth century, when we observe "the relatively sudden emergence of models of subjective vision in a wide range of disciplines" (Crary 1995: 46). The emergence of models of subjective vision in art history takes place roughly during the period from 1810 to 1840, during which time dominant discourses and practices of vision break with the classical regime of visuality, locating vision within the density and materiality of the body, thus rendering vision faulty, unreliable, and arbitrary. As Jonathan Crary writes,

> [I]t is possible to see one aspect of modernity as a continual crisis of attentiveness, to see the changing configurations of capitalism pushing attention and distraction to new limits and thresholds, with unending introduction of new products, new sources of stimulation and streams of information, and then responding with new methods of managing and regulating perception. (1995: 47)

Preceding visual modernism, vision was understood as merely one layer of a body that could be captured, shaped, and directed by a range of external techniques. This perception of vision shifts during the era of visual modernism, with the onset of a new regime of faciality. The notion that regimes of faciality can alter modes of being and belonging serves as the point of departure for this chapter. In what follows, I explore the convergence between the cinematic close-up used by Srinivas Krishna in *Lulu* (Canada 1996) and theories of the face-to-face encounter. To elucidate what is meant by the allusion to the face, I draw from the work of Emmanuel Levinas, for whom the face-to-face encounter is a crucial dimension of ethical responsibility.

For Levinas, the encounter with the face symbolizes a relationship with absolute alterity that decries subsuming the other into the same in a totalizing conceptual system that comprehends self and other. In the work of Levinas, the other remains enigmatic as the irreducibly other, prior to all ontological claims of being "at home" in the world. By rendering complex the face-to-face encounter through the assertion that the other must always remain other, Levinas's thought leads us in the direction of a new articulation of community, where the encounter with face as the face of the other alters what it means to be-in-common politically, ethically, and culturally.

As I demonstrate throughout the chapter, however, the face also acts as an emblem of resistance to community, for the face displays not only your irreducible alterity, but also my horrific reaction to that alterity. A poignant example of such a response to the face of the other occurs in Milcho Manchevski's *Before the Rain* (Macedonia 1994). This encounter with the face takes place in a restaurant in London where a counter-revolutionary from the Balkans opens fire. As the gunfire calms and the people begin to slowly regain consciousness, the camera pans to Anne, cradling her husband's head in her arms. "Your face, your face," she moans, looking at his face, half blown off. In a film concerned with the effects of war and ethnic cleansing on a transnational sensibility, this encounter with the face is less reminiscent of Levinas's notion of the face-to-face encounter, than of Kurtz's "The horror, the horror."

Before the Rain signals yet another shift in the regime of faciality, suggesting that in the midst of the havoc of late-twentieth-century violence, colonialism has come full circle; consequently, the ethics of the encounter can no longer be securely located anywhere, not even in the face,[1] which threatens to repulse us. The face has become the stranger that nauseates us, the one we turn from. "Strangely," writes Julia Kristeva, "the foreigner lives within us: he is the hidden face of our identity, the space that wrecks our abode, the time in which understanding and affinity founder" (1991: 1).

It is the horror of the face as exemplified in Manchevski's *Before the Rain* that serves as the point of departure for a reconceptualization of the face in this chapter. While I turn extensively to Levinas's work on the face to clarify what might be understood as an ethico-politics of the face, I concurrently initiate a critique of Levinas's theory of the face. This critique is based on the fact that, too often, we turn away from the foreigner, nauseated by the features of his or her difference, horrified by our relationship to the foreigner's alterity, which threatens our tenuous membership "at home" within the homogenous community of the same. This chapter is therefore written as a tightrope between the Levinasian face-to-face encounter, which, despite its ethico-political resonance, seems to be a somewhat utopic rendition of our relationship to the other, and what I consider to be a more radical engagement with the face.

As outlined in the previous chapters, an alternative ethic of the other blurs the boundaries of the nation. This chapter challenges national discourses such as those outlined in the previous chapters—the politics of identity, liberal pluralism, multiculturalism—which depend on the domestication of the face of the other. I argue that it is time we become aware of the mechanisms we employ daily to "save face" in our interactions with "the other." I decry all attempts to *comprehend* the other. I do so through a reading of Srinivas Krishna's *Lulu,* which is a film that resists all attempts at constructing "a people," alerting us to the impossibility of domesticating the language of the other. Krishna's film underscores that, even within the vocabulary of the nation, the language of the other can be heard, a language that speaks of the horror, the horror.

An emphasis on the horror of the face can be understood as another way of destabilizing the vocabulary of the nation. This chapter is an attempt to locate, within philosophy, the necessity of the face as the singularity that propels the thought of the ethical, of community, and, necessarily, of the political. It is the face that ensures us both of our apparent commensurability and of our enforced difference, suggesting that the other can be conceptualized as such only when he or she is recognizable within the limits of what can be understood as community. When the other escapes or exceeds such a thinking of community, the other is immediately cast outside, not simply because he or she defies similarity, but because he or she cannot be imagined at all. Within the national imaginary, this unimaginable other is the one we must at all costs avoid, both as ourselves and beyond ourselves.

The horrific other ensures the end of community as the locus of similarity and democratic consensus. This nauseating other alerts us to the distortions in our own features, in our language, in the grammar we celebrate as the line of communication toward democracy and multiculturalism. This nausea in the face of our own otherness, in the face of the other as other, brings to light a different mode of conceptualizing the other within the spatial and temporal imaginaries we accept as our own. This nauseating other perhaps offers not only a reflection of our own incommensurability, but also an awareness of the inconsistencies within the system, both philosophical and political, in which we claim to locate and house the other.

In a double-voiced attempt to face the other within political philosophy and to envisage the face of the other as the horrific instance of the Eurocentric gaze, I turn to Levinas's theory of the face-to-face encounter first and then to Deleuze and Guattari's work on faciality. I explore in detail a few of the pertinent aspects of Levinas's thought to underscore the ways in which a Levinasian perspective is vital in any engagement with the other. Then, I suggest that Levinas's work does not take us far enough in the direction of incommensurability. This second argument is underscored by a critical reading of the concept of community as theorized by Jean-Luc Nancy, juxtaposed with Krishna's *Lulu*. The elaboration of the question of the ethical with respect to the other not only expands the previous discussion concerning identity and territory, it also serves to further emphasize the incestuous link between nation, identity, territory, and ethnic singularity. By turning to the face as the ethical (im)possibility of politics, this chapter foregrounds the necessity for a modus of reflection that escapes the bounded scope of the national by illuminating the contradictions within the imaginary of the nation when the nation is faced with an other it cannot comprehend.

Face to Face

Srinivas Krishna's film *Lulu* begins with the hidden presence of an in-store security video camera, waiting poised for any sign of movement or deviation. Perceived from the perspective of the security device, *Lulu*'s main character, Khuyen—known throughout the film as Lulu—is always already detected, witnessed, and tried by the gaze that confirms her difference. Always watching, the movement-detector catches every glance, capturing Lulu from above, segregating her as the other, recording her face on its archive. This first encounter with the face in *Lulu* invites us to see Lulu as a face that must be secured, where security depends on the pretense of insecurity. Paradoxically, however, as we shall see, Lulu's face also represents that which dismantles the security system, thereby effecting a rewriting or a de-facing of the political.

The initial securing of the face in *Lulu* would seem to suggest that the face is a mute or passive object. This representation of the face is contrary to Levinas's theory of the face-to-face encounter, where the face is a repository for a communication that is always already in progress. As Levinas outlines, the presentation of the face does not disclose an inward world previously closed, adding a new region to comprehend or to take over (*à comprendre ou à prendre*). Rather, it incites conversation beyond the given that language already places in common between us. Accordingly, in opening myself to the face, I realize that "language does not take place in front of a correlation from which the I would derive its identity and the other its alterity" (Levinas 1969: 215). Rather, implicit within the face-to-face encounter is language's resistance to the imposed semantic differentiation between self and other.

The encounter with Lulu's face seems to connote quite the contrary, however, since Lulu's face is not only objectified, but also silenced by the security devices. Does this mean that the face in *Lulu* is the representation of a certain *imposed* muteness that can be remedied through a face-to-face encounter that reestablishes the other as other and thereby resolves this initial objectification, or, conversely, that the face functions wholly outside the ethical relation of the Levinasian face-to-face? I would suggest the latter: the face in *Lulu* alerts us to a completely different way of facing the face, and, in so doing, of facing language as the ethical relation. For as we shall see, in *Lulu* the face is never wholly without language, even when language remains the barrier between the face and comprehension.

The relationship between language and the face is an excessive one. Levinas suggests that the face-to-face encounter necessitates a mode of saying that endlessly obligates me to the other as other, a multiplicity in being that refuses totalization, taking form instead as an ethical relation that forever precedes and exceeds the egoism and tyranny of ontology. Levinas's concept of the face-to-face encounter is a departure from the Heideggerian notion of being-with *(mitsein)*, where the focus invariably remains of the concept of "being" and alterity is subsumed to the same. The proximity of the face-to-face encounter cannot be enveloped into a totality, but produces instead a relation to infinity, whereby the face signifies the philosophical priority of the existent over Being. Levinas rejects the Heideggerian grammar of the self-other relation, substituting being-alongside to an encounter in-front-of that reinforces the fundamental separation between self and other. In this move, Levinas attempts a thinking of the other that, contrary to the tradition of Greek thought to which Heidegger remains indebted, is most irreducibly not ontological.

In a departure from Heidegger's notion of *aletheia* as the unconcealment that exposes Being, Levinas suggests that the opening does not open to truth and Being, but instead to otherness, where no category or totality can be enclosed and where "experience . . . can no longer be described by traditional concepts, and . . . resists every philosopheme" (Derrida 1978: 83). Levinas takes seriously the notion that the philosopheme always announces the specter of the sovereign. As Derrida notes, describing Levinas's project:

> Without intermediary and without communion, neither mediate or immediate, such is the truth of our relation to the other, the truth to which the traditional logos is forever inhospitable. This unthinkable truth of living experience, to which Levinas returns ceaselessly, cannot possibly be encompassed by philosophical speech without immediately revealing, by philosophy's own light, that philosophy's surface is severely cracked, and that what was taken for its solidity is its rigidity. (1978: 90)

Levinas attempts to think a community of nonpresence, where the face represents absolute difference, inconceivable in terms of logic, yet that which I eagerly turn toward. Rejecting the Heideggerian notion of being-in-common, substituting a position "in-front-of," Levinas reinforces the relation that is absolute between self and other, proposing an ethical relationship whereby the "I" is questioned through the appearance of the other. This experience of alterity culminates in the face, which is "the way in which the other presents himself, exceeding the idea of the other in me" (1969: 50). This other, represented through the face-to-face encounter, is the one I cannot evade, comprehend, or kill, the one before whom I am called to justice.

The call to justice guarantees that the other's face can never fully be absorbed. For Levinas, the self that is called to justice is always the other. Ethics for Levinas is not only an overcoming or abandonment of ontology, it is the deconstruction of ontology's limits and its comprehensive claims to mastery. The ethical is based not on a Heideggerian notion of *Dasein*'s truth of Being, but on the relation I have with the other and in the unique demand made to me by the other, whom I face. Subjectivity is my subjection to the other. The face-to-face relation enacts a disruption or interruption of the Said; consequently, I am addressed by the other in a way that calls me into question and obliges me to be responsible. In other words, the face-to-face encounter Levinas proposes is an attempt to disrupt totalitarian politics through the introduction of an ethic that leads to an interrogative demand for a just polity.

The political other in Levinas is evoked as *le tiers: le tiers* is the passage from ethics to politics, or from the other to the third. As Levinas writes: "It is not that there first would be a face and then the being it manifests or expresses would concern itself with justice: the epiphany of the face as face opens humanity" (1969: 213). The immediacy of the ethical is always mediated politically. *Le tiers* has always already entered the ethical relation, troubling and doubling it into political discourse. The question that is returned via *le tiers* is the question of justice:

> Justice is necessary, that is, comparison, coexistence, contemporaneousness, assembling, order, the visibility of faces, and thus intentionality and the intellect, the intelligibility of a question, and thence also a co-presence on an equal footing as before a court of justice. (Levinas 1981: 158)

Justice, as the translation of ethics into politics, is the moment when I am in relation to the other for whom I am infinitely responsible. It is the moment when I face the other as other and know myself to be an other like all others. At the level of justice, I and the other are co-citizens of a common *polis* where commonality is always a relation of nonpresence.

While Levinas's thought motions toward the ethical in compelling ways, the encounter between Levinas's understanding of the face and *Lulu*'s visualization of the face raises various shortcomings within Levinas's work, not least of which is the question of whether we can speak of the ethics of the face when what is at stake is not a responsible encounter with the face of the other, but a consumption of the other through his or her face. A critique of Levinasian ethics is relevant not only to a reading of *Lulu* but also to the rearticulation of the political because it warns us not to use ethics—or the face—as an uncontested system that promises complete emancipation from the strictures of the national. We must be attentive to the fact that ethics can be as conducive to the erection of strict national borders as it can be instrumental in transgressing them.[2] As we shall see, the confrontation between Levinas and *Lulu* suggests that the ethic of responsibility outlined in Levinas's face-to-face encounter is always, despite its best intentions, in some sense associated to ethics as a discourse on which the metaphysical philosophical tradition depends for its constriction of time, space, and alterity within the ethico-political limits of the self-same.

Despite these reservations, the question of the ethics of the other in Levinas cannot simply be dismissed, whether one adheres to Levinas's notion of the face-to-face or seeks to move beyond it. Levinas's work on ethics is located at a historical, philosophical, and political juncture. Consequently, any attempt to move beyond Levinas involves an attempt to draw a new map of the historical, political, and philosophical realities of our time. For instance, a reply to Levinas might entail finding a correspondence between the ethics of the face that emerge in Levinas as a response to Hitler's totalitarian politics and the new regime of faciality represented in contemporary society's computerized and digitized faceless encounters with an alterity that can no longer be securely located anywhere, much less in a face-to-face encounter.

Levinas's model is based on the assumption that the ethical relation is always one of asymmetry, where a certain creative antagonism ensures that justice is carried through in the sight of the other's face. Such a model depends on the conceptualization of politics as that which is proper to "a people" who live within the secure borders of a political community, which is usually understood to be the modern territorial state. Within the Levinasian model, no critique is raised of the territorial limits of alterity. Levinas's model does not challenge the question of the ethics of the enclosure, does not question the fact that the sovereign has access to different modes of seeing, and ultimately of facing, than does he or she who must obey the law, either within or outside the policed borders of the nation-state. Who is the other, for instance, whose face is never invited into the fold, who, in other words, is never allowed to face me? To contend with these questions, Levinas's topos of the *polis* must be further challenged not only by a deconstruction of the ethical as such, but with the knowledge that the plural economies of value in an increasingly globalized world disrupt and alter the orientation between self and other.

The regime of faciality (or face-lessness) spurred by plural economies of value alerts us to new ways of understanding the encounter. It forces us to reexamine what an ethics of the face-to-face entails in our technology-driven existences, wherein we seldom encounter the face of the other in our daily transactions. It also foregrounds the selective aspect of all encounters, inciting us to inquire who (if anyone) is invited to take part in our face-to-face encounters, and by whom? According to Levinas's model, there is no other until I face, until I choose to locate, through his or her face, this other, whose features are then reflected onto my face. A challenge to this model entails exploring the consequences of the *inability* to face the other and the resultant horror of this face-lessness, horrific because it foregrounds the moment of exposure to the other as the instance of the potential negation of the other's (and my) face. The erasure of the other's features establishes a fierce hierarchy between self and other, whereby it is the self who chooses either to face or to turn away in horror. In the work to follow, I suggest that it is through an appreciation of a regime of face-lessness that negotiates the horror of the other that we can begin to articulate a social order that calls for a different understanding of the ethical and, by extension, of the political.

It is by now apparent that what troubles me about Levinas's notion of the face is the assumption that all faces are created equal, that is, the suggestion that you will always be willing to look at my face. What of the encounter that disfigures? What of the moment when I realize my face is not yours, is not white enough? What of the horror of my face? What ensues from an encounter that is repulsed by the face, that refuses to face? Does Levinas's face-to-face encounter assure us of a different organization of the political, or does it simply replicate the bounded community of those whose faces we welcome at the expense of those whose faces are incommensurable, disquieting, different?

"From its very beginnings philosophy has been stricken with horror by anything that is other and remains other, as if it had an incurable allergy to it," writes Levinas (1987: 211). How is it that the face adequately subdues this relation to the horror of the other? And, if it is indeed possible to subdue this horror of the other, what are the consequences of domesticating this horrific encounter with ourselves? My aim here is not so much to refute Levinas's theory of the face as to expand it to its potential limit, addressing the uncanniness within the figure of the face as expressed through Krishna's *Lulu,* where the face reaches a moment of inexorability and redundancy in the wake of the encounter with the security system.

For Levinas, the meeting with the face of the other results in a rupture of context. This is theorized as the condition of possibility of language. It is from this experience that the meaning of speech and expression must be sought. This eruption of language occurs through the confrontation with alterity. According to Levinas, ethical communication is always conducted in the language of the other: the face discloses itself through language as other. The muteness of Lulu's initial "face" displaces this theory, however, following much more closely in the tracks of Deleuze and Guattari's work on faciality. In their work on the face, Deleuze and Guattari reject the Levinasian vocabulary, locating the face not within a linguistic system, but instead within a normative signifying matrix in what they call the white wall/black hole system. Within this framework, the white wall can be understood as the backdrop onto which signification is inscribed. The apparition of the subject onto this white wall results in an interruption of the white wall by the black hole of consciousness. Stratified within this linguistic model, we find ourselves looking into "a broad face with white cheeks, a chalk face with eyes cut in for a black hole" (Deleuze and Guattari 1987: 167).

According to Deleuze and Guattari, the face is the signifying semiotic that guarantees stratification. In other words, the face upholds the power of the sovereign. Within the regime of faciality, the face as sign is overcoded, guaranteeing the uniformity of its enunciation, the unification of its substance of expression, and the control over its statements, all within a regime of circularity. The face thus becomes coterminous with state philosophy: all individuated enunciation remains trapped within dominant significations, and all signification is associated with dominated subjects. The face can therefore be theorized as the outcome, or the presentation, of the systems of signification and subjectification; the face is the horror of representation within their circularity.

For Deleuze and Guattari, faces are not individual. Rather, they "define zones of frequency or probability, delimit a field that neutralizes in advance any expressions or connections unamenable to the appropriate significations" (1987: 168). The face is a redundancy, a constructed wall the signifier needs to bounce off. The face is the frame or screen of signification's intelligibility: "[t]he face digs the hole that subjectification needs in order to break through; it constitutes the black hole of subjectivity as consciousness or passion, the camera, the third eye" (1987: 168). Thus, whereas the head is included in the body, the face is not:

> The face is produced only when the head ceases to be a part of the body, when it ceases to be coded by the body, when it ceases to have a multidimensional polyvocal corporeal code—when the body, head included, has been decoded and has to be *overcoded* by something we shall call the Face. (1987: 170)

The face becomes a face within the regime of the state apparatus when it is identified and represented as a broad face with white cheeks, a chalk face with eyes cut out for a black hole. The face becomes facialized when the face can adequately function as the locus of signification, of meaning, and of understanding within the stratified apparatus of state philosophy. For Deleuze and Guattari, the personification of the image of a white chalk face with eyes cut out for a black hole is demonstrated through the close-up. They describe the close-up as the taut skin on which the black holes of emptiness are gouged. Onto this taut skin are superimposed the features of the face, defying, through their uni-dimensionality, the tacticity of textured experience. Deleuze and Guattari use this image of the close-up—which is more a metaphor for the manner in which the face functions within western metaphysics than an actual close-up—to draw our attention to the fact that the representation of the face in state philosophy guarantees the solidarity of encounter only to those whose faces measure within its parameters. Hence, Deleuze and Guattari warn that "the face has a great future, but only if it is destroyed, dismantled. On the road to the asignifying and asubjective" (1987: 171).

Theorized according to the Deleuzo-Guattarian regime of faciality, the face is not that which reveals my alterity, but that which measures the coherence of the dominant signifying systems: if you speak my language, I face you as the other you are, unthreatening, similar in your difference. Seen in this light, the representation of Lulu's face begins to make sense. Lulu's face is captured by the security system not so that the dominant social order learns to appreciate her face's difference, but to assign it a category in order that it operates well within the systems of signification and control that will attempt to classify, comprehend, and police its alterity.

(Ef)facing Community

Lulu begins with a close-up of Lulu and frames all subsequent characters throughout with similar, center-screen close-ups. Rarely do we see characters' faces looking at each other within or across the shot. The film captures each character as the incommensurability of his or her singularity, unreflected by the other. The face in *Lulu*—in particular Lulu's face—emerges as the measure of difference that defies the seduction of being-in-common, leaving us instead with a memory of the face's difference and its inevitable collapse within the disappearing frame. The face in *Lulu* rejects all assimilation, even as the representation of the other as other, requesting instead its own demise as the insurance against its consumption by the governing body politic. The face in *Lulu* remains ephemeral, appearing only long enough to communicate across the frame, deconstructing itself in the moment when there is a temptation to appropriate the face as the embodiment of the discourse of *the* other.

Adjacent to the faces that connote difference and incommensurability, the context of the film also defies categorical interpretation: *Lulu* narrates a marriage between a white Canadian called Stephen (nicknamed

Lucky) and his picture bride, the Vietnamese Khuyen, whom Lucky calls Lulu because he cannot pronounce her name. Clive, the Jamaican-Canadian who comes to stay with them after he is released from prison, complicates the relationship between Lulu and Lucky by becoming involved with Lulu. Meanwhile, Clive offers death insurance to those who are willing to sell their bodies to a pharmaceutical company after their death, while Lucky is involved in an operation that delivers stolen meat carcasses for profit to a local restaurant dedicated largely to the homeless, run by a kind of inner-city, ethnically mixed Mafia.

Within the film, all main characters are of different ethnic origin, and there is never a sense that theirs is a common journey. Quite the contrary: *Lulu* undermines the mythic narrative of immigration that offers either the promise of the security of commonality among displaced migrants or assimilation within the "national identity." No one is at home in *Lulu*, not even the white character, Lucky. This is one of the striking characteristics of the film. *Lulu* not only resists any adherence to a dream of location and community—where the face of the other would be absorbed either within his or her immigrant environment or in the elusive dream of Canadian identity—it also resists the temptation to decry the homeless other a victim of circumstance. Each character in the film plays his or her game of appropriation and consumption, whether in the trafficking of dead first- and third-world bodies, in the usurping of the Canadian's marriage certificate as the passport to a new life, or in the dream of a subservient picture-bride wife.

The story of the film foregrounds the eerie incommensurability of its characters, each of them racially different and alone. The close-up further reinforces the limit between each character, suggesting that there can be nothing in common between them except the need to be incommon. And yet, something more is at stake in *Lulu*, which I explore via Nancy's work on the inoperative community, linked with Deleuze and Guattari's theory of faciality. What I suggest is that *Lulu* engages in a rethinking of community through a de-facing of the face, where the face is no longer the parameter for encounter but the moment of deconstruction. For although the face in *Lulu* is continually foregrounded through the close-up, it is ultimately disembodied and dismantled. Levinas's face-to-face encounter is not possible because, in the end, there is no face to encounter. Or, articulated slightly differently, the face we encounter is always the demise of our own face.

Deleuze and Guattari argue that "the face has a correlate of great importance: the landscape, which is not just a milieu but a deterritorialized world" (1987: 172). The close-up of the face reveals a landscape that we recognize as a pedagogy through which we understand the face as both the other and the same. Through the lens of the landscape, the face is familiarized: white wall, black hole. The face becomes the sublation of identity and territory. Both the face and the face-as-landscape guarantee our complicity in the narrative that suggests that the face cannot be universal unless by universal we are referring to the face of the White Man. Within this signifying matrix, the face as landscape—that is, the landscape we *recognize* as the face—is that of the White Man, with the broad white cheeks and black holes of his eyes.

The face we see most often in *Lulu*, framed more than once in the reflection of the mirror, is Lulu's face. And what we see is her attempt to create that face. Meticulously, Lulu applies makeup, streaking her face with pale foundation, drawing out the features of her ethnically different face by whitening it. Facing her reflection, we watch as she attempts to recognize the face that nonetheless remains foreign, alien, incommensurable. She smiles a stilted smile, more a grimace than a smile, frowns, and smiles again, as though attempting to paste a look onto her features that will allow her to be assimilated within the maze of the white faces that surround her.

Lulu's attempts do not provide her with the elusive white face. Rather, they emphasize her facelessness in the discourse of the faciality of the White Man. However, through the awareness of the impossible bridge between difference and similarity symbolized in Lulu's whitening of her face, Lulu does initiate an interruption of the signifying system, calling forth the possibility of an altered community imagined through a different discourse of the face. This rearticulation of community is a meticulous process that can be achieved neither unilaterally nor indefinitely. For every deterritorialization of the face implies a reterritorialization:

> The deterritorialization of the body implies a reterritorialization on the face; the decoding of the body implies an overcoding by the face; the collapse of corporeal coordinates implies the constitution of a landscape. . . . The face is a politics. (Deleuze and Guattari 1987: 181)

The complexity inherent in the dismantling of the face resides in the realization that de-facing is always the rendering-political of the face, where de-facing can be understood as the moment of the eradication of the imperial landscape. The (ef)facing of the face is a political commitment to expose the white wall of the signifier as that which we have come to recognize as the White Man's face: "The face, what a horror" (Deleuze and Guattari 1987: 190).

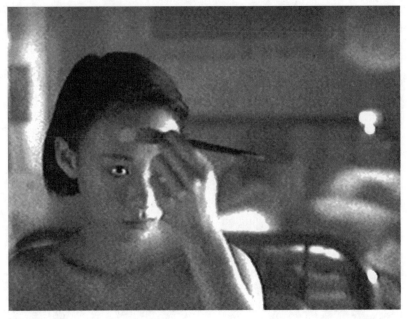

Still from Srinivas Krishna's film *Lulu*.

Locating the face as that which no longer carries with its features the promise of uninterrupted communication with the other opens the way for a rethinking of community. In *The Inoperative Community,* Jean-Luc Nancy takes as his point of departure what still speaks in a term like "community" when we assume the closure of the metaphysics of subjectivity. Nancy's concept of community refutes the promise of immanence, proposing instead a community of alterity or incompleteness, of *désoeuvrement* or worklessness, an idling, unoccupied, out-of-work community that refuses to create itself as a finished work.

Without relying on a signifying order assured by and for a subject, and without any communion of the subject with itself, without any accomplished self-presence, Nancy works out a thought of difference in political terms that continues to speak to us despite its loss of philosophical meaning. Although Nancy's inoperative community is reminiscent of Levinas's notion of the community of nonpresence, it resists the utopia of the face-to-face encounter through a continuous breach of the myth of being-in-common. Nancy's inoperative community thus expands on Levinas's argument while critically exploring the limits of faciality.

Srinivas Krishna's *Lulu* exemplifies the inoperative community in what I perceive to be an ongoing engagement with a radical difference in

Still from Srinivas Krishna's film *Lulu.*

Canadian cinema, a difference that is linked to a willingness to witness fractured alterity that communicates falteringly, haltingly, and facelessly within and beyond the time and space of the nation. In *Lulu*, Krishna deconstructs the notion of "being together," opting instead for a complex web of difference where the characters respond to each other without trying to comprehend each other. Krishna attempts, through *Lulu*, to create a political milieu that speaks back to the nation by rejecting community as a subsistent ground or a measure for being-in-common. By imagining a community that would refuse to become the object or the *telos* of a politics, Krishna inflicts a blow on the nation's body politic, piercing its liberal consensual apparatus. Krishna's work thereby positions the inoperative community as a vital tool in the deconstruction of national identity.

Nancy's inoperative community is based on a propelling of Heidegger's concept of *Dasein* beyond its ontological determination into the ecstasy[3] its being-toward-death promises. Uncannily surprised and rendered vertiginous by the fact of being, *Dasein* discovers—through the *Da* as the site of its exposure—the fact of its abandonment: it discovers that it is *Da-sein*. *Dasein*, and the experience of the revelation of *Dasein*, mirrors the death of the other (which is always inherently *Da-sein* as being-toward-death); consequently, the other calls the subject beyond itself and delivers it to its freedom. The individual *Dasein* first knows community when it experiences the impossibility of communion or immanence (the self-presence of individuals to one another in and by their community) before the dead other. Hence, it is in ec-stasis that *Dasein* discovers the possibility of community. When death presents itself as not ours, the very impossibility of representing its meaning suspends or breaches the possibility of self-presentation and exposes us to our finitude. It is thus through its assumption with mortality that *Dasein* first encounters the other, and it is only through the other and by way of that which the other communicates of its mortality that *Dasein* knows its own mortality.

Face to face, skin to skin, limit to limit, rethinking community consists in this sharing and compearance *(com-paraîssance)* of finitude. Within an inoperative community, singular beings give themselves to the other without a bond and without communion, distant from any notion of connecting or joining, of common or fusional interiority. The inoperative community takes place in what both Blanchot and Nancy refer to as *désoeuvrement*, that which, before or beyond the work, withdraws from the work and which, no longer having to do with either production or completion, encounters interruption, fragmentation, and suspension. The inoperative community is, in a sense, resistance itself, that is, resistance to immanence, given to us with being and as being, well in advance of our projects, desires, and undertakings.

In *Lulu*, death marks an interruption in the concept of being-in-common, signaling a breach in the myth of eternal fusion. This is apparent in Clive's response to his mother's death. After having dealt with the surprise and trauma of her passing, Clive takes his mother's body to Dunkel Initiatives, a pharmaceutical company that buys dead bodies to recycle them. "What are you going to do with her?" Lucky asks the doctor. "First we take the heart, the liver, and the brain—they go for medical research," the doctor replies. "Then we take the pituitary gland, the ovaries, and the remaining organs and they go for pharmaceutical drugs.... Then we take the skeleton and we clean it up—we boil it. Then we take the hair to a wig-maker." Rather than becoming the site for nostalgia, the body is made useful; it is recycled, discolored, purged of its identity. Finally, rendered faceless, the body is given to the other. Through this soul-less (anti)communal death, an alternative notion of community is evoked, a community of the postmodern world in which the living are (ef)faced with/by death (or recycled life) every time they buy a wig or go to the pharmacy.

In *Lulu*, the interrupted community takes shape through *Dasein*'s exposure to ec-stasis. It is through death—where death is understood as the finality that undermines all attempts at being-in-common—that the characters in the film are invited to shift outside the limits of ontological discourse. By resisting community, the characters are capable of transgressing the oppressive narrative of national identity. The inoperative community instantiated by this renunciation of commonality envisions an other who is not contained within a territorially exclusive imaginary. This other exists as the representation of the singular being that delights in the contingencies that prevent a community from basking in the myth of ethnic, ethical, political, or cultural homogeneity.

The inoperative community refrains from classifying alterity. It does, however, recognize the fact that lovers form the extreme though not external limit of community. Intercalated, the shared texts of lovers offer what belongs to no one and returns to everyone: the writing of the other as other. However, as lovers begin to attempt to shape the other into the mold of possession, the inoperative communities risk being overcoded with dreams of a cohesive being-in-common. Such a moment of (dis)possession is demonstrated in *Lulu* as Lulu and Clive lie in bed, basking in postcoital bliss. Clive confides to Lulu that he remembers a dream in which he was making love to a woman he couldn't see, who could see him. "It felt like I was finally coming home," he tells Lulu. "You're like that dream." While Clive's dream reinforces the sense in which Lulu is rendered faceless in the moment of their ecstasy, it also suggests that Clive is in the process of attaching a face to Lulu. The ecstasy of their interrupted community that depended on their willingness to remain singular is in danger of being overcoded by Clive's desire for a unity he defines as "home."

Lulu fears this dream of commonality would only substantiate the other's desire to classify and consume her face. She is not interested in providing the men who desire her with this promise of domesticity. She therefore proceeds to endanger Clive's life by revealing him to Lucky as her lover: moments before Lucky's entrance into the bedroom with a gun, Lulu grabs hold of Clive's testicles and pull him onto her. The irony here is that, in the end, Lulu provides not the home Clive seeks but his emasculation. A connection is thus established between emasculation and the myth of commensurability that suggests that when we adhere to the limiting narratives of the nation-state, we forfeit our power to engage in the ecstasy that would lead us outside the confines of the nation.

Lulu plays no games of recognition or cohesion. Lulu's only desire is to separate herself from a world that seeks to commodify her face. Hence, we can assume that Lulu's final words—"He loves me"—refer less to a desire to fall into Clive's narrative than to an appreciation of the dangers inherent in an ecstasy that risks transforming itself into an ontology. Both Lucky and Clive are beaten by their desire to contain Lulu, who confidently walks away from them into her constructed, interrupted anti-communal community. Trapped by their desire for commonality, the men who desire Lulu are remembered through their impotence and their broken bodies, unlike Lulu, who escapes relatively unscathed. The breach between Lulu as the initiator and the men as passive victims is apparent in scenes such as the one in which Lulu raises then drops Lucky's limp penis onto his sleeping body, and in the fight scene where Lucky attempts to kill Clive with blank bullets.

The Being of the absent community, envisioned here as Lulu, is an un-Being who seeks not recognition but contestation. For Lulu, subjectivity is not confined to ontology. Ontology remains focused on the face as the image of being-other. To interrupt this racism that delves deeply into the Eurocentric, territorial, philosophical consciousness, Lulu contests all notions of Being, thereby de-facing herself. By rejecting the face and everything it represents, Lulu begins to ex-ist, ec-static, on the division that marks the encounter with the other, recognizing herself as exteriority. This act of composition entails a decomposition that calls not only for her effacement from the metaphysics of subjectivity, but also for the (ef)facing of those who would attempt to include her in their community of difference, thus attempting to assimilate her face.

The End of Myth and the Beginning of the Political

If the resistance to community as being-in-common is experienced through a renunciation of the myths that seek to solidify the boundaries of our commonality, where myth is understood as "the staging and setting to work *(mise en oeuvre)* of a 'Volk' and a 'Reich,' in the sense that Nazism gave to these terms" (Nancy: 1991, 46), it is important to explore further the ways in which *Lulu* refutes any possibility of an originary founding myth. This is particularly apparent with Clive and Lulu, who appear and compear without offering any sense of a coherent outcome, of a shared story, or even of an entangled narrative. I've often wondered whether it is this very lack of myth, be it a myth of the nation or a myth of the immigrant, that resulted in the bleak reception of the film at the Toronto Film Festival in 1996, due to which *Lulu* never achieved distribution.[4]

Unlike Krishna's earlier film *Masala* (Canada 1994), *Lulu* offers no image of a community to which a distinct label of "otherness" can be ascribed. There is no redemption in *Lulu*, no sense of a promise of commensurability, no location within a bounded and secure space. As a consequence, each character is alone in his or her (horrific) difference, occupying space in a transitory and haphazard fashion. There is no sense of an arrival or a departure, of the insurrection of a home or an attachment to the environment as a territorially constrained space. Krishna neither lauds the concept of Canadian national identity, nor does he celebrate the migrant's commonality. He makes the film no "other" is allowed to make without losing face. Krishna attempts something only the White Man is allowed to do. As a result, *Lulu* is a film that cannot be categorized, distributed, explained, or exploited. Sadly, the result is that it is forgotten, placed alongside those others of whom it speaks, the disenfranchised.

One could argue that, for those who claim the political as that which is proper to a people living within the secure borders of a community understood as the modern territorial state, where myth remains emblematic of the coherence of the nation-state as stable entity, *Lulu*'s time has not yet come; consequently, *Lulu*'s focus on the interrupted community as a renunciation of the mythic narrations of the nation may be premature. Whether or not we choose to recognize them, however, such interrupted communities do take place. As *Lulu* demonstrates, even within the boundaries of the nation-state, narration can act as resistance, articulating different modes of political existence, foregrounding the mythic community of the nation in its inevitable demise.

There is *Lulu*'s paradox: *Lulu* portrays something the nation may not be able to comprehend, while at the same time demonstrating the futility of comprehension. This paradox is apparent in the film's reception as well. Both as a film and as a threatening cultural representation of society's fear of the other who will not be assimilated into the same, *Lulu* resists the dominant discourse of the nation, refusing to "place" itself within the canonical Canadian cultural imaginary. The film is then discarded by the critics on the basis of these very criteria of inclusion (and subsequent exclusion) from the Canadian canon.

The conflict between alterity and cultural belonging is foregrounded in *Lulu*, which emphasizes the necessity that we rework our relationship to alterity beyond the conceptual framework of the nation-state. This rewriting involves a departure from a mythic articulation that rules over time and space. Leaving myth behind implies undermining the narratives of national identity and belonging that segregate the other as stranger. To effect an interruption of the nation, it is necessary to subvert all communities that rely on the face as it is represented through state philosophy. This is a challenge that can be dealt with seriously only through the (ef)facing of the ethical, which, by extension, involves a de-facing of the political and the national. As a consequence of such a de-facing, ethical alternatives to national politics emerge, which take as their point of departure not the territorial identity of the self-same, but the incommensurability of a community that responds not to the face of the other as other, but to my facelessness. In this regard, *Lulu* is caught between the mythic consciousness it denies and the postethical or post-politico-national chronotope it seeks.

To better understand how the renunciation of myth can result in a rearticulation of the political, it is useful to turn to Nancy's theorization of myth. Nancy clarifies the conjunction between myth's demise and the inoperative community. He suggests that comprised within the concept of myth is the imposture of a modern world that has exhausted itself in the fabulous representation of its own power:

> The idea of myth alone perhaps presents the very Idea of the West, with its perpetual representation of the compulsion to return to its own sources in order to re-engender itself from them as the very destiny of humanity. In this sense . . . we no longer have anything to do with myth. (Nancy 1986: 46)

As full, original speech, at times revealing, at times founding the intimate being of a community, myth is that through which the world makes itself known. Neither dialogue nor monologue, myth is the unique speech of the many who come thereby to recognize one another, communicating and communing through the telling of their story. In this regard, myth is always the myth of community.

Despite the currency of myths as the basis for most national narratives today, we should be suspicious about myth at this historical juncture since mythic politics must remind us, among other things, of the terror of Hitler's fascism. Hence, Nancy argues that we cannot once again risk a relation to myth. Myth always evokes a polarity between narrative cohesion—which implies national unity, ethnic singularity, and historical linearity—and an unfinished scripting or genealogy. To speak of myth with the idea of rearticulating the political is therefore to speak of its necessary interruption. And, since wherever there has been myth there has also been community, to interrupt myth is also to speak of the interruption of community. As Nancy writes:

> If myth is a myth, community is reabsorbed into this abyss along with it or is dissolved in this irony. This is why lamenting the "loss of com-

munity" is usually accompanied by lamenting the "loss" of the power of myths. (1991: 57)

If the absence of myth marks the common present-day condition, this condition, rather than constituting community, undoes it.

What is shared at the limit of the interrupted community is not communion, nor is it a sense of common identity. What is shared is sharing itself. This sharing announces a rethinking of the ethics of the political. It is only in the face of the retreat of politics—where politics is understood as the governing voice of the metaphysics of subjectivity—that the political can be retraced. Such a rescripting of the political—through a renunciation of myth as the coherence of our notion of community—allows us to critically reenvisage philosophy's preoccupation with the ethical. As Simon Sparks explains, drawing on the thought of Nancy and Philippe Lacoue-Labarthe,

> the political marks the place where the distinction between philosophy and non-philosophy, between philosophy and its unthought, becomes blurred. This place, the place of the political, would always have the character of a limit. . . . The political is both at the limit of philosophy and forms its limit . . . the philosophical describes the limit and identity of the political. (1997: xvii)

A breaching of the problematic of the political allows us to rearticulate the limitations of philosophy's account of the ethical. It is within this rewriting of the political that we begin to relocate ourselves within a differentiated notion of community. This is not to suggest that we achieve closure, however. The rewriting of the political must be an ongoing process, as is the desire to be incommon.

Staging a departure from the mythic solidarity of such policed enclosures as the nation-state, or ontology itself, involves a rethinking of the political that allows us to negotiate, among other things, the centrality of figuration within our conceptual frameworks of being-in-common. Within the vocabulary of community as being-in-common, the figure continues to be seen as the identity principle: the human Subject (i.e., the White Man) continues to see himself as "an original *mimeme;* as the mark of an originary fiction at the heart of metaphysics" (Sparks 1997: xxiv). As Nancy writes: "This question forms today the contour, if not the aporia, of the actual paradox of the meaning of the political: Is there still meaning without figuration or configuration?" (1997: 142). The challenge is to think the political beyond the identity principle of myth at the heart

of which resides the figure. We must reconceptualize the political beyond
the ethics of the face. Yet, as Nancy and Lacoue-Labarthe warn, this cannot be considered a simple procedure, for we are not immune to figures
and "it is not certain . . . that one can ever avoid a grounding gesture"
(1997: 133).

It is essential that we reexamine what we consider to be the figural within the configuration of the mythical that sustains our politico-
national imaginaries. In other words, what we must seek is an exploration of how the figural dominates the myths we accept and encourage
as the centerpieces of our being-in-common. In *Lulu*, this dilemma of
the figural can be observed through Lulu's attentiveness to her face as
that which allows or denies her access into the national imaginary. Lulu's
ultimate rejection of the figural is her renunciation to myth of the other
as theorized within the vocabulary of the nation-state. In the wake of
figurality, Lulu de-faces the tradition of the face by introducing the face
as ephemeral. In *Lulu*, the postfigural might be aptly conceptualized as
the rendering-ephemeral of the face of the political. *Lulu* suggests that
by acknowledging the ephemerality of the face, we may be capable of
resisting the grounding narratives of mythic belonging and politico-
national attachments. The face as the ephemeral instance of facelessness
in *Lulu* alerts us to the necessity of shifting the articulation of the political toward a postfigural chronotope in which our sense of time and space
would no longer be dominated by the notion that we are a community of
compatible figures or faces.

Despite *Lulu*'s allegiance to a postfigural chronotope, Lulu's continual
return to the mirror to paint her face acts as a warning that we remain
vigilant. The specter of the figural remains, even if it is now cast as
ephemeral: even in face-lessness, we cannot completely be rid of the
face. Hasn't political philosophy, in the name of the figure, more often
than not reproduced, or simply recast, the very practices of exclusion it
has sought to overcome, usually in the name of marginality, excess, and
diversity, even in the name of otherness itself? How is ephemerality or
facelessness different? As Golding laments: Rather than having produced
a counterculture or a counterphilosophy, rather than having inaugurated
a subversion of the ethics of similarity, hasn't the recasting of the vocabulary of alterity simply left us with

> a kind of "shopping list" of so-called subjective "other" identities—be
> it woman, Jew, immigrant, person of colour, s/m dyke, whore, etc.—
> gathered together in opposition to the so-called objective "dominant-

power" forms of identities, often named male, white, heterosexual, middle or ruling class? (1997: xii)

The practice of de-facing must be envisioned critically at every turn. We must pay serious attention to the ways in which new narratives of containment and comprehension take form. We must remember that writing often retreats into the library of mythic accounts of the White Man's most recent battles for self-empowerment, where the figure invariably remains, as white and mighty as always. Writing the other against myth—as an interruption of myth—involves acknowledging the seduction of the figural, remembering all the while that otherness is not something substantial, but "simply and only a cosmetic wound: a very thin, virtual, and in this sense 'impossible' limit" (Golding: 1997, xiii). As *Lulu* aptly demonstrates, it is only when this perceived otherness, my own wrinkled surface, admits to itself that it is but a surface—a pluralized, contagious, seductive, cosmetic surface—that I, as other, can begin to acknowledge the interruption of myth as the bleeding into uncontainable identities and incommensurable communities.

The interruption of myth through a writing of *différance* performs community as disjunctive, opening a space for an other ethics. If the absence of myth marks the common present-day condition, this condition, rather than constituting community, undoes it, thereby also deconstructing the ethics that depends on a stable and coherent conceptualization of territory and identity. At this juncture, an other ethics emerges, a face-less ethics that relies not on the bounded structures of a politico-philosophical tradition of territorial integrity and metaphysical subjectivity, but on a passion for the community that propagates itself, unworked *(désoeuvrée)*. This interruption of ethics turns community toward the outside instead of gathering it toward a center, transforming the center into the geographical locus of an indefinitely multiple exposition.

An engagement with the interruption of the myth of the other renders Krishna's *Lulu* an example of the interruption of community. Within the film, there is a critique of the necessity to mythologize the other by recording his or her difference as a juxtaposition to (and passport to) the narrative of the nation. What is revealed in this encounter with the scripting of the other is the impossibility of gathering alterity into the national imaginary. This sense of futility is revealed in the exchanges between Lulu and the filmmaker, Miguel. Himself a refugee, Miguel attempts to record Lulu's story to create a history of the other. "Now the history of my country doesn't include me anymore," the filmmaker tells

Lulu. "You sound like my father," she responds, referring to a man who has not been capable of negotiating the shift from Vietnam to Toronto. "I interviewed him—I interviewed refugees from all over the world," Miguel responds. "I want people to know about us. They should hear our story. We just mope around, wallow in our misery, nobody can understand us. That's why I need your testimony, photographs, mementos from home." The relationship Lulu develops with Miguel is both informative and transformative because, on the one hand, it alerts her to the seduction of subsuming all narratives into the vocabulary of the nation, while, on the other hand, it clarifies Lulu's position as resistant to *both* the notion of assimilating herself as a "refugee" *and* as a "national citizen."

Through her refusal to narrate herself as other, Lulu inaugurates a multiple exposition of herself that decries assuming a singular subjectivity within a bounded and policed imaginary. Lulu's compearance constitutes her very being, where compearance implies ef-facing the other as other. This effacing of the other can be understood as the interruption of the narrative of the national. In this interruption there is no longer anything to be done with myth, where myth always implies completion or fulfillment. Lulu arrives at this realization through her interactions with Miguel. In her attempt to come to terms with her status as a refugee, Lulu begins to narrate her own story. This narration causes Lulu to distance herself from Lucky and his notion of love as possession and being-in-common. It is not surprising, therefore, that Lucky resents Miguel's presence in Lulu's life: he is terrified he will lose Lulu as a result of her telling her story. For Lulu's narrative has always and will always be the story of how Lucky believed he could purchase her face.

Lulu's story—the trafficking and consumption of third-world bodies for the pleasure of "lucky" first-world men—is an articulation that seeks the interruption of community, ethics, politics, and national identity. Lulu must distance herself from everything that constitutes a platform for the commodification of her face and her body. Most of the solicitation of bodies in *Lulu* takes place through the institution of Dunkel Initiatives, a name that evokes images of darkness, shadiness, and unlawfulness. Dunkel Initiatives effaces the other through the trafficking of bodies, offering money for the compensation of the body after death, a practice that suggests that the body—and its alterity—can be consumed and recycled for profit.

Lulu's rewriting of her narrative can be understood as an attempt to distance herself from the underground meat-carcass operation that employs all the men in her life, even her father, who is convinced by Clive to sell his body to Dunkel Initiatives after his death. It is imperative that Lulu rewrite herself into an interrupted community in which her body is no longer a commodity of exchange and return and her face no longer the necessary locus of an encounter with the White Man. It is at this limit where the body is no longer the site of commodification, where the story no longer speaks of identity and national community, that the defacing of politics permits a rearticulation of the political.

Defacing the Nation

Nancy's community is not a locus of similarity, of faces we encounter easily and comfortably. It is a place of dissension, a space of encounter that reminds us of our responsibility toward the maintenance of an incoherence that has the capacity of rendering us both impotent and entranced with respect to and as the other. This encounter does not take place face to face, but skin to skin, where the skin is the filament of our writing, of our narration, of our incapacity to house the other, once and for all. The inoperative community assures us that the other is not containable, not foreseeable. The other escapes spatial containment, foregrounding the horror of our myths, the myths that compel us to believe that we can face the other and contain him or her in our stories of national coherence and domestic aspirations.

This dissonance within the schematic of the ethics of encounter renders Krishna's *Lulu* uncategorizable as a film, caught somewhere between me and you, territory and boundlessness, the white, the black, the yellow, the powdered, the faceless face. Rather than offering an ordered representation of the other, *Lulu* negates the possibility of a being-in-common, replacing it with a dynamic scenario of love, deceit, desire, and death. *Lulu* is aware of the seductions and shortcomings of national myths, but does not give in to them. Rather, *Lulu* offers an articulation that lodges a fracture in the national vocabulary that sustains the hierarchy between alterity and similarity, between native and immigrant, between life and death.

Lulu stages a critique of narratives that attempt to contain the other. There is no absolute other, *Lulu* proclaims, for we are all others, horrific and nauseated, different and common, seductive and loved, face to face with ourselves, always attempting to efface ourselves, our difference, our similarity. As *Lulu* demonstrates, if what we want to encounter is our own incommensurability, the ethics of the face are inadequate. We must delve beyond the face, beyond the white wall/black hole landscape, beyond the myths that allow us to believe that there can be a narration that maintains the other in his or her place of difference. This can be achieved through an appeal to a different ethics of encounter. A rethinking of the ethical must not only foreground the inconsistencies in the imaginaries that sustain our dis-eased nations, but must also facilitate a withdrawal from the spatial organization of the nation and its narratives. For "ethics," as Nancy writes,

> along with "logic" and "physics," appears only within philosophy, whose history and end are metaphysical. To appeal to an ethics is to remain within the closures of this end. It is not even to suspect the possibility, and still less the possible necessity, of challenging this closure. (1997: 33)

Challenging the closure of metaphysics requires, among other things, that we place the study of ethics beside organizing discourses such as politics—where politics refers to the sovereign organization of the territorial, the identical and the national, thus developing an awareness of how these discourses are parasitical, how they feed on each other in the name of the sovereign (be it philosophy, law, or the White Man) to sustain a metaphysics of subjectivity. Placing the ethical and the political side by side in the name of a critical engagement with alterity, a tension emerges that calls for a deconstruction of the ethical. An ethics-under-deconstruction in turn signals a rearticulation of the political.

Ethics-under-deconstruction as a rewriting of the political challenges hierarchical assumptions inherent in the national vocabulary. Dichotomies such as self and other, national citizen and immigrant, homed and homeless, are called into question, thus rendering abject the subject/object opposition. The abject in this case can be conceptualized as the specter of the unhomely, which arises with a massive and sudden emergence of uncanniness, subverting the political qualifications of the subject. The abject severs our relationship to the dominant (symbolic) order, propelling us into the unknown: the abject can be understood as the state of mind in which one's foothold in the world of self and other disintegrates, leading us toward a potential psychosis where "the 'I' blurs and is not yet" (Kristeva 1982: 120). This experience of abjection is profoundly unsettling, for it emphasizes a cataclysmic renunciation of the stable categories of identity.

The shift from object to abject involves a rearticulation of the bounds of the political, since alterity functions as a stable signifier within the imaginary of the nation. To realize this shift in political thinking, the nation as stable entity must be dismembered, allowing the captive bodies in its midst to reorganize themselves. This can only be undertaken through a renegotiation of the terms of inclusion and exclusion within the uneasy language of the nation: the nation must be addressed in a vocabulary that resists its territorial imperatives. Abjection is a dynamic process that operates through convulsions. In the case of the national body-politic, abjection can be visualized as the consequence of the entry of "others" into the body of the nation, who both occupy and disturb the identity and territory that was reserved for the coherence of the national imaginary. To retain its coherence, the nation rejects these abject parts of itself, defined as other or excess, thereby engendering the mythic consolidation of a homogeneous national identity.

However, as Kristeva argues, the abject invariably reemerges as that which constitutes and opposes the self, whether of the individual or the nation-state, confounding both the self's and the nation's boundaries, thus condemning the nation to continual redefinition. The other as abject symbolizes the horrific and terrifying dissolution of both the self's and the nation's perceived integrity. Despite its resistance to the abject, the nation is forced by the abject to instantiate interrupted communities that act like sores on the nation's epithelium. Faced with this threatened return of the abject as prohibition that dissolves the national self into undifferentiable physical parts, the self/nation attempts to close and police its boundaries by effacing the other.

In *Lulu*, rendering faceless is a form of abjection from the objectifying narratives of the nation-state. Lulu's intransigence with respect to the attempts made by the White Man to assimilate her within the metaphysics of subjectivity can be understood in this vein. Lulu expresses a desire to be *abject* rather than *object*, based on the presumption that, unlike the objectification that ensues with the consumption of (third-world) bodies and faces, the return of the abject affects all levels of the hierarchical spectrum, exposing each self to its horrific limitations and excesses as an other. The abject de-faces the White Man by bringing him face to face with his own *Unheimlichkeit*, with the strange familiarity of his horrific features: white wall/black hole.

Counternarratives of the nation, such as *Lulu*, foreground the inevitable return of the abject within the body-politic of the nation. In so doing, they ensure a continual displacement between the presumed secure categories of self and other, national citizen and immigrant initiating a resistance to the metaphysics of subjectivity in an era of figurality that continues to be dependent on the strictures of a political philosophy that reinforces a territorially and racially bounded ethics. Offering a challenge to the politics of similarity, cinematic events such as *Lulu* provide the possibility of initiating a dialogue in the name of an ethico-politics-under-deconstruction that allows us to conceptualize an alternative to the exclusive ethico-politics of the nation-state. For as Homi Bhabha reminds us, "the political unity of the nation consists in a continual displacement of the anxiety of its irredeemably plural modern space" (1994: 149). The horror, the horror.

In the final chapter, I extend the discussion of horror to the separatist politics in Quebec, expanding my analysis of the politics of alterity to an exploration of the manner the other is constructed in and through language. In Quebec, while dwelling necessarily implies a dwelling-with-the-other, dwelling also carries within its political etymology the imaginary imposition of a unique cultural identity. For those who cannot imagine identity as unique, what remains is the challenging task of inventing a language that deviates from that of the overarching nationalist politics condoned in both the "soft" and the "hard" sovereignist circles. With reference to what Derrida calls the "monolingualism of the other," I explore the link between identity and territory in the separatist imagination. Returning to my initial question about how we construct vocabularies of belonging, I ask whether it is possible to write languages that challenge the transition from the local into the global. Attentive to a shift from the politics of being-in-common to a politics of being incommon, I work with the films of Robert Lepage, asking once more where an errant politics might lead us in the transformation of our wor(l)ds.

5. Dwelling within the Language of the Other

We have attained political maturity and we are now ready for economic emancipation . . . now is the time for us to become masters in our own house.

—Jean Lesage, premier of Quebec (1962)

Claude Jutra's internationally acclaimed film *Mon Oncle Antoine* (Canada 1974) begins with the words, *"Dans la nation de Quebec."*[1] These are heated words that speak to the emotional connection between identity and territory that resides at the heart of the Quebecois nationalist and separatist imagination. According to the current political vista, these are fictional words, words that speak more to a desire for a future not yet mapped than to a past already deciphered. What I hear in Jutra's words is the endeavor to imagine a separate nation that always already existed. Some would argue that Quebecois separatist politics are about this reclaiming of a past. These people would assert that Quebec has always reigned as a *polis* quite separate from the rest of Canada. My concern in this chapter is not to trace a genealogy of nation-ness with respect to Quebec's cultural and political legacy, but to explore how the fiction of belonging naturalizes a certain reading of history.

The relationship between history and the nation merges into focus in the reclaiming of a past. This involves staking a claim on the archive of official memory that secures itself as the narrative of the nation as cohesive entity. To naturalize such a claim on the nation's memory, it is necessary to identify history as that which establishes a certain dominion over the future by way of the past. This traversal of time necessitates a certain forgetting—in Lauren Berlant's terminology, a "paramnesia"—which involves a selective consciousness that identifies and naturalizes only certain aspects of political life to the detriment of others (in Golding 1997). When history is taken to task in the name of the legacy of a nation, however, this selective memory of the past risks becoming unraveled. One result of such an unraveling is that both history and the national imaginary begin to emerge as an infinite conversation, an unworked work *(oeuvre désoeuvrée)* no longer contained by "the masterwork" whose teleological narrative inevitably inscribes past hurts into future resentments.

Writing history as an unworked work involves exploring the language of the other who exists in the gap where territory and identity no longer coincide. In this gap, we discover an altered imaginary in conflict with the idea of the nation as the sovereign territory that houses "a people." Throughout *Ephemeral Territories,* I have sought various terminologies to assist me in the un-writing of the vocabulary of the nation. Another helpful tool in this process of the dissemination of the nation's vocabularies of belonging is Michel Foucault's concept of "effective history." Effective history challenges traditional historiography by adopting a critical stance vis-à-vis the construction of narratives of the past, alerting us to the ways in which any writing of history is complicit in evoking a hierarchy of events that prioritizes not only certain peoples, but also certain chronologies.

Effective history stages a resistance to the notion of linear time, suggesting that historical experience be understood in terms of rupture, discontinuity, arbitrary shifts, and confluences, rather than according to the implicit cosmogonic assumption in historiography that the origin of an historical state of affairs can be found, and, if located, that the origin can shed ultimate meaning on that state of affairs. As Foucault (1984a) argues, the presumption of immanent rationality is a theoretical fiction historians and philosophers of history employ to defend against the arbitrary and multiplicitous (non)foundations of historical experiences that resist conceptual categorization. Taking issue with the historical narratives that presume that the multiplicity of present historical phenomena can be derived from a single origin, Foucault uses the concept of effective history to demonstrate a reversal of the historiographic trope of the Fall, suggesting that in the beginning was multiplicity, not homogeneity.

Genealogy is Foucault's historiographic articulation of effective history. Genealogy can be understood as the writing of the necessary departure from historiography's teleological narratives. Genealogy focuses not on the grand events or grand narratives of "history," but on the minute details and aberrations historiographers prefer to ignore. It is not genealogy's task to go back in time to restore an unbroken continuity, nor does genealogy seek to recover forgotten memories or to demonstrate that the past actively lives in the present, secretly animating it, having imposed a predetermined form on all its vicissitudes. Genealogy rejects the "meta-historical deployment of ideal significations and indefinite teleologies," opting not for the discovery of a forgotten identity, eager to be reborn, but for a complex system of distinct and multiple elements that cannot be mastered by the powers of synthesis (Foucault 1984a: 77).

Faced with genealogy's dynamic constellations, historical accounts boasting national homogeneity based on unmarred stories of origins and straightforward teleologies find themselves subverted by the very narratives they seek to contain. As divergent genealogical narratives come into contact with the nation's myths of origin and homogeneity, and the sovereignty of the nation as the body of a national narrative is threatened, incentives are invariably carried out to polish the stories of containment that perpetuate the nation's myths of belonging and cohesion. On the surface, the teleological narrative of history often prevails. For example, in Canada, the reliance on the linear narrative of history in the telling of the story of "a people" results in the continuing conflation of identity and territory for the promotion of a unified "national identity." Similarly, in Quebec, we witness the perpetuation of a myth of ethnic homogeneity as a central pillar in the quest for sovereignty.

Despite the appearance of Canadian nationalism as a benign pursuit and the popular belief that Quebec's drive toward sovereignty is harmless, genealogical readings of both these nationalisms warn us that nationalism is a parochial investment in history and, as such, a dangerous and even potentially violent solicitation of a narrative of homogeneity. Vocabularies of nationalism are informed by staid and stagnant traditions that perpetuate racism and discrimination, languishing in a nostalgia based on fractured dreams of lost unity where the other who cannot be assimilated is posited as a threat to history and its dreams of uniformity.

In this chapter, I search for political vocabularies that speak back to the nation. To do so, I revisit the history of the sovereignty movement in Quebec. I find Robert Lepage's films instrumental to this task, for they offer genealogical rereadings of the politics of the nation in Quebec, entering into the debates of historical *appartenance* and delving beyond these debates to a vision of a contextual politics that encompasses both the local and the global. Lepage's films provide a rare glimpse into a complex political and cultural question, proposing new ways of invoking a rapprochement of the local and the global. Lepage's films emphasize the manner in which Quebec politics remains ensconced in the fissure between history and genealogy. There is, in Quebec sovereignty politics, both a desire to be open to a global/local politics of difference and the need to hold on to a racial politics that silences alterity. This is apparent in many facets of political life in Quebec, though never as obvious as through the politics of language, where being "Quebecois"—as opposed to being simply "French-Canadian" or "Francophone"—relies on what is too often a linear historical narrative spoken in the discernible accent of the Quebecois *pur-laine*.[2]

My focus for this chapter is on a genealogical reading of the politics of language in Quebec as seen through the lens of two films by Robert Lepage, *Nô* (Canada 1998) and *Le Polygraphe* (Canada 1996). I begin my exploration of the politics of language in Quebec with an inquiry into the difference between being Quebecois and being Francophone in Quebec to draw attention to the complexity inherent in the use of the French language as a political tool for sovereignty politics. I am puzzled by the notion that, despite the fact that difference always already resides within language, the claim to language in Quebec is one that rests on the assumption of similarity. The dissension between what it means to speak as a Quebecois as opposed to simply speaking as a Francophone results in a conflictual politics that creates a rift between language as the means to convey a sense of origin and language as a tool that challenges us to communicate across borders and nationalities.

I suggest that language inspires, by its very polyvocality and intertextuality, a certain dissonance in the articulations of community, potentially violating the uniformity of the community as nation. This dissonance within language paradoxically haunts attempts to choreograph the Quebec "nation" once and for all in the name of a politics of language. For the voices that speak in a multitude of accents in Quebec invariably alert us not only to the various interpretations of what it means to live in Quebec and speak French, but also to the varied linguistic and cultural consequences of espousing a concept of sovereignty that is based on a politics of language-as-conformity.

This is the topic of Robert Lepage's film *Nô*, in which even the title alludes to the polymorphous aspect of language, referring both to Japanese theater and to the "no" vote in the Quebec referendums. Through readings of both Lepage's *Nô* and *Le Polygraphe*, I focus on the limitations and dangers of a discourse of sovereignty. I suggest that sovereignty is a discourse that, by its very nature, results in the attempt to marginalize the language of the other. Concurrently, I draw attention to the ways in which the contemporary cultural imagination in Quebec—as demonstrated through the films of Robert Lepage—can effect a resistance to linear narratives of cohesion and monovocality.

I present not a history of Quebec, but a genealogy of an era that positions language as the center of its national truth. In so doing, I foreground not the ills suffered in Quebec at the hands of les maudits Anglais,[3] but the ways in which the language debate in Quebec exposes a politics of resentment and exclusion that discriminates against the other who does not see himself or herself reflected in the dominant narratives of the quest for sovereignty. There are many "others" in Quebec, and many versions of the debate for sovereignty. I do not attempt to answer to this plurality, nor do I necessarily speak against the desire for self-determination. If self-determination is the goal, then let it happen not in the shadow of a political agenda that is written in the vocabulary of the nation. Let us imagine instead a different way of "being at home" based on a political vocabulary that celebrates difference in Quebec, in the rest of Canada, and in the world at large.

Dwelling With/In: Robert Lepage's Nô

The last few months of 1998, shortly preceding the reelection of Lucien Bouchard, premier of Quebec and leader of the Parti Quebecois,[4] showed a resurgence of the debates on Quebec sovereignty, which, over the past three decades, have haunted both sides of the Quebec-Canada border, resulting in an apparently unresolvable conflict. In a poll of Quebecois, statistics showed that if a referendum had been held at the end of February 1998 on the issue of Quebec sovereignty (accompanied by a partnership with the rest of Canada), 49 percent of decided voters would have voted yes, while 51 percent would have voted no. At a referendum on Quebec independence, 34 percent of Quebecois would have voted yes, while 66 percent would have voted no.

Heated political discussions continue to take place both inside and outside Quebec in light of these figures, fueled by comments such as those made by Quebec premier Robert Bourassa in 1990, who declared that "English Canada must clearly understand that, no matter what anyone does, Quebec is and always will be a free and distinct society, capable of taking responsibility for its own destiny and development."[5] It is as a result of such comments, spurred by the politics of the Parti Quebecois throughout the 1990s and the subsequent reelection of Bouchard's separatist government, that the long-standing debate on the subject of Quebec sovereignty continues to prevail over most political discourses in Quebec, often eclipsing other important issues.[6]

Robert Lepage's film *Nô* participates in this political debate. Lepage initiates an encounter with Quebec sovereignty politics through a depiction of the events leading up to the first Quebec referendum. In *Nô*, Lepage uses as his lens the events of the October Crisis in 1970—the violent revolution of the *Front de Liberation du Québec* (FLQ) and the subsequent military rule imposed on the province of Quebec by Prime Minister Pierre Trudeau—the Quebecois presence in the representation of Canada in the World Fair in Osaka, Japan, and the referendum in May 1980. What makes Lepage's film particularly interesting is not the actual reenactment of these events, but the link he draws on the one hand between language and revolution in Quebec and, on the other, between the events on Quebec soil and in Osaka. Broadening the conflict in Quebec by exposing it to an international stage, Lepage recasts the events of the early 1970s in a more global context, offering us a complex version of the often restrictively localized narrative of Quebec's battle for sovereignty. Without falling back on rehearsed stories of victimization and national usurpation, *Nô* demonstrates in a refreshingly creative manner the situation that has led to the current political climate in Canada.

Quebec has long sought a suitable political status vis-à-vis the rest of Canada, demanding greater powers from Canada's federal government in areas such as economy, culture, social policy, language, law, and education. This desire for self-determination extends as far back as the early confrontations between the French and the British settlers in Upper and Lower Canada.[7] The focus for this chapter, however, is on the more recent history of the sovereignty movement in Quebec, which can be traced to the inception, by René Levesque—who would later head Quebec's first pro-sovereignty government—of the *Mouvement souveraineté-association* in 1967, which, the following year, became the Parti Québécois. This rise to political power coincided with the Quiet Revolution, which took form as Quebec society underwent the slow transformation from religion to secular life, shifting from a rural to a successful urban society. Henceforth, Quebec sovereignty has figured as a central platform in the program of one of Quebec's two main political parties, altering the balance between federalist and pro-sovereignty forces in the province of Quebec and elsewhere in Canada.

During the Quiet Revolution, the ratio between private and public action, between the "people" and the public institutions of state and economy, are understood as having been transformed. Gagnon and Allor argue that the key cultural significance of the social changes inaugurated by the Quiet Revolution has been nothing less than the production of the "Cultural" field itself as both the legitimating agency of government and as an emergent regime of social power. . . . This production of the "cultural" involves the elaboration of new forms of knowledge about the peuple québécois and hence new articulations of social difference within the population. (1996: 8)

Spurred by the Quiet Revolution, Quebec's cultural field became a motivating factor for the creation of new definitions of a secular Quebec, reinforcing a desire for differentiation (both cultural and linguistic) from the rest of Canada. The cultural field is seen both through the lens of state intervention into the production, circulation, and consumption of cultural materials, and as the broader public space responsible for the contesting of the outcomes of cultural development.

Michelle Gagnon and Martin Allor argue that "the 'distinctiveness' of Québec within the Canadian confederation at the present moment is not simply due to the effects of nostalgic narratives of the two 'founding peoples'" (1996: 20). It is a complex result of conjunctural rearticulations of the relation between culture and the state as well as between the state and civil society in Quebec, where the cultural has, since the Quiet Revolution, been elaborated as the productive center of both the social and the political. This situation sets the stage for Lepage's *Nô*, which takes place at two historical junctures in Quebec, October 1970 and May 1980.[8] Lepage tackles the political events adjacent to the quest for sovereignty through a rare lens: humor. *Nô* refrains from espousing a moralistic or apocalyptic tone while relating the often contradictory sides of the story as voices intermingle from Quebec to Vancouver to Japan to Ottawa.

In *Nô*, Lepage describes the quest for sovereignty as a "project" that has reverberations that span the globe and the country. In simple terms, this "project" can be understood as the desire to legalize, for Quebec, a cultural and political identity that is separate from that of the rest of Canada. In more nuanced terms, the inception of the notion of the "project" allows Lepage to locate sovereignty as both the possibility of an event and as the search for a unifying endeavor. This classification of sovereignty as "project" grants sovereignty its place within the political spectrum while concurrently alerting us to the fact that sovereignty is but one method of working together for a common goal.

The complexity of sovereignty as "project" is most palpable in the final scene of *Nô*. In this scene, Michel and Sophie are watching the outcome of the 1980 referendum on television, visibly disappointed by the "no" outcome. "People who have a collective project are always somewhat at a disadvantage compared to those who have none. It takes more energy to change social and political forums than to do nothing," Michel remarks. "At the same time," Sophie responds, "those who voted 'no' have their own collective project. They believe in Canada." "But surely no one can imagine that it's settled," replies Michel. "It's like a couple who is desperately trying to find a common interest. It's sterile—there is no common identity." "Are you talking about us, as a couple?" Sophie asks. "It's that we have no project for the future," he responds, "no posterity, no goal."

This final dialogue in Lepage's *Nô* situates the quest for sovereignty as a project that takes place both inside and outside the home. The politics of sovereignty as outlined by Lepage is about the desire for a common identity, a desire that is propelled as much out of a need for attachment on a personal level as it is for cohesion on a collective level. On the one hand, *Nô* suggests that we can consider the "project" of sovereignty as Michel's seemingly benign personal desire to conceive a child of the "Quebec nation" with Sophie to combat the postreferendum doldrums. On the other hand, we can understand the project of sovereignty as one that has devastating local and global consequences, such as the dropping of the atom bomb on Hiroshima and Nagasaki. Hence, Lepage's emphasis on post-Hiroshima Japan, where the battle for sovereignty maimed a generation.

The juxtaposition between the desire for sovereignty in Quebec and the effects of sovereignty on Japan is dramatized through the use of a time-image that cuts from Michel and Sophie's desire to have a baby in postreferendum Quebec to Hanako's testimony regarding her experience as a child of the bombing of Hiroshima.[9] Sovereignty in Lepage's film is thus conceptualized at once as the offspring of a dissatisfied future generation in Quebec and as the perpetrator of the figure of the mutant in Japan, whose future is undermined by a bomb deployed in the name of the security of the nation-state. Sovereignty, in these terms, spans a vast territory, from the comfortable Quebecois and Canadian homes—whose televisions reveal both the apathy and the celebrations as a result of the lost referendum on the night of May 20, 1980—to the uprooted and often painful lives of a generation of Japanese who are the unlucky victims of a world war fought in the name of state sovereignty.

Such are the sad and perverse ironies foregrounded in Lepage's *Nô*, a film that, through humor and sarcasm, spans one of the most painful decades of Canadian and Quebec history, reminding its viewers of the catastrophic events of the FLQ crisis that unfold during the Osaka World Fair of 1970. Lepage creates a cacophony of juxtaposition using these two interrelated though completely separate events to demonstrate the political ironies in both locales. In Osaka, Canada is being represented theatrically by a group of Quebec actors performing a French play by Feydeau, in preparation of which the Quebec actors have had to rehearse the French accent. As Sophie sarcastically tells the Canadian cultural attaché: "We are a colonized people. *Vive le Quebec libre!*" These moments are interspersed by the terrible events taking place in Quebec, where a government minister is killed by the FLQ revolutionaries, leading Prime Minister Pierre Trudeau to institute the War Measures Act.

A famous dialogue between Trudeau and a reporter is interspersed within the reenactment of these events in Lepage's film: "With your army troops, you seem to be combating them almost as if it was a war," the reporter challenges. "And if it is a war, does anything they have to say have validity?" "Don't be silly," Trudeau interrupts, "we're using some of the army as peace agents . . . so that they are more free to do their job as policemen." "At any cost?" the reporter asks. "How far would you go?" "Just watch me," Trudeau responds. Lepage uses Trudeau's involvement in the events of the October Crisis to demonstrate the violence and short-sightedness inherent in all politics of sovereignty, be they federalist or separatist. Trudeau's stance vis-à-vis the political events of the October crisis are reflected in his deployment of federalism, where federalism, as a sovereign vocabulary of governance, is portrayed as being no more emancipatory—and no less violent—than the language of sovereignty proposed by the revolutionaries in Quebec. In *Nô*, the fight for "freedom" is revealed not, in the end, as a productive battle for the liberty of voice, language, and culture, but as a reversal of freedom into violence.

In August 1998, the Supreme Court of Canada ruled that Quebec cannot unilaterally separate, yet it affirmed that the Quebecois have the democratic right to determine their own future as long as they do so within the law. In a unanimous ruling lauded for its lucid account of Canadian federalism, the Supreme Court declared that for Quebec to leave Canada, a majority of Quebecois must say yes to a clear question as well as negotiate the terms of Quebec's separation with the rest of Canada. The Supreme Court's ruling also obliges the other provinces to negotiate in good faith with Quebec. In response to this ruling, the minister of Intergovernmental Affairs, Jacques Brassard, pointed out that the high court had indeed recognized the legitimacy of the sovereignty movement in the province. If Quebec were to vote yes on a referendum,

Quebec and the federal and provincial governments would be obligated to negotiate secession. If the rest of Canada refused to negotiate in good faith, and if Quebec could convince other nations to recognize it, Quebec might have a case for separation on the international stage.

The response to the ruling of the Supreme Court was not unilateral, though most Canadians who publicly responded to the decision were pleased to hear Quebec could not secede without intervention from the other provinces. Some were angered that the Supreme Court ruling would oblige them to negotiate with Quebec if a future referendum vote favored leaving Canada. At this point in the race for Quebec sovereignty, what is most apparent, however, is the listlessness of the response: "The fact that the ruling is so widely considered fair and balanced almost guarantees it will scarcely register with Canadians already bored by two decades of constitutional staring contests with Québec" (Evenson *Globe and Mail*: 30 November 1998). As one anonymous commentator noted:

> It's not a central issue, and unless one simple aspect (of the ruling) is drawn out and the rest ignored, it won't register. Listening to the radio this morning I heard people say this was a victory for federalists and this was a victory for separatists. I think it's a victory for obfuscation.

What can be singled out from these events is the manner in which the model of the sovereign nation has become naturalized as the only viable mode of political governance. The adoption of the rehearsed language of state sovereignty has the inevitable effect of short-circuiting the process of rethinking the political outside the parameters of the territorial nation-state. That is to say: the political in Quebec finds its articulation only in certain enunciations. Consequently, the language of sovereignty, whether of the *oui* or of the *non,* becomes the only way of understanding culture, politics, and belonging. Sophie's miscarriage in front of her bombed home in the midst of the FLQ crisis reflects this situation, emphasizing the infertility within the political vocabulary that remains limited by the discourse of the nation. As the blood pours down her legs, the police officers—inattentive to the bleeding—arrest her in the name of federalism, as though guaranteeing that no creation can come of the quest for Quebec sovereignty, from either the federalist or the separatist camps.

Indeed, the past thirty years have shown not a creative process between Quebec and Canada, but a constitutional wrangling that has defied the possibility of exploring alternative venues for a rethinking of the political. Rather than attending to nationalism's dangerous exclusionary practices, what has continued to be evoked is the victimhood of an oppressed people, as much on one side of the border as on the other, where territorial sovereignty has remained the only vocabulary for self-determination. This has resulted not only in a stalemate with respect to Quebec and the rest of Canada, but in growing dissension amid the native peoples and the immigrants, both of whom continue to be marginalized in the ongoing debate concerning state sovereignty.

The dream of the sovereign nation as that which offers the promise of constitutional liberty and democracy, be it in Quebec or in Canada as a whole, reaches at the heart of the troubling contradictions of modernity, alerting us to the myopic quality of our political time, where national sovereignty is evoked as the only modus operandi of the political. Quests for self-determination become battles for state sovereignty, as can be observed not only in the tense negotiations between Canada and Quebec, but also in the debates between the Quebecois and the Cree population in northern Quebec. This situation is summed up well by Connolly, who writes:

> In late modernity, the nostalgic idealism of territorial democracy fosters the nostalgic realism of international relations. . . . The nostalgia is for a time in the past when the politics of place could be imagined as a coherent possibility for the future. (1995: 135)

National politics are politics of homesickness. In the case of Quebec, the lament is narrated in the name of a nostalgia for a lost place and a fulsome past that never was, in longing abeyance to a dream spoken in the unwavering vocabulary of community, nation, and "a people."

Within the Quebec sovereignty debate, the politics of language figure as a central motif, encapsulating all the injustices and desires at the heart of the identification of the Quebecois with the Quebecois "nation." While the centrality of language is not new to battles for sovereignty—ethnic cohesion and linguistic singularity continue to be associated with racial purity and cultural assimilation in many areas of the world—in Quebec, the focus on language has taken on a life of its own. Here, language operates not only as the potential harbinger of sovereignty—that which ultimately defines all Quebecois as a people and therefore guarantees their "nationhood"—but, paradoxically, language also acts as the potential nemesis that will ultimately prevent a consensus. This is the case because of the rift between those who speak the "real Quebecois French," the *Québécois de souche*,[10] and those who are merely French-Canadian. This rift is complex, for it both defines the Quebecois as "a people" and widens an ever-increasing divide between French-Canadians and Quebecois, potentially alienating immigrants, native peoples, Francophones inside and outside Quebec, and English-speakers in Quebec.[11]

In Quebec, language acts as the sovereign who, "in a permanent state of exception, declares that there is nothing outside language and that language is always beyond itself" (Agamben 1998: 21). To speak, on the one hand, is to speak the law, as Michel reminds the revolutionaries in *Nô:* "Our first form of resistance is language, the way we speak it, the words we use, the words that are not the words of our colonizers. We must transcend to the language of the sovereign." Although Michel arrives at an important interpretation of the role of language, what he leaves out is that language can never function simply as a symbol of belonging, be it belonging within the politics of the colonizer or those of the sovereign. Language cannot be assimilated. As Derrida writes, "I have one language, yet it is not mine" (1998: 2). Like the sovereign who is always both inside and outside the political order, language operates as that which we dream of calling our own when we seek to use it to oppress or repress the other, and as that which eludes us when we attempt to define ourselves according to its laws.

Language—all speech, all writing—is a promise and a desire, an expectation without a horizon, a moment in passing. To attempt to hold language captive, as an extension, for instance, of the vocabulary of sovereignty, is to ignore the possibility that there may be alternative models of political governance by choosing the state of exception as the only moment of self-determination. This is demonstrated ironically in *Nô* in the scene where Michel proclaims the potential of language in the face of his colleagues' incomprehension. For them, language and revolution are two completely separate issues. As a result, it is the playwright with writer's block, not the revolutionary-in-action, who composes the list of demands to be given to the journalists, a list that is eventually blown apart by a bomb that was programmed accidentally for noon Japan-time rather than Montreal-time.

Language is a promise of communication that offers no guarantees. Language always leaves a residue we cannot control. Language opens onto a politics that questions the rights to property, territory, identity, hospitality, and belonging, while at the same time playing the trickster by trying to seduce us into thinking that language itself is that which allows us to speak of property, sovereignty, and ethnic superiority. Such is the paradox of language: it is used both to imprison and colonize a people, and to set them free. As Derrida writes, within language's violent circularity, "'colonialism' and 'colonization' are only high points *[reliefs]*, one traumatism over another, an increasing buildup of violence, the jealous rage of an essential *coloniality* and *culture...*" (1998: 24). Regardless of its persistent charms of seduction, assimilation, and cohesion, language cannot be comprehended as a totality. Rather, language alerts us to the incoherence of the law, any law, and to the resultant paradoxical effects of sovereignty, where the language that is spoken in the name of the sovereign, despite the use of the "correct" accent, of the "right" words and syntax, nonetheless reappears as the language of the other whom we are attempting to assimilate or exclude. As Derrida writes, "[My] language, the only one I hear myself speak and agree to speak, is the language of the other" (1998: 25).

Despite language's ruse, "[e]very culture institutes itself through the unilateral imposition of some 'politics' of language. Mastery begins, as we know, through the power of naming, of imposing and legitimating appellations" (Derrida 1998: 39). On the one hand, then, language acts as the rational voice of sovereignty, while on the other hand language subverts the quest for sovereignty through its subtle but invasive mechanisms of disruption and contagion. The pretense of monolingualism—the desire that only one language be spoken—is therefore another name for the dictatorship of the sovereign who operates in the guise of the appellation of a law that originates from the political utopia that claims that language is the origin and the content of that law:

> The monolingualism imposed by the other operates by relying upon that foundation, here, through a sovereignty whose essence is always colonial, which tends, repressively and irrepressibly, to reduce language to the One, that is, to the hegemony of the homogeneous ... effacing the folds and flattening the text. (Derrida 1998: 39–40)

Even when we speak only one language, this language eventually returns (us) to the other, for it is a language *for* the other, *from* the other, spoken *by* the other. Hence, language is never natural, habitable, original, or proper. We cannot inhabit it, nor can we attempt to locate language as the grounding concept of home, where home remains the promise of the project of common identity. Even if we persist in our desire to locate language as the seat of an exclusive national identity based on a fissure between "us" and "them," we cannot remain completely deaf to the fact that "our" language is also spoken by the "other," whose location within the discourses of home, nation, security, and sovereignty may diverge from our own. Eventually, therefore, language cannot but remind us that all culture is the culture of the other. As Derrida writes, "The *of* signifies not so much property as provenance: language is for the other, coming from the other, *the* coming of the other" (1998: 68).

Within Quebecois separatist politics, language continues to be articulated as the signifier of timed-place. Language operates as the sovereign body that functions as the guarantor of similarity: language remains the vehicle for the propagation of the nostalgic myth of a cohesive past that speaks of ethnic purity and cultural unity in Quebec. The nation that Quebec sovereignists seek is a return to the myth of the nation-state as an ethnically singular entity, wherein language follows a linear trajectory that does nothing more than translate the law of the sovereign. Multiculture, in this case, is seen as an encroachment on the singularity of *the* Quebecois, where the other is invited only upon the promise of assimilation. What is disregarded in this scenario is the fact that any notion of a multiplicity of cultures involves a struggle wherein the dialogic polyvocality of language is audible.

Robert Lepage's films seek a departure from atavistic notions of the Quebecois nation through an emphasis on the cultural polyvocality of Quebec. Resisting the temptation to set up a dichotomy between cultures, or creating a language impasse, Lepage undermines the notion of ethnic purity perpetuated by those who would attempt to calcify Quebec in the name of singularity. For Lepage, culture is cultivation in the sense that it evokes an interruption of itself, opening itself onto the other, thereby de-idealizing both itself and the other. Lepage is attentive to the opportunity to see the other not as an already familiar and thus cognitively and practically dominated other, but as the other who reveals him- or herself through singularity and incommensurability. Lepage thus creates an unworked work, one that speaks not of cultural fusion, but of dissent and incoherence, voicing a rejoinder to the political rather than replicating the stale articulations of the language of history, sovereignty, and the nation.

An exemplary confrontation between language and sovereignty in the name of an albeit unsuccessful rearticulation of the political is explored in the scene referred to above, where two revolutionaries and a playwright are discussing the revisions to the list of demands to be presented to the media by members of the FLQ. A debate takes place between Michel, a playwright who hasn't produced a play in three years because he refuses to work for "the institutions that are financed by a fascist government" (referring to the federalists) and two "revolutionary" members of the FLQ. As explained above, in an interception of the list of demands compiled by the revolutionaries to be delivered with a bomb, Michel questions their use of language. "You can't print this," he tells them. "Why the hell not?" they ask, pressed for time with a bomb scheduled to explode in a few hours. "It's . . . it's not clear," the playwright tells them. "There are . . . spelling mistakes . . . , syntax errors, formulations which are clearly too French." "We're not addressing ourselves to intellectuals, but to the people," one of the members of the FLQ responds. "You need a certain intellectual rigor," argues Michel. "At the moment when we need to use the power of words, all of a sudden language has no importance." "It's a fucking list of demands!" one of the revolutionaries exclaims, "not a fucking play!" "I thought this was all about language," Michel replies. "Is it for the advancement of a cause or to explode a bomb?"

What Lepage underscores is the ambivalence within any politics of language. Language is both an ally and an informant, since language, as Derrida has shown, is never something that is given without reserve. Language cannot, once and for all, fulfill the promise of territorial integrity and cultural belonging. This is exemplified once again in one of the final scenes in *Nô*, where a sentence is misleadingly translated and language is exposed in all of its indeterminacy. Speaking about Rimbaud's demise, Hanako speaks of the epoch in which he stopped creating. *"C'est dommage qu'il se soit tue,"* she says. "It's sad that he killed himself," Errol translates. "No," she laughs, *"je n'ai pas dit tué, j'ai dit tue*—I didn't say killed, I said silenced." Not only does Lepage draw our attention here to language's variability, he also demonstrates in a very concise manner the effects of inaugurating a politics of language in the name of the coherence of a people. The language politics in Quebec, Lepage seems to say, have resulted in inaugurating a silence that could easily be misunderstood as the death of the other.

Dwelling With/Out: Movements of the Global

Lepage suggests that language is a pivotal element in the articulation of the political. Rather than simply focusing on the politics of language "at home," the realms of the local and the global are interwoven in Lepage's films; thus, the politics of language extends beyond the immediate concerns of a local (Quebecois) politics. In Lepage's *Nô*, for instance, there is a continuous juxtaposition between Osaka and Montreal, even though the encounter between language and politics is staged primarily *within* the nation; consequently, what is emphasized is a domestic politics of difference. In Lepage's *Le Polygraphe* the politics of language is also extended to an inter- and transnational arena. This oscillation between the local and the global within Lepage's films is what allows Lepage to broaden his political spectrum and delve beyond the boundaries of Quebec identity to address the consequences of the discourse of Quebec sovereignty.

A bridging of local and global politics does not imply that language somehow becomes incorporated in either the local or the global arenas as a stand-in for identity and cultural cohesion. Language remains ephemeral in the sense that all utterances are fleeting, spoken in many places at once. Language inaugurates both appearances and disappearances. Language personifies the slipperiness of the political: language cannot be captured as a system, but must instead be continually rearticulated to be understood in the context of the present. Lepage's films underscore this ephemerality of language by pointing to the manner in which language functions within a contextual politics (the bridging of the local and the global) that potentially subverts territorial sovereignty, exposing the incongruities, seductions, and misunderstandings inherent in all state-centered discourses.

This is not to say that the nation-state has lost currency or that language does not concurrently function within state-centered discourses in the name of a homogenous ideal of identity. In fact, in many cases, despite the impulses of globalization, we continue to experience the strengthening of national borders, as can be seen in Quebec. One response to this problematic is to dissect the local, finding fissures within its systems of governance, foregrounding examples of the ways in which the local is constituted by uneven development and dialogue between constituencies. The local as a site of resistance offers a glimpse into the deterritorialization of the sovereignty of the nation-state, where deterritorialization is not to be read as an absence of space or as a mode of territoriality that opposes the dominantly inscribed spatiality of the modern sovereign state. Deterritorialization is understood as an exponential acceleration and proliferation of both the space of the state and the space of the interstate—or, in this case, the relationship between the local and the global: deterritorialization is a transfusion, since it transcends the moment of contact, of the state and the interstate.

Within deterritorialization, smooth and striated spaces are interlocking and mutually parasitic planes, or plateaus, of conceptual and spatial organization that, far from being distinct, owe their (figurative, if not ontological) nature to their continuous collisions and to the fact that they are repeatedly "forcibly wedged " into one another (Deleuze and Guattari 1987: 474–75). According to the logic of deterritorialization, the local in dialogue with the global potentially figures as a layering of space that resists the discourse of the state apparatus through the articulation of new modes of the political. Setting the global and the local side by side emphasizes the necessity of refiguring "one-way models of domination to the social formations of modern nation-states," activating "multiple lines of social invention, contestation, mobility, reimagining, coalition, and flight" (Wilson and Dissanayake 1996: 2). A global/local nexus emerges as a result of new economic and cultural zones of transcultural hybridity, which, in turn, effect a rewriting of the logic of the nation-state and a subsequent remapping of space and time.

A dialogue between the local and the global is at work in Lepage's films. Through a focus on the global in the narration of local events, Lepage encourages a certain deconstruction of the discourse of nationalism on the home front and state sovereignty in the intra- and international arenas. He achieves this destabilization of the nation-state by integrating moments of political hesitation (effective history) within the discourse of the local while concurrently exploring the politics of space in the global arena. In other words, Lepage effects a contextualization of time and space that calls for a contextual politics. He incites us to confront the constructed character of all events, replaying cinematically the importance of engaging with the ephemerality of time and space.

This ephemerality is foregrounded through a rejection of the model of a singular system of organization and representation for the reinvention of the political and a replacement of this model by the assertion that the political spans events. The political, for Lepage, is not simply a system of governance that operates in time and space. The political is a rearticulation of language that results from the simultaneity and collisions of the events of everyday life. Like the ephemeral, which is defined as that which "lasts only one day," the political for Lepage is a vehicle of transition, a moment when time and space are reconfigured in abeyance to the next moment.

In Lepage's films, we are introduced to domestic and foreign political encounters. Lepage effects this translation of time and space by embracing the specificity of the local and superimposing it onto global events that also retain their unique character. Lepage resists generalizing about the visceral effects of a local politics on the global front. This is captured beautifully in a scene I will describe shortly, where an event that takes place in Quebec City in *Le Polygraphe* is intercut with images of one of the characters crossing the policed border from East to West Germany. In this scene, neither event is given narrative precedence. Rather, these events complete one another, complicating the notion of a linear sequence of time. Politics thus becomes not that which takes place either strictly "at home" or "elsewhere," but that which is articulated through the simultaneity of events. Through such juxtapositions, Lepage theorizes the political as a genealogical account of accidents, rather than a historical continuity that assumes a strict hierarchy of times, locations, and spaces. For Lepage, the political is not that which occurs singularly in Quebec or in Berlin. The political is conceptualized as that which marks the *interconnection* between events that take place in Quebec *and* in Berlin.

Language figures as the pivot for the rearticulation of both local and global politics in Lepage's films. The centrality of language is underscored in *Le Polygraphe* through the specter of cultural translation. Language's integrity as the law-abiding voice of state sovereignty is deferred through the process of cultural translation, drawing attention to the impossibility of an "original" (linguistic) event. To explore this in more detail, a short exposition of the story of *Le Polygraphe* is necessary: *Le Polygraphe* is centered on a murder that occurred a year previous and is now being filmed within the film. In the midst of this rewriting of the past, the central character, François, is faced twice with the lie detector, even though the police already know who the killer is: a woman they are protecting because of her father's diplomatic immunity. While these events are taking place, François is busy writing a dissertation on "cultural alienation and the loss of identity in the context of political exile," with a focus on the divided East and West Germanys. At the same time, his closest friend and neighbor, Lucie, is acting (in the film within the film) in the role of the woman (François's ex-girlfriend) he is accused of having killed. Concurrently, Lucie falls in love with Christof, an East German who defected to Montreal during the cold war.

The emphasis throughout *Le Polygraphe* is on the global/local nexus. This is not to say, however, that Lepage turns a blind eye to the complexity of the nationalist politics "at home." On the contrary: Lepage is keenly aware of the effects of nationalism on the home front. He simply does not see the politics "at home" as separate from the politics "elsewhere." Lepage relies on the global/local nexus to demonstrate the ways in which the political is rearticulated through a global/localization that destabilizes at once the boundaries of the nation-state and the contours of "home." Lepage is keenly aware of the need to imagine a trans- or postnational imaginary where national identities and political allegiances are potentially undone.

Through encounters with languages and cultures in the plural, Lepage's films reflect a different organization of the political. What ensues from this articulation of resistance is not only the foregrounding of cultures that are otherwise rendered inarticulate within the discourse of the nation, but a renewed emphasis on the ways in which difference can be visualized both culturally and politically. If we are to critically reenvision and rewrite the vocabulary of the political through a renunciation of the language of the nation, it is imperative not only that we find cultural instances that instantiate a reenvisioning of the nation, but that we learn to read them accordingly, attentive to the ways in which new vocabularies of the political take form. In *Le Polygraphe,* a performative critique involves embracing the option of responding to the continuous practice of translation evoked throughout the film, rather than attempting to draw together a linear account of the film, thus imprisoning the film within a politics it renounces. It is necessary to emphasize not the (in)coherence of the text, but the impossibility of clearly discerning the intelligibility of the text.

The injunction to take part in the construction of a politics is a central aspect of Lepage's films, and, in particular, of *Le Polygraphe,* where Lepage purposefully renders unstable our relationship to the present and the past, forcing us to engage in our own reading of genealogy's simultaneities. This challenge is cast out in many ways throughout the film, one of which is through the confusion of the diegetic and the nondiegetic events in the film; consequently, we are incited to repeatedly ask ourselves what is happening at the various strata of filmic experience. Lepage undertakes such a juxtaposition of time and space at the level of the characters as well, continuously requiring them to alter their relationship to the events of the past due to a deferred translation of these events in a present that does not adhere to a linear continuity in either time or space. Even the lie detector is incapable of offering an accurate reading, which suggests that every moment exacts its own reading of the "truth." Truth as a wavering discourse becomes a metaphor for the elusiveness of cultural and national identity.

Lepage characterizes the construction of the political as a performative exercise. Bhabha writes:

> In the production of the nation as narration there is a split between the continuist, accumulative temporality of the pedagogical, and the repetitious, recursive strategy of the performative. It is through this process of splitting that the conceptual ambivalence of modern society becomes the site of *writing the nation.* (1994: 145–46)

Drawing on Bhabha's distinction between the pedagogical and the performative, I follow Lepage's lead, emphasizing the potential of the performative to subvert bounded discourses. Placing the reader of Lepage's films in a position of power, I suggest that the cultural critic *can* alert us to ways in which cultural texts undermine the homogenizing tendencies of the nation-state.[12] Whereas the *pedagogical* founds its narrative authority in the tradition of the people, the *performative* intervenes in the sovereignty of the nation's self-generation. Confronted with the nation split within itself, a performative reading evokes the liminal space that is internally marked by minority discourses, heterogeneous histories of contending peoples, and the tense locations of cultural difference.

It is not only through the writing but also through the reading of counternarratives of the nation that we can begin to deconstruct the totalizing boundaries of the nation-state, initiating an engagement with the dislocations of the local in the global and vice versa. It is important to resist explicating the text in an effort to contain the text within a historical continuity. To do the text justice, we must instead embrace the ephemerality of the text, not to situate the text beyond the political, but quite the contrary—to evoke the ephemeral as the voice of errant politics. In other words, we must resist attempting to *comprehend* the ephemeral in the sense both of understanding it and of holding it captive.

Dwelling with the Other: Histories Written in Blood

As critical readers who seek to uncover not the pedagogical elements of cultural texts but culture's performativity, we are left with the arduous task of locating within texts examples of the subversion of the national imaginary, a task that involves composing a counternarrative to sovereignty through the elaboration of alternative modes of political governance. This is not a simple endeavor. As Walker and Saul Mendlovitz remind us, "[W]e have become so used to thinking about political life as if state sovereignty is the only guide to what is possible that it even informs our understanding of what alternatives there might be" (1990: 2). Through performative readings of counternational texts such as those of Robert Lepage, however, we have at our disposal examples of alternative enunciations of the political that do not rely on the limiting discourse of state sovereignty. In his films—and, indeed, throughout all his work—Lepage responds to the challenge of creating culture in the plural by seeking to undermine state sovereignty, evoking a compelling and disquieting relationship between the forces of political sovereignty and those of cultural elaboration.

Le Polygraphe begins with François being interrogated while strapped to a polygraph. The camera looks down on François, who is captive in a windowless room. Imprisoned by what the police would like to call "the truth," a truth they already know to be a lie, François becomes enmeshed in the tendrils of his unstable narrative as he begins to count on the lie detector to distinguish between what is true and what is false. "The results are inconclusive," the police commissioner tells him after the test. "What do you mean, inconclusive? Did I do it or not?" François yells. "You tell me," the commissioner replies. But François does not remember, and as the scene closes, we see him still connected to the lie detector, incapable of finding the (right) way out. Concurrently, we watch Lucie at her audition, where she is asked to improvise a tragic situation for the mute role of the murdered woman. The scene shifts from the audition room to the subway platform, where we see Lucie panic at the sight of a person throwing him- or herself onto the tracks. Already, narrations are spatiotemporally confused.

In a following shot, we watch as François sits in front of his computer, attempting to download an image of the Brandenburg Gates from the Internet. "Insufficient memory," the computer flashes. Simultaneously, we encounter Christof, the East German who fled the socialist regime and is now a successful medical doctor in Montreal. Insufficient memory becomes the gnomon around which a tale of forgetting takes place. Simultaneously, through the figures of François and Christof, we are introduced to a paramnesic tendency to repress the heterogeneous and conflicting experiences, be they those concerned with political regimes or those that involved violences committed at home. As the story unfolds, memory, as paramnesia, becomes the vehicle for the potential subversion of cultural, national, and political "certainties."

Memory's transformative potential can be cultivated only if we refrain from succumbing to a nostalgia that seeks to relive the past at the expense of the present. An adherence to the past invariably results in the will-less unfolding of a web of ressentiment. Such a practice of ressentiment is carefully avoided in Lepage's work. Memory, as explored in *Le Polygraphe*, is closer to Nietzsche's notion of forgetting as a means to the will to power, a theory that emphasizes the necessity of letting go of memory as nostalgia in order not to succumb to the ill will that results from the refusal to partake in the contingent world of the present. Such a politics of forgetting enables a critical reassessment of the past while it paves the way for the discourses of the present that transgress accepted understandings of time and space, thereby privileging discourses of simultaneity and juxtaposition that subvert the closed and static narrations of continuity on which territorial and historical containment depend.

In an adjacent scene, while the camera shoots François from above sitting in the bath with his head down, looking desolate, the news on the radio situates us: we are in the fall of 1989 and Mikhail Gorbachev is arriving in East Berlin on an official two-day journey to mark the fortieth anniversary of the German Democratic Republic. The commentator explains: "It's a highly sensitive trip to an East-bloc country that has stubbornly refused to embrace perestroika and glasnost . . . yet the crowds gave him a hero's welcome." In the following scene, through a small window, we see François slumped in a chair, crying. The relationship between the local (François) and the global (the end of the cold-war era) is presented at once as strangely congruous and fiercely separate, for the global is both impossibly distant from François's current concerns and terribly close to him as the subject of his dissertation. Such simultaneous alienation and conjunction persists throughout the film, as *Le Polygraphe* relies on dichotomies to underscore the effects of the global on the local, though the ending of the film suggests that we must eventually discard the closed circuit of the dialectic to face the confusing contradictions of a world in flux.

One important scene that shifts between the local and the global occurs toward the beginning of the film, while François defends his dissertation proposal and Christof simultaneously performs an autopsy of a murder victim. In this scene we are thrust into a simultaneity of times and spaces, facing at once the discourse of the institutional (Quebec as university, both in the guise of a political-science department and of a medical seminar), the political (François's presentation on Berlin and the simultaneous unfolding of a visual narrative of Christof leaving East Berlin), and the physical (Christof's autopsy of a murder victim). In this pivotal scene, no clear-cut separations are made between the categories of the political, the physical, and the institutional. This scene incites us instead to juxtapose the discourses of the global (the situation in East Germany) and the local (the murder of a woman and subsequent accusations aimed at innocent people).

The scene begins with an establishing shot of Christof in an auditorium undertaking the autopsy of a murder victim and follows with an establishing shot of a similar auditorium, where François is defending his thesis proposal. During this scene, the camera often moves around in a circle, resulting in a dizzying effect of vertigo, suggesting that there is no way of situating ourselves comfortably within a contextual politics.

Within contextual politics, we are always situated between contradictory discourses, whether they be concerned with truth or lies, with the global or the local, with the present or the past. It is of this ephemeral contextuality that Christof and François speak, simultaneously, separately:

> We determined that the victim's wounds were caused by an elongated, pointed object that pierced the skin and penetrated the subjacent tissue. / *After the fall of the Third Reich, of which it was the capital, Berlin was reduced to a pile of rubble and misery.* / The victim's wounds were extremely broad, and considering that they were caused by such a thin instrument, we can surmise that the form and depth of the lesions were altered during the struggle / *The victors* / by the repeated entry of the blade, / *cut the city into American, French and British sectors. As for the Soviets, they erected a 40 km wall* / cutting him on the left hand and right arm with a stab to the rib cage that perforated the lung. We can surmise that the fatal blow was given here / *in the middle of the city [slide of the Brandenburg Gates].* / between the fifth and sixth ribs, / *The Wall of Shame, as the West Germans call it [Christof crossing through the border between East and West Germany], was erected to stop the flow of Berliners,* / provoked by the severing of the septum. / *a symbol of the division between capitalism and communism,* / The septum is a thin wall located in the center of the heart that blocks the passage / *from East to West.* / from the left to the right ventricles. / *But the passage is strictly one way [Christof at Friedrichstrasse, the last subway station between East and West Berlin]* / because a sophisticated system of gates that open and close *[Christof is ushered through the gate]* / controls the flow of Westerners / unoxygenated blood / *and keeps East Germans [Christof walks through the gate]* / oxygenated blood [Christof showing his (West German) passport] / *from passing the other way.*

A lot is happening in this scene, not least of which is the metaphorical superimposition of the opening/closing of the heart and the erection of the wall between East and West Germany. This exchange is brought to fruition through the narration of the murder case at the center of *Le Polygraphe,* which can be seen as an allegory for the closure of circulation between East and West. The murder case requires a discourse of truth that is its own undoing because any discourse of truth requires a politics of memory that can result only in a lack of oxygenation, since memory that resides in nostalgia holds us captive in an idealized prison house of our own making.

The narration of *Le Polygraphe* happens in a "meanwhile" mode that negotiates the complex and contradictory experiences of cultural translation and political migration. The language shifts from English to French to German. To be understood, characters from various parts of the world speak in languages that are not their mother tongues. Lepage thus makes an effort to characterize Quebec as *one* place among a multilingual global political community, staging a departure from the strict language politics of Quebec's political platform for sovereignty while at the same time offering an intimately local narrative of the events in a few people's lives within a small community. Rather than suggesting that the concerns of the local cannot be thought outside the realm of the particular, Lepage offers a narrative that links local events (the murder of a woman, the escape of a man from East Germany) to the globalizing forces of the late twentieth century (the fall of the Berlin Wall) in an effort to understand political exile.

We hear the news of the fall of the Berlin Wall on the radio at the same time Lucie plays with Christof's *matryoshka*, toward the end of the film.[13] Referring to the *matryoshka*, Christof tells Lucie that he likes to think the dolls "represent the truth as hiding another truth as hiding another truth and on and on and on." This interaction—as Christof meticulously fits the pieces of the doll back into place—seems to point to the fact that Christof is not yet ready to accept truth as *différance*, and thus he must keep the dolls, the narratives of truth, tightly in one place: "They're supposed to be on display like that . . . fitted in . . . ," he explains. Later, we learn that the *matryoshka* is the only possession he took with him during his exodus from East to West. As long as he is not yet ready to confront his paramnesia, the doll will remain closed in on itself.

Christof does eventually disclose his past, though disclosure does not happen easily, or without consequence. With the collapse of the Berlin Wall, the need for silence on Christof's part is diminished. Yet the years of imposed forgetting have left Christof with deep scars infected with unexplained emotions, truths, and lies, rendered all the more excruciating by the suicide of his wife shortly after the fall of the wall. Nonetheless, Christof does face his demons, though not without implicating those "at home," where "home" is conceptualized as an amorphous space in-between. As can be expected from Lepage, who insists that the political is a communicative discourse, *Le Polygraphe* emphasizes not only the complexities within the "emancipation" of East Germany, but also the reverberations of global politics on local constituencies. This is demonstrated through a confrontation between François and Christof that takes place in the midst of the confusing aftershocks of the end of the cold war.

After hearing the news of the fall of the Berlin Wall, François goes outside to the roof of his building to attempt to erase the Russian script painted in red letters on the wall. Christof stands in the background. "History is written in blood," Christof reads, his knowledge of Russian a surprise to François, who immediately confronts him about his German past. Christof evades François's questions. As they speak, François attempts to erase the script. Yet he is incapable of erasing the words that have underpinned his academic and personal life during his years of research on the subject of the cold war. This confrontation that ends in an anger that cannot be efficiently articulated leaves us with the suggestion that histories continue to be written in blood.

In the end, we recognize the language on the wall as a pertinent reminder of the reverberations of the politics on the home front. Language remains a contentious issue. For language politics in Quebec *is* a history written in blood, both with respect to the legacy of a past colonized by *les maudits Anglais* and a present attempt at colonization by *les maudits Français*. On the other hand, by attending to the language on the wall, Lepage also seems to imply that we now have the opportunity to assess the limitations of a history that seeks to constrain identity in the name of language, ethnicity, and nationalism. In a move to introduce a concept of effective history that would replace the historical narratives that contain Quebec within the imaginary of a nation, Lepage evokes language (the fact that words cannot be completely erased even as languages shift to accommodate new political utterances) to translate the local into a politics of the global.

This is not to suggest that Lepage does not take local politics seriously. Lepage understands with remarkable lucidity the paradoxes of a politics of language that lays claim to the "truth" of a people. As François aptly explains in a lecture to his students, there can be no "truth" of a people as long as populations continue to create contingent genealogies that resist history's stolid narratives of linear progress, for these very genealogies incite confusion and inconsistencies within the world order, impeding, among other things, the "politics of reconciliation," in Germany as in Quebec. François explains:

The Germany of the twentieth century has seen many changes. It has been devastated, divided, and rebuilt, and, more recently, reunited. The question is whether Germany will be able to achieve reconciliation. While the majority of Germans are glad the wall's down, many feel nostalgic for a time when they could blame their misfortunes and anxieties, whatever in the system didn't work, on the wall. So, within this reunited Germany we are faced with a dichotomy.

As François's explanation of the world order at the end of the twentieth century draws to a close, the camera pans across the room to a succession of bored-looking, youthful faces. "All right," François tells them, "I'll give you an example," and we are led once more into a narration of simultaneities as we watch Lucie and Christof saying good-bye to each other at the airport while we listen to François's monologue:

> Imagine you've just been through a major ordeal and you feel you need to be alone. So you decide to go away. As you board the plane you suddenly feel vulnerable. You start to panic. Since you cannot go back you must have trust [Christof being scanned by the metal detectors at the airport] and confront your fears [x-ray of Christof's bags]. Thus, in our increasingly heterogeneous societies, trust is the only route to reconciliation. This is hard: though we claim to be able to see the thoughts and the feelings of human beings, the soul remains a mystery [Christof watching as an attendant unpacks and takes apart the *matryoshka*], hiding another mystery, and on to infinity.

Lepage ends *Le Polygraphe* with the notion that we must delve beyond the dichotomy or dualistic thinking that characterizes modernity and is a symptom of the era of nationalism. We must do so by critiquing the politics of reconciliation that act as an attempt to "understand" the mysteries and contingencies of effective history. As Lepage argues, we must face the local/global nexus as a discourse that does not disclose the truth—be it of nationalism, territory, or identity—but as that which pries the truth apart, exposing the contradictions that result from articulations of the global in the local, and vice versa.

This is aptly demonstrated by Christof's final frenzied moments at the airport, as he quickly throws the pieces of his dismembered *matryoshka* into his bag despite his previous keen desire to put her back together. The airport as the final locus of time and space in *Le Polygraphe* acts as a metaphor for the local/global nexus: it is both the zone of displacement and the bounded and policed intersection between sovereign states. At the airport, the x-ray machine functions as the polygraph that reminds us that every movement we make toward both the local and the global is necessarily also a movement that involves a potential lie concerning our motives, our origins, our territorial imperatives, and our relationship to state sovereignty and nationalism. Yet, as the x-ray machine displays in color images of the effects of people's lives, we are also reminded of *our* influence on the nature of the images, texts, and languages we produce. After all, it is we who pack our bags.

This choice—the willed gatherings of our personal effects in a world in flux—demonstrates the contextuality of our existences as citizens of late modernity. "Late modernity is a distinctive political time without a corresponding place of collective political accountability," writes Connolly (1995: 159). *Le Polygraphe* does not deny modernity's shortcomings. Instead, it visualizes, through the colorful images of our packed bags, the pluralization of political spaces of action through attention to the global/local nexus. Following *Le Polygraphe,* we might imagine, for instance, a democracy that engages in a dialogic reciprocity of the local and the global and attends to the specificities of the multicultures that coexist within its changing frameworks.

Faced with the sovereignty debates in Quebec and the consequent resurgent nationalisms across Canada and Quebec, cultural texts such as those of Robert Lepage invite us to choose the narratives through which we define and express ourselves. These texts remind us that it is our choice whether we conform to a politics that endangers life through the qualification and disqualification of political subjects in the name of language, race, ethnicity, or gender. We *can* envisage a multicultural polydemocracy that resists the politics of sovereignty, thus becoming aware of the dangerous limitations of all discourses of sovereignty that conflate identity and territory and narrate the other in the vocabulary of the selfsame. Oppressive narratives of sovereignty do not offer the promise of a renegotiation of the political. Narratives of sovereignty impose constraints on our articulations of territorial and linguistic difference and on our ability to visualize this difference.

Conclusion
Water from the Rock

There is politics as soon as there is time.

—**Geoffrey Bennington**

Language, writes Bakhtin, is "populated—overpopulated—with the intentions of others" (1986: 42). In the name of incommensurability and difference, sovereignty and dominion, language articulates all of our modes of being-in-common and being incommon. All attempts to re-engender our various cultural and political vocabularies take place through a radical reconception of the manner in which the political is articulated through language. Throughout *Ephemeral Territories,* I have made an attempt to subvert territorial definitions of the political through a dissemination of the vocabulary of the nation. I have sought to reformulate, through language and its effects of representation, the basis for a theory of the political (an errant politics) that seeks to move beyond the strict enclosures of territorial sovereignty and national identity.

Ephemeral Territories is orchestrated around St.-Exupéry's notion of the ephemeral. Situating culture as a pivotal element in the subversion of the national, I have demonstrated how the ephemeral can call forth a process of deterritorialization when the ephemeral is situated in conjunction with the cultural. Approaching culture as the ephemeral that speaks to and makes demands on the nation, I have explored the manner in which cultural texts exact a performative response from the nation while challenging its pedagogical utterances. In *Ephemeral Territories,* the ephemeral refers to the aspects of culture that permit culture to remain incomplete, uncertain, unstable, and, ultimately, indefinable.

Ephemeral Territories is a work against politics insofar as it recognizes politics as a metaphysical utterance that privileges the dichotomies on which the discourse of the nation-state relies. It is against politics as long as politics continues to be imagined and understood as the overarching signifier. It is against politics when politics is situated as the championing voice of an exclusionary metaphysics. *Ephemeral Territories* is, therefore, by necessity, a reenvisioning of the possibility of talking about politics. It is not a hermeneutic exploration of the meaning of life, for it does not return to itself. Rather, *Ephemeral Territories* is a musing on the necessity of rethinking what we mean when we make "political" utterances. Is there an utterance that isn't, in some sense, political? And, if not, how can we learn to speak in such a way as to create the possibility for difference within our political vocabularies? These are questions that persist throughout *Ephemeral Territories,* questions I do not seek to answer in a tone that would betray either certainty or finality, questions that, in accordance with the vision of a politics-to-come, must remain open.

The two gestures with which I frame *Ephemeral Territories*—politics and deconstruction—are potentially antithetical. Politics, as a metaphysical construct, secures vocabularies for its own reinstatement. In the name of governmental organizations, national institutions, and official cultural texts, politics silences undecidability in favor of the dream of a concrete vision of governmentality. Politics thus becomes a moral discourse oriented toward its own end. Deconstruction, on the other hand, prizes undecidability. Unlike politics, deconstruction does not institute a narrative. Deconstruction demonstrates the manner in which hierarchized binaries are institutionalized in the history of Western thought. Hence, deconstruction is the very practice of politics' (un)readability.

We do not actively deconstruct. Rather, we show metaphysics in deconstruction. Hence, when I affirm a rearticulation of the political in the name of deconstruction, I begin the necessary task of exposing metaphysics' unraveling. In other words, a rearticulation of the political is a moment in the exposure of politics' debt to metaphysics. Insofar as a rearticulation of the political is the very gesture through which politics exposes itself as a construct of metaphysics, a rearticulation of the political *becomes* a deconstruction of politics. For deconstruction is a

> radical appeal to a future (the coming of the undecidable future event) which will never be a present . . . , although it always happens *now.* This appeal to an irreducible futural future (the interminably a-venir . . .) suspends deconstruction always this side of any ethical or political doctrine or programme. (Bennington 2000: 16)

To speak of a rearticulation of the political is therefore, at best, a tenuous endeavor that involves, every step of the way, a conscious effort not to fall back to the soothing imaginary of "being-in-common," which remains the central tenet of a metaphysical politics. We must, instead, continually have the courage to reconstruct our homes, returning to the idea of the ephemeral, to the promise of finitude, which offers nothing more (or less) than the temporality of incommensurability (being incommon).

In and of itself, the political is not radical. The political only becomes radical the moment its metaphysical genealogy is interrogated. The metaphysical aspect of the political resides in its reliance on a vocabulary of absolutes that proclaim its ability to "change the world." Is this claim so different from my own, my desire to imagine a polity that exceeds the bounds of territorial imperatives of identity? Do I not, as well, long for a "different" world? How does a rearticulation of the political ensure that it doesn't simply become a rearticulation of the very politics it seeks to undermine? A rearticulation of the political as I imagine it departs from the metaphysical concept of politics insofar as it beckons toward an interpretive politics, that is, a reading of the political that does not precede the writing of cultural texts, but is informed by them. As *Lulu* articulates so well, we are incommon through our own readability, and it is this readability that offers the promise of life as reinvention.

What is at stake, then, in *Ephemeral Territories* is the naming of the political as a practice of *reading*. Reading inaugurates a politics-under-deconstruction. Reading is an interpretive gesture always to come that challenges my subjectivity-in-process. The margin opened by readability is the possibility of the rearticulation of the political. Tracing a path to an opening, reading can also be formulated as a proposal for an encounter with the other. The text is the other to whom I turn not for comprehension, but for the challenge of exposing my own difference. The political is cast as this reading of the other that insists on the ultimate indecipherability of him or herself. Reading is not just a tranquil act of deciphering, but an exposition of the irreducibility of the other (as text, as world, as human being). Reading is politics-in-the-making.

I read to make reading possible. I read to exceed my duty as a citizen. I read to claim my position as a stranger. In *Ephemeral Territories* I read, and through this practice of reading, I expose a politics-to-come that exceeds and challenges categories of national politics such as citizenship, sovereignty, immigration, multiculturalism, homelessness, and racism. I explore the manner in which, within the vocabulary of the nation, the citizen constructs him- or herself in opposition to the other. I challenge the politics that sustain a notion of citizenship that depends on the nurturing of a figure of the citizen that rejects the other, where citizenship is defined as the form of collective affiliation that is "situated primarily in the juridical network of the (imaginary) international system of state sovereignties" (Shapiro 2000: 1).

I read in order to find the voice, the language, the text, aware that this very search is an implicit aspect of the voyage toward a rearticulation of the political. I read to negotiate the relationships of dominion sanctioned by a traditional notion of politics. I read to subvert hierarchies such as citizen/stranger, homed/homeless. I read to reread. I do not read to condemn texts, because I know that reading must always remain an exploration beyond familiar political vistas. I read to imagine a dialogical chronotope that is not indebted to the vocabulary of the nation.

Bennington writes that

> the deconstructive operation of apparent oppositions is the only possible 'ground' upon which metaphysics could ever claim to identify itself in the first place. Derrida can thus be said to repeat metaphysics differently. (2000: 11)

There is no "beyond" of metaphysics, only a continual *différance* of its terms. The ephemeral can be contextualized as one of these mechanisms of *différance*, for the ephemeral both defers and differs. It defers insofar as it does not lay claim to more than the present, the moment, the finite. It differs in that it prizes that which is other to the confining, stultifying encapsulation of time and space within a regulatory discourse of containment. Within the vocabulary of the ephemeral, the "beyond" cannot extend past today. It is in texts-in-the-making that the ephemeral lives, now.

Faced with the finitude of the political-as-ephemeral, I make decisions. These are timely decisions, made against the grain of time, impatient decisions because time is always already too short. "Politics happens in time, against time," writes Bennington. In the quickness of time, a rearticulation of the political is the injunction to make decisions that are not based on preprogrammed scenarios. Decisions are not given, as Derrida (1990) reminds us, they are taken. Politics, when it begins to drift away from its metaphysical determinations, can be thought of as a timely process of "taking" decisions, of reading texts in which reading itself is understood as a task that celebrates the ephemeral. The political is happening now. The political cannot be deciphered. It is lived, articulated, and rearticulated in the moment of its undoing. Because of its ephemeral qualities, the political cannot be properly theorized, but must instead "strive to keep open the event of alterity which alone makes politics possible and inevitable, but which political philosophy of all colours has always tried to close" (Bennington 2000: 33).

It is here, at the junction between politics, reading, and the ephemeral, that the (impossibility of the) ethical emerges. Where do we imagine ethics in a scenario that foregrounds politics as an articulation of *différance*? Isn't ethics, perhaps even more so than politics, entrenched within a metaphysical discourse that always already delineates what it construes as the unbridgeable distance between self and other? The deconstruction of politics cannot propose an ethics. "Ethics" is a theme and an object of deconstruction to be deconstructed, rather than a subject of its admiration and affirmation. Ethics is metaphysical through and through and can therefore never simply be assumed or affirmed in deconstruction.

Nonetheless, something is called for in relation to the other. Does not the horror we experience, face to face with the impossibility of subsuming the other into the same, bear the name of ethics? Perhaps, but only if we locate ethics as the ephemeral companion to a politics-always-under-deconstruction. In this case,

> "ethics" too might provide deconstruction with resources repressed or left unexploited by its metaphysical determination, and these resources might then be shown to be more "powerful" than that metaphysical determination, in excess of it. In which case deconstruction might after all be describable as ethical, and perhaps as ethics itself. (Bennington 2000: 35)

An ethical act worthy of its name is always inventive—inventive, not in the sense of re-creating a metaphysics of freedom and emancipation, but in the sense of espousing a response and response-ability to the other. Such an ethics cannot be located outside the reading of the text: I am ethical only insofar as I am actively reading the other's text. There is no escaping from "complicity" with the tradition (national borders continue to delineate our subjectivities), hence I must rigorously and inventively negotiate that very complicity. The horror, the horror.

In the (horrific) relation to the face of the other, I begin to invent a politics, an ethics, when I am willing to acknowledge that my gaze is distorted by the presence of those outside the immediate relation of face-to-faceness. This is a departure from Levinasian thought, which suggests that the nonsymmetrical dual relation is the primary receptivity that defines the ethical relation as the face-to-face. For Levinas, the other has a radical prior claim on me. I do not exist first, and then encounter the other. *Ephemeral Territories* seeks an infiltration of this dual gaze. I call for an acknowledgement of the dizzying nausea with which we must often contend when we face the ephemeral moment when all "pure" relations of alterity are dismantled. The imposing presence of the third party haunts the face-to-face relation, contaminating the purity of the properly ethical relation. The acknowledgment of this contamination (the horror!) is necessary if we seek to avoid the danger of re-inscribing an absolute violence in the name of a pure encounter with the other.

The ethos of a politics-in-the-making rests on the assumption that ethics is constitutively pervertible. This perversion cannot be preordained, however, nor can it be constituted as such. Hence the horror, for what is unknowable in most cases horrifies us. This unknowability must be maintained, for absolute knowledge of the subversions within the discourses of ethics and politics would immediately evacuate their specificity in favor of an administrative or bureaucratic application of cognitive rules. Ethics as a rearticulation of the political involves making singular decisions on the occasion of singular events. When the decision is already made, a particular understanding of the sovereignty of the deciding subject is celebrated. On these occasions, we return to a metaphysical deployment of both ethics and politics.

Every singular decision I take (every reading of the other's text) involves the recognition of the other that tells me something about myself, insofar as it is I who am actively engaging in the reading of the ephemeral. The other is not absolute: my politics cannot exist beyond the surprising, delightful, painful exigencies of the now. I decline the notion of the absolute in my ethical relation with the other, a relation that is mediated by the contaminating presence of the other's other. I am lost in the multiplicity of encounters that read me as I extend myself toward them, in a political (and ethical) gesture: *tout autre est tout autre* (every other [one] is every [bit] other).

To "decide" on politics is a violent act—violent, not only because it scars language's readability, but because the decision to "decide on politics" can never accurately be calculated. Violent, because it will always risk reinstating the very violence it seeks to exceed. There is no "beyond" that successfully erases violence: "Presence as violence is the meaning of finitude, the meaning of meaning as history" (Derrida 1978: 133). Violence marks every practice of reading, every gesture toward writing. Not even the ephemeral is exempt from violence: as the little prince painfully realizes, within the ephemerality of his rose lies a potential rancor at a life lived only today. He is stung by the rose's thorns, as we are each time we cling to the metaphysics of presence.

Still,

we cannot do away with the concept of the sign, we cannot give up this metaphysical complicity without simultaneously giving up the critical work we are directing against it, without running the risk of erasing difference in the self-identity of a signified reading to itself its signifier, or, what comes to the same thing, simply expelling it outside itself. (Derrida 1978: 281)

Hence, in my practice of imagining a rearticulation of the political, I continue to "give meaning" to signs such as "politics" and "ethics," "nation" and "home," even as I attempt to divest them of the "meanings" that identify them within a metaphysical tradition. Perhaps it is enough, for the moment, to acknowledge this dangerous game of give-and-take.

This is the demand placed on me by the ephemeral: I must be willing to renegotiate my terms even when the terms at my disposal risk revealing the most vulnerable moments in my reading. For isn't vulnerability always that inaugural moment that betrays the dream of community, of gathering, even in the name of difference? As Derrida warns:

Be they affirmed, denied or neutralized, these 'communitarian' values always run the risk of making a brother come back [to haunt us]. Perhaps we must make a note of this risk so that the question of the 'who' [who is my friend?] can no longer allow itself to be politically forced via the schema of being-common or being-in-common (even a neutralized being-common or being-in-common) into a question of identity (individual, subjective, ethnic, national, State, etc.). (1997: 298–99)

Or, in the words of Bennington,

There is no political which doesn't dream of putting politics to rest in light of the dream of an "after-politics" (that is nothing but a pre-politics, or nature); every law aspires to render the possible necessary, but, and here is the *hic*, the political, that which is but the possible within the realm of possibility, the radically possible which is another name for the impossible, is also that which prevents us from putting an end to politics.

Wandering the vistas of life, I opt for a politics that escapes the ephemeral accommodation I no longer call home, seeping from the arid discourse of the nation like water from the rock.

Notes

Introduction

1. Deconstruction here does not imply a critical endeavor in and of itself. Rather, deconstruction consists in "dislocating, displacing, disarticulating, disjointing, putting 'out of joint' the authority of the 'is'" (Derrida 1995b: 25). Deconstruction refers both to the strategies that disturb and unsettle, as well as the context in which those strategies are required to operate. In *Ephemeral Territories*, the deconstructive engagement is one that involves rereading the text to garner its metaphysical groundings.

2. The metaphor of the stutter is one Gilles Deleuze (1994) employs to illustrate the ways in which language can not only be interrupted but also reinvented. The stutter destabilizes language's parameters, foregrounding the contingent nature of language's enunciations. The cultural can be conceptualized as a performative utterance that potentially inflicts stuttering into the language system that sustains the nation (Deleuze 1994: 23–25).

1. An Excess of Seeing

1. Racine fastens the pages of the dictionary onto mirrors. As a result, the "missing words," such as territory, reflect our own faces as we read the definitions of the missing signifiers. Furthermore, light is reflected and refracted by the mirrors, making it (potentially) difficult for us to read the definitions, reflecting our own (failed) attempts at "understanding" and categorizing the artwork.

2. The members of what became the Group of Seven began to associate in Toronto between 1910 and 1913, although the Group itself was not officially founded until the time of their first exhibition at the Art Gallery of Toronto in 1920. The original Group was composed of Franklin Carmichael, Lawren Harris, A. Y. Jackson, Franz Johnston, Arthur Lismer, J. E. H. MacDonald, and F. H. Varley. Tom Thomson, who died before the inception of the Group, was never an official

member. It has often been suggested by the members of the Group, however, that Thomson's art and relationship to the northern landscape was both an inspiration and a driving force for the Group of Seven.

3. Previous to the Group of Seven, art in Canada was indebted primarily to British and Dutch landscape painting. The landscapes of the Group of Seven were a departure with respect to artistic genre. They added a critical perspective to colonial art by refusing to adhere to British and Dutch principles of landscape painting, stating that the depiction of a different or "new" landscape was necessary to the inception of a Canadian nationalist imaginary. These nationalist, anticolonialist leanings, as well as the new renditions of the artistic vision of the land, caused uproar within the upper-class art circles of the early 1920s. By the 1930s, however, the Group of Seven had secured a faithful following, which, in many cases, hasn't abandoned the Group's vision of Canada to this day.

4. There are a few instances of critiques of the nationalism propagated by the members of the Group. Newton MacTavish's response to the Wembley exhibit of 1924 is a rare published example of a critique of the Group's nationalism. In *The Fine Arts in Canada,* he writes: "Much conflicting opinion is expressed from time to time as to nationality in art. . . . For that reason the term 'Art in Canada' is used purposely in this book. . . . [T]he writer is not convinced that there is anywhere any art that is peculiarly Canadian" (quoted in Hill 1995: 159). In a letter to FitzGerald dated 15 March 1933, Brooker also provides a critique of the Group's nationalist leanings: "I am a little afraid that a strong nationalist bias, which always gets into the utterances of the old Group, either public or private, is going to continue very strong in the new Group. Comfort and I . . . did stress that painting, even by Canadians in Canada, need not necessarily be confined to any sort of nationalistic tradition" (quoted in Hill 1995: 286).

5. In the *Toronto Daily Star,* shortly after the Group of Seven's 1925 exhibition, under the pseudonym "the Observer," Salem Bland writes that he found revealed in the work of the Group of Seven "the Canadian soul. . . . I felt as if the Canadian soul were unveiling to me something secret and high and beautiful which I had never guessed—a strength and self-reliance and depth and a mysticism I had not suspected. I saw as I had never seen before the part the wilderness is destined to play in moulding the ultimate Canadian" (quoted in Hill 1995: 158).

6. Of course, there are exceptions to these myth-making practices that can be traced as early as the beginning of the century. One example is the work of Emily Carr, which, in many ways, problematizes the use of the landscape by the members of the Group of Seven and their obfuscation of the native presence. Although a contemporary of the Group, Carr was never formally admitted into the Group itself.

Carr's work reveals an attempt to sever ties to her Victorian British surroundings. Her subject matter was largely relegated to native artifacts—most notably totems—that she painted in an attempt to record a disappearing culture. As she notes in *Dear Nan:* "The Indian people and their art touched me deeply. . . . I was going to picture totem poles in their own village settings, as complete a collection of them as I could" (1990: 211).

7. This publication accompanied the recent exhibition (1995–1997) of the work of the Group of Seven, which took place at the National Gallery of Canada, the Art Gallery of Ontario, Vancouver Art Gallery, and the Montreal Museum of Fine Arts.

8. Because of the continued dominance of the Group of Seven in English Canada, Canadians were tardy in their involvement in modern international abstractionism. The Painters Eleven were among those who struggled to create art in the wake of the Group of Seven that wasn't nationally oriented, preferring abstract art to depictions of the landscape. Their 1952 exhibition, *Abstracts at Home,* suggests there is more than one way of seeing Canada through art. Despite their inventive work, however, expectations of an art that mirrored that of the Group of Seven's quest for national identity prevailed. As Brooks writes, "[C]ritical acceptance was still framed in terms of a new representation of the nation, though now a representation which included Canada as a member of an international community" (1992: 52).

9. A plane of consistency allows for a deviation from the strict codes of territoriality toward a becoming-deterritorialization that takes into account distributional articulations rather than anchorages, compositions rather than unities, and rhizomes (and . . . and . . . and . . .) rather than trees (to be, to be).

10. The favored metaphor for multiculturalism in Canada is that of the mosaic, as contrasted to the image of the melting pot in the United States.

11. In *Souvenirs of the Self,* Yoon's body becomes a measure of national identity, drawing out the awkwardness of naturalized assumptions about who is "at home" in Canada. As Germaine Koh writes: "The project is not a simple argument for inclusion; rather, it is a matter of denaturalizing these constructed nationalist models by bearing witness to the limited (racialized, for example) ways in which subjects appear within them" (1998: 183).

2. Beyond Accommodation

1. The woman does share in the *polis,* but only to the extent that it is appropriate to her confinement in the household. Her relationship to the public realm, therefore, is that of a "necessary condition" rather than its "integral part." Moral goodness and reason are attainable only through participation in public life, and this involvement is reserved for free, adult males. See Jean Elshtain (1982).

2. Metaphysics is understood as "a tradition of thought defined in the pursuit

of security; with the securing, in fact, of a secure *arche,* determining principle, beginning or ground, for which its under-standing of truth and its quest for certainty calls. Security, then, finds its expression as the principle, ground or *arche*—for which metaphysical thought is a search—upon which something stands, pervading and guiding it in its whole structure and essence" (Dillon 1996: 13).

3. *Espacement* is visualization of the trace and of *différance.* This writing of *différance,* which both defers and differs, explores the strange movement of the trace that cannot operate within the modified presence that linear time essential-izes. No longer operative within the phenomenological experience of a presence that speaks linear time, spacing speaks the articulation of space and time as the becoming-time and the becoming-space of space. See Jacques Derrida (1974).

4. Nicole Fermon argues that "republicanism and democracy [in Rousseau's notion of the household] require a particular sexual economy between sexual politics and what is conventionally referred to as the political, the world of the state, its regulations and bureaucracies" (1994: 442).

5. Biskupin is a central motif in *Fugitive Pieces.* This archaeological site is both the space where Athos meets and saves Jacob and the story Athos spends the rest of his life trying to narrate to redeem his dead colleagues. An archaeological site from which an ancient civilization was being uncovered "whose houses faced the sun," Biskupin was not only destroyed by the Nazis but also claimed by the *SS Ahnenerbe* as belonging to Germany (as proof that ancient civilizations were part of Germany's history).

6. An ethics of responsibility refers to the work of Derrida and to Levinas, both of whom stress the necessity of not subsuming the other into the same. Levinas conjoins the ethic of responsibility with the encounter with the face of the other. He suggests that the place of the nonviolent relation with radical alteri-ty that is ethics is the face, that is, the apparition or the trace of the other, where the other exceeds the idea of the other in me. In *Fugitive Pieces,* however, as in *Lulu* (see chapter 4), the face symbolizes not the emancipation of alterity, but the potential encounter with the horror of the sovereign.

7. For a detailed explanation of the Deleuzian time and movement images, see the analysis of *Rude* and *Eldorado* in the following chapter.

8. Abouali Farmanfarmaian draws a useful link between the home, the fami-ly, and the nation. See Abouali Farmanfarmaian (1992). See also Patricia Molloy (1999).

3. Where the Zulu Meets the Mohawk

1. Canada is an interesting case with respect to this notion of unitary culture because the lack of such a culture is precisely what leads to an incessant preoc-cupation through the media of Canada's "national identity." This preoccupation,

which can be located throughout Canadian history and can be explained in various ways—with respect to the hegemonic American presence, to the colonial legacy, etc.—finds its way into cultural critique via a preoccupation with issues of "Canadian-ness." As a result, questions such as "How Canadian is Cronenberg?" and "How do we ensure that Deepa Mehta's films are Canadian if they are produced with Indian funds?" become habitual.

Responding to this state of events, Charles Levin writes: "[Canada] is the sort of country whose federal government feels obliged to rent billboards and newspaper space to advertise the flag. Everything about Canada is vague, ambiguous or unknown. . . . It is difficult to convey precisely the atmosphere of a country like Canada because it is in a perpetually uninterpretable state of being. Everything about Canada is undecidable. . . . Product neither of tradition nor revolution, Canada is a kind of political transplant—in effect, the first parasitic nation—created by the decree of a foreign parliament fed up with the administrative headache of running an ambiguous country" (1996: 209–10, 217).

2. Cornel West argues that "white supremacy is *constitutive*, not additive to the makings of the modern world. . . . [A]ntiblack racism is *integral*, not marginal to the existence and sustenance of American society. . . . [R]ace matters in regard to what it means to be modern, American, and human in our contemporary world" (1998: 301).

3. Walcott writes: "Erasing all evidence of any other presence (First Nation and Black) is crucial if the myth of the two founding peoples is to hold the crumbling nation of Canada together in the face of Quebec's impending separation and declaration of nation status" (1997: 44).

4. Virgo's *Rude* is one of the first instances of "Canadian" blackness reflected on Canadian screens by a black Canadian filmmaker. This, in addition to the fact that Canadian films have a staggeringly small audience compared to American films, results in the image of "American" blackness being much more current in Canada than its Canadian counterpart.

5. The usage of "citizen" as the marker for the national subject is not intended to suggest that the "citizen" is a singular entity. It is, rather, to emphasize, within the current vocabulary of the nation-state, that to be homed usually depends on the link between the citizen and the state.

6. These words are spoken at the beginning of *Rude* by the deejay.

7. Luke's artwork differentiates him from his junkie friends. Despite the violence that reigns in their worlds, no one touches Luke's wall, even when he is sent to jail. "Maybe it's because they know you painted it and you're not finished," Luke's wife ventures when he returns from jail to find his wall intact. Creativity seems to be one way out of the destruction of the inner city.

8. Both *Rude* and *Eldorado* use blue, yellow, and orange predominantly. In

Rude, the city is represented through shades of blue and yellow, with yellow as the color of the rising (Easter) sun, Jessica's (Luke's police-officer wife) home, and the lion of Judea, all images of freedom and resurrection. All narratives dealing with Maxine and her aborted child are framed in blue, suggesting that blue is the color of painful histories and memory. Red is the color of the drug world and the inner-city violence. In the final scene of the film, yellow, red, and blue come together as Luke and Jessica resist and finally kill Yankee, who is the embodiment of white-supremacist domination. As the sun rises, however, shades of red and yellow are combined, suggesting that the current rendition of history is also a potentially violent one.

In *Eldorado,* Rita dyes her dress red, as though red were not the color of violence per se, but a powerful color that represents the desire to act. Blue is often the color used to depict homelessness, as well as the face of Gaspard/Lloyd. Roxan's apartment is yellow.

9. In *Eldorado,* the cello player is always associated with Rita, an artistic counterpart that plays a similar role to Luke's wall in *Rude.* Through the music, Rita is invited to relive the pain of her past. At the end of the film, the cellist plays his sad notes as Rita walks along the tracks with Lloyd. This scene suggests that there will always remain a discrepancy between the organic—the story of Rita and Lloyd—and the crystalline, the fragmentation of the timeline through the sounds of the music. It is this very fragmentation that offers the possibility of an alternative to the stifling narratives of causality grafted onto the movement-image.

10. With gray smoke marking circles around her unidentified face, Rude speaks: "Don't recognize my voice, can't see my face, my face is isolation isolated by a fragile, infantile fantasy. Many sleep with eyes open, cope with the pain that stains the brain. Don't recognize my voice, can't see my face . . . feel the blood race, treading water, a tragic existence is a co-resistance, fight with spiritual persistence . . . a kiss of dysfunctional illusion, silence plus noise, confusion, sweet and sour delusion, laws of survival, resist the self, rival self-righteous primal desire to see, to flee, to find the blind center of identity, reality, two-dimensional sensuality, to touch you is not to know you, don't recognize my voice, can't see my face . . . oh, what a tragedy . . . another voice swallows an island . . . don't recognize my voice? If I shall rise from my sublime demise. . . ." Rude's words are important markers of the way in which the film seeks to disrupt the perceived stability between the black body and its effects in a white-supremacist society, where the black body evokes disruption.

11. The troubling link between the state and the Church is hinted at in Rude's words (a link that also comes up with respect to the discourse of sovereignty in Quebec, as outlined in the final chapter). For a detailed analysis of modernity's debts to God, the state, and man, see David Campbell (1998). Campbell writes:

"Contrary to the traditional historical narrative's supposition of a complete rupture between the social functions of the church in the Middle Ages and the political effects of the state in the modern era, . . . common across time and space was the role of the church and the forms of 'state': in securing identity amidst disorder. . . . [I]n so far as the emerging 'state' forms came to predominate in mediating claims of identity, they were replicating that function performed earlier by the church" (1998: 48).

The allusion to Christianity in *Rude* suggests a continuity between the search for the state "as home" and the return to a narrative of God. The explicitly religious symbols of Easter, sins, and trumpets in *Rude* suggest adherence to the discourse of the Church while state sovereignty is rejected: the Church continues to be seen, in some sense, as the potential for emancipation. This ambiguity in the film is emphasized in Rinaldo Walcott's critique of the film. As Walcott argues, it is dangerous to rely on the model of the Church for a departure from the racist politics of sovereignty, especially since, in many cases, the postnational politics of religion are likely to sustain the very racism *Rude* attempts to subvert.

12. Supplementarity, a notion that Derrida uses (1974), is relevant here. For Derrida, the supplement is both the surplus that adds itself and a plenitude that enriches another plenitude: it is the fullest measure of presence because it cumulates and accumulates presence. And yet, the supplement also supplements, adding only to replace, intervening in-the-place-of and thus filling (if it fills) a void. The discourses of the racial other, the homeless, the migrant, and the refugee can each be understood as supplementary to that of the nation-state, both in the sense that they are outside the nation's parameters and in the sense that they reveal the lack within the nation's promise of identity and coherence. Their supplementarity reveals the necessity of their presence to the nation's fulfillment.

13. We must, however, remain attentive to the fact that the differentiation between pluralism and pluralization does not preclude the possibility that pluralization can be fundamentalized, since both pluralism and pluralization participate in the same political matrix, wherein a set of general presumptions prevail concerning the terms of national security, gender difference, law and justice, the shape of the economy, reason, identity, and the political.

14. One of the ways in which *Rude* and *Eldorado* complexify the discourse of multiculturalism is by drawing attention to the fact that immigrants are also, in many cases, responsible for the specification of the other. In other words, the discourse of immigration is not simply one that traces a clear binary between the political powers of a nation's narratives of inclusivity at the top and the immigrants down below. Rather, hierarchies are often established and fiercely guarded *within* immigration populations.

4. Face-to-Face with the Incommensurable

1. Before delving into the face-to-face relation, it is useful to note the ambiguity in the interpretations of the face-to-face encounter within Levinasian scholarship. As Robert Bernasconi writes: "The question is: what status is to be accorded the face-to-face relation? . . . Some interpreters understand it as a concrete experience that we can recognize in our lives. Other commentators have understood the face-to-face relation to be the condition of possibility of ethics and indeed of all economic existence and knowledge" (1989: 23).

2. One of Levinas's blind spots with respect to the ethics of the other is his relationship to the Palestinians. When asked, "Isn't the other above all the Palestinian?", Levinas referred to Palestinians as enemies. "There are people who are wrong," Levinas replied (in Bernasconi 1991). In response to the resulting confusion concerning Levinas's relationship to the exclusionary practices of the nation-state, Shapiro writes: "Evidently, Levinas's attachment to the venerable story of state sovereignty, and even to a Hegelian spiritualization of states as instruments of spiritual reconciliation, collides with his commitment to an unqualified respect for alterity and makes him veer away from his commitment to an ethical bond that precedes all such ontological and spatial attachments. In his perspective on Israel, his model of alterity seems ultimately not to heed the Other's stories of self and space" (1997: 185).

3. I refer to ecstasy both as ec-stasis (being outside of) and as the passion it usually connotes. I want to suggest that it is only when being is outside itself, in exteriority, that we can begin to think a community of nonpresence where the other is not reduced to the same.

4. The only review in *The Globe and Mail* of Krishna's *Lulu* (and its only introduction to the public, other than its brief screening at the Toronto Film Festival) expresses disappointment with the film: "One of the more acute disappointments of this year's Perspective Canada program, Srinivas Krishna's second film has all the kinetic energy and visual sumptuousness of 1991's head-turning *Masala,* but none of that film's humour, wit or precise satiric focus. . . . While *[Lulu]* probably has something to do with the displacement of community and self in the global village, *Lulu* is too incoherent to warrant the effort required to interpret it. Here's hoping the talented Krishna has merely come down with a bad but fleeting case of sophomore curse" (September 12, 1996).

5. Dwelling within the Language of the Other

1. *"Maîtres chez nous"* was the 1962 campaign slogan of the Quebec liberal party, signaling not a mandate for separation from Canada, but an acknowledgment of the government's commitment to economic nationalism in Quebec.

The shift from religious to secular nationalism began as early as the 1930s, with the founding of the *programme de restauration sociale* and the inception of a new political party, the Action Libérale Nationale (ALN). During this period, French-Canadian progressives were coming to terms with a departure from the church and larger-scale industrialization and urbanization. It is important to remember, however, that the church was the one institution that Quebec controlled from the Union period onward. The church therefore offered Quebec a certain financial independence from Ottawa. As Roberto Perin argues, the distinct society we recognize today in Quebec was primarily the creation of the church, not the state (1992: 36). For more on the geographical imperatives of nation-building with respect to Quebec politics, see David Kaplan (1994). Kaplan argues that a sense of spatial identity may not coincide with territory currently controlled by the group, but always coincides with the territory a group aspires to control. He writes: "The existence of a defined territory, whether or not under actual control, undergirds all conceptions of nationalism. . . . [N]ationalist movements thus politicize space and create geographically demarcated homelands over which nationalists claim sovereignty" (1994: 586). Kaplan draws an analogy between spatial ideology and territorial ambition, whereby territorial ambition refers to the need to attain and protect land by whatever means necessary. The Quebecois spatial identity of the late-nineteenth and early-twentieth centuries reflects a reliance on the church. During this period, the mass of the Quebecois were organized at the level of the parish. Each parish consisted of religious and educational institutions intended to focus community life. Urbanization altered this conception of spatial identity. The longing for a state therefore follows directly in the wake of the decline of the role of the church in Quebec.

2. The Quebecois accent and dialect has long stood as a badge of identity, segregating the Quebecois from the "French" as well as from the other Canadians who are identified as "French Canadians."

3. Literally translated: "The cursed English." This phrase is often used with reference to the rest of Canada.

4. Lucien Bouchard resigned in early January 2001.

5. http://www.premier.gouv.qc.ca/project/historia.html, p. 1.

6. This, despite that Canadian prime ministers Pierre Trudeau and Brian Mulroney were elected from Quebec and that the federal parties that form the Canadian government have traditionally had substantial support and many parliamentary seats from Quebec.

7. It is possible to locate dissension in Quebec with respect to the rest of Canada as early as 1763, when the Treaty of Paris was signed. This treaty officially ceded Quebec to the British, making no concessions to the cultural uniqueness

of the Quebecois, who were then known as the *Canadiens*. This situation worsened over the course of the following centuries to the extent that, some argue, the Quebecois lost their affiliation to the state. In an influential essay written on the cusp of the Quiet Revolution, Michel Brunet (1958) deplores this situation, suggesting that French Canadians were forced to reject the state as an instrument for the promotion of their collective well-being.

8. In 1976, the Parti Québécois was voted in for the first time. It pledged to hold a referendum on Quebec sovereignty. In this first referendum, held on May 20, 1980, nearly 60 percent of Quebecois voted against giving government a mandate to negotiate an agreement on political sovereignty comprising an economic association with Canada. Despite the referendum defeat, the Parti Québécois was reelected in 1981, when Premier René Lévesque agreed to take part in negotiations to repatriate Canada's constitution, which was enshrined in an Act of the British Parliament, passed in 1867. These talks were unsuccessful; therefore, the repatriation of the constitution was passed without the signature of Lévesque. Quebec has since remained bound by a federal agreement it never signed.

The federal elections on September 4, 1984, brought to office the Progressive Conservative Party led by Brian Mulroney. Succeeding the Liberals under Pierre Elliot Trudeau, the new government adopted a less intransigent attitude toward Quebec's demands. The Conservatives pledged to find a compromise acceptable to all provinces to bring Quebec back into what Mulroney called the "Canadian family." The five conditions set by Quebec for a renewal of the constitution were as follows: (1) recognition of Quebec as a distinct society; (2) veto power over constitutional amendments; (3) guarantees concerning the appointment of Quebec judges to the Supreme Court of Canada; (4) the right to financial compensation for provinces that opt out of federal programs; (5) full control for Quebec over immigration within its territory. These recommendations led to a series of negotiations that culminated in the 1987 Meech Lake Accord, which was annulled before coming into power due to a lack of support in Manitoba and Newfoundland. As a result, Quebec was not successfully brought back into the constitutional fold.

The Charlottetown Accord followed the Meech Lake Accord and was similarly unsuccessful. The accord treated Quebec as merely one among ten provinces, sidestepping the long-standing principle of two founding peoples in Canada, one of French origin and the other of British origin. The Quebecois rejected the Charlottetown Accord by a vote of 57 percent on the grounds that the federal proposal did not in any way meet Quebec's historic demands. Outside Quebec, the deal was turned down by 54 percent of the voters; many judged it made unacceptable concessions to Quebec.

After failing to break the constitutional deadlock and bring Quebec back into the constitution, the Conservative government, having reached the end of its term, called a federal election in October 1993. The Bloc Québécois, a pro-sovereignty party that ran candidates at the federal level, won fifty-four seats. The support received by the Bloc Québécois in the federal elections confirmed the renewal of the pro-sovereignty movement in Quebec. Its revival was further substantiated in September 1994, when the Parti Québécois returned to power after ten years of Liberal rule. The new government, led by Jacques Parizeau, immediately declared its intention to hold a referendum on sovereignty.

The Parti Québécois chose October 30, 1995, as the date for the second sovereignty referendum. The referendum question was phrased as follows: "Do you agree that Quebec should become sovereign, after having made a formal offer to Canada for new Economic and Political Partnership, within the scope of the *Bill Respecting the Future of Québec* and the agreement signed on June 12 1995?" With a record 96 percent turnout, Quebec voters rejected the government's proposal to secede by a slim margin of 50.6 percent to 49.4 percent.

9. Hanako relates the fact that, as a child of the atom bomb, she is not desirable to Japanese men, who fear she will bear a mutant child.

10. The terms *Québécois de souche* and *pur laine* both refer to the ideal purity of genealogical descent in Quebecois lineage.

11. Language has been the main platform for the sovereignists since the Quiet Revolution. The first legislative act, Bill 63, was passed in 1968. Bill 63 sanctioned the existing principle of free choice with respect to language in Quebec, but sought to promote the teaching of French in the English school system to ensure that all the peoples of Quebec, whatever their origin, be able to speak French. This bill was received with indignation by many Quebecois nationalists.

In 1974, Bill 22 was adopted. Bill 22 established the priority of French in Quebec society, forcing immigrant children to enter the French school system. In 1977, Bill 101, also known as the "Charter of the French Language," was passed. This time, only children with at least one parent who had studied in an English-language primary school in Quebec were allowed to enter the English school system. This move enraged many immigrants, particularly those of Italian descent, who had chosen to enter their children in English-speaking schools. Later, Bill 178 was passed, placing strict limits on the use of English for commercial signs.

12. Bhabha's use of the pedagogical as a tool that represses the performative has been countered by those who explore the radical potential of pedagogy. I nonetheless draw on Bhabha's formulation, since I believe it is a lucid way of understanding the ways in which dominant discourses are passed through the generations, as a result of which these discourses become naturalized. However,

my stance does not imply that these pedagogies cannot be challenged through the instantiation of radical pedagogies that undermine dominant ideologies through performative means.

13. The *matryoshka* refers to the Russian doll that has many replicas of itself inside its outer shell. It is passed down through generations to women.

Bibliography

Agamben, Giorgio. 1998. *Homo Sacer: Sovereign Power and Bare Life.* Trans. D. Heller-Roazen. Stanford: Stanford University Press.

———. 1997. "The Camp as the Nomos of the Modern." In *Violence, Identity, and Self-Determination.* Ed. H. de Vries and S. Weber. Stanford: Stanford University Press.

Anderson, Benedict. 1983. *Imagined Communities: Reflections on the Origin and Spread of Nationalism.* New York: Verso.

Anzaldúa, Gloria. 1987. *Borderlands/La Frontera: The New Mestiza.* San Francisco: Spinsters/Aunt Lute.

Appadurai, Arjun. 2000. "Grassroots Globalization and the Research Imagination." *Public Culture* 30, no. 1.

———. 1998. "Full Attachment." *Public Culture* 10, no. 2.

———. 1996a. "Sovereignty without Territoriality: Notes for a Postnational Geography." In *The Geography of Identity.* Ed. P. Yaeger. Ann Arbor: University of Michigan Press.

———. 1996b. *Modernity at Large.* Minneapolis: University of Minnesota Press.

———. 1990. "Disjuncture and Difference in the Global Cultural Economy." *Public Culture* 2, no. 2.

Baker, Ernst, ed. 1962. *The Politics of Aristotle.* New York: Oxford University Press.

Bakhtin, Mikhail. 1990. *Art and Answerability: Early Philosophical Essays.* Austin: University of Texas Press.

———. 1986. *Speech Genres and Other Late Essays.* Trans. V. W. McGee. Ed. C. Emerson and M. Holquist. Austin: University of Texas Press.

———. 1981. *The Dialogic Imagination.* Trans. M. Holquist. Austin: University of Texas Press.

———. 1973. *Problems of Dostoyevski's Poetics.* Ann Arbor: Ardis Press.

Balibar, Étienne. 1996. "The Nation Form: History and Ideology." In *Becoming*

National: A Reader. Ed. G. Eley and G. Suny. Oxford: Oxford University Press.

———. 1995. "Culture and Identity (Working Notes)." In *The Identity in Question.* Ed. J. Rajchman. New York: Routledge.

———. 1994. "Racism as Universalism." In *Masses, Classes, and Ideas.* Trans. J. Swenson. New York: Routledge.

Balibar, Étienne, and Immanuel Wallerstein. 1991. *Race, Nation, Class: Ambiguous Identities.* Trans. C. Turner. London: Verso.

Bammer, Angelika, ed. 1994. *Displacements: Cultural Identities in Question.* Bloomington: Indiana University Press.

Bennington, Geoffrey. 2000. *Interrupting Derrida.* London: Routledge.

———. 1992. "Frontiers: Two Seminar Sessions." *Oxford Literary Review* 14, no. 1–2.

Berger, John. 1972a. *Ways of Seeing.* Harmondsworth, England: Penguin Books.

———. 1972b. *Selected Essays and Articles.* Harmondsworth, England: Penguin Books.

Berger, John, and John Mohr. 1969. *A Fortunate Man.* Harmondsworth, England: Penguin Books.

Berlant, Lauren. 1998. "Live Sex Acts [Parental Advisory: Explicit Material]." In *In Near Ruins.* Ed. N. B. Dirks. Minneapolis: University of Minnesota Press.

Bernasconi, Robert. 1991. "Skepticism in the Face of Philosophy." In *Re-Reading Levinas.* Ed. R. Bernasconi and S. Critchley. Bloomington: Indiana University Press.

———. 1989. "Re-Reading Totality and Infinity." In *The Question of the Other.* Ed. A. Dallery and C. Scott. New York: State University of New York.

Bhabha, Homi. 1999. "Arrivals and Departures." In *Home, Exile, Homeland: Film, Media, and the Politics of Place.* Ed. H. Nacify. New York: Routledge.

———. 1997. "The World and the Home." In *Dangerous Liaisons.* Ed. A. McClintock, A. Mufti, and E. Shohat. Minneapolis: University of Minnesota Press.

———. 1995. "Freedom's Basis in the Indeterminate." In *The Identity in Question.* Ed. J. Rajchman. New York: Routledge.

———. 1994. *The Location of Culture.* London: Routledge.

———. 1992a. "The World and the Home." In *Nationalisms and Sexualities.* Ed. A. Parker, M. Russo, and P. Yaeger. New York: Routledge.

———. 1992b. "Postcolonial Authority and Postmodern Guilt." In *Cultural Studies.* Ed. L. Grossberg, C. Nelson, P. Treichler. London: Routledge.

———. Ed. 1990. *Nation and Narration.* London: Routledge.

Billingsley, Robert. 1976. *Changing Visions: The Canadian Landscape.* Edmonton Gallery and AGO.

Blanchot, Maurice. 1993a. *The Infinite Conversation.* Trans. S. Hanson. Minneapolis: University of Minnesota Press.

———. 1993b. *La Communauté inavouable.* Paris: Les Editions de Minuit.

Bottomley, Gillian. 1992. *From Another Place: Migration and the Politics of Culture.* Cambridge: Cambridge University Press.

Brah, Avtar. 1996. *Cartographies of Diaspora: Contesting Identities.* London: Routledge.

Brooker, Bertram. 1973. *Bertram Brooker 1888–1955.* Ottawa: National Gallery of Canada.

Brooks, Sharon. 1992. *"Abstracts at Home": Against the Ideals of Nationalism.* M.A. Thesis. York University.

Brubaker, Roger. 1996. *Nationalism Reframed: Nationhood and the National Question in New Europe.* Cambridge: Cambridge University Press.

Brunet, Michel. 1958. *La Présence Anglaise et les Américains.* Montreal: Beauchemin.

Butler, Judith. 1996. "Universality in Culture." In *For Love of Country: Debating the Limits of Patriotism.* Ed. J. Cohen. Boston: Beacon Press.

———. 1995. "Collected and Fractured: Response to Identities." In *Identities.* Ed. K. Appiah and H. L. Gates Jr. Chicago: University of Chicago Press.

———. 1993. *Bodies That Matter: On the Discursive Limits of "Sex."* New York: Routledge.

———. 1990. *Gender Trouble: Feminism and the Subversion of Identity.* New York: Routledge.

———. 1987. *Subjects of Desire.* New York: Columbia University Press.

Campbell, David, and Michael Dillon, ed. 1993. *The Political Subject of Violence.* Manchester: Manchester University Press.

Campbell, David. 1998. *National Deconstruction.* Minneapolis: University of Minnesota Press.

Caputo, John. 1993. *Against Ethics.* Bloomington: Indiana University Press.

Carr, Emily. 1990. *Dear Nan.* Vancouver: University of British Columbia Press.

———. 1929. "Modern and Indian Art of the West Coast." In *Supplement to the McGill News* (June).

Caruth, Cathy. 1995. "The Insistence on Reference." In *Critical Encounters: Reference and Responsibility in Deconstructive Writing.* Ed. C. Caruth and D. Esch. New Jersey: Rutgers University Press.

Caygill, Howard. 1997. "The Shared World—Philosophy, Violence, Freedom." In *The Sense of Philosophy: On Jean-Luc Nancy.* Ed. D. Sheppard, S. Sparks, and C. Thomas. New York: Routledge.

Chambers, Iain. 1994. *Migrancy, Culture, Identity.* London: Routledge.

Clark, Kenneth. 1949. *Landscape into Art.* Boston: Beacon Press.

Connolly, William. 1995. *The Ethos of Pluralization.* Minneapolis: University of Minnesota Press.

———. 1993. *The Augustinian Imperative: A Reflection on the Politics of Morality.* Newbury Park, California: Sage.

———. 1991. "Democracy and Territoriality." *Millennium* 20, no. 3.

———. 1988. *Political Theory and Modernity.* London: Basil Blackwell.

Crary, Jonathan. 1995. "Unbinding Vision: Manet and the Attentive Observer in the Late Nineteenth Century." In *Cinema and the Invention of Modern Life.* Ed. L. Charney and V. Schwartz. Berkeley: University of California Press.

Critchley, Simon. 1993. "Retracing the Political: Politics and Community in the Work of Philippe Lacoue-Labarthe and Jean-Luc Nancy." In *The Political Subject of Violence.* Ed. D. Campbell and M. Dillon. Manchester: Manchester University Press.

———. 1992. *The Ethics of Deconstruction: Derrida and Lévinas.* Oxford: Basil Blackwell.

Critchley, Simon, and Robert Bernasconi, ed. 1991. *Re-Reading Levinas.* Indianapolis: Indiana University Press.

Dalby, Simon. 1997. "Contesting an Essential Concept: Reading the Dilemmas in Contemporary Security Discourse." In *Critical Security Studies.* Ed. K. Krauss and M. C. Williams. Minneapolis: University of Minnesota Press.

de Certeau, Michel. 1988. *The Writing of History.* Trans. T. Conley. New York: Columbia University Press.

Deleuze, Gilles. 1994. "He Stuttered." In *Gilles Deleuze and the Theater of Philosophy.* Ed. C. Boundas and D. Olkowski. New York: Routledge.

———. 1993. *Difference and Repetition.* New York: Columbia University Press.

———. 1990. *Pourparlers, 1972–1990.* Paris: Les Editions de Minuit.

———. 1989. *The Time-Image.* Trans. H. Tomlinson and R. Galeta. Minneapolis: University of Minnesota Press.

Deleuze, Gilles, and Félix Guattari. 1987. *A Thousand Plateaux.* Trans. B. Massumi. Minneapolis: University of Minnesota Press.

Der Derian, James. 1993. "The Value of Security: Hobbes, Marx, Nietzsche, and Baudrillard." In *The Political Subject of Violence.* Manchester: Manchester University Press.

Derrida, Jacques. 1998. *Monolingualism and the Language of the Other, or the Prosthesis of Origin.* Trans. P. Mensah. Stanford: Stanford University Press.

———. 1997. *Adieu à Emmanuel Lévinas.* Paris: Galilée.

———. 1995a. *On the Name.* Trans. D. Wood, I. Wood, and J. P. Leavy Jr. Stanford: Stanford University Press.

———. 1995b. "The Time Is Out of Joint." In *Deconstruction Is/In America: A*

New Sense of the Political. Ed. A. Haverkamp. Trans. P. Kamuf. New York: New York University Press.

———. 1994. *Specters of Marx.* Trans. P. Kamuf. New York: Routledge.

———. 1992a. "Onto-Theology of National Humanism (Prolegomena to a Hypothesis)." *Oxford Literary Review* 14, no. 1–2.

———. 1992b. *The Other Heading.* Trans. P. A. Brault and M. B. Naas. Indiana: Indiana University Press.

———. 1990. *Du Droit a la philosophie.* Paris: Galilée.

———. 1981a. *Dissemination.* Trans. B. Johnson. Chicago: University of Chicago Press.

———. 1981b. *Positions.* Trans. A. Bass. Chicago: University of Chicago Press.

———. 1978. "Violence and Metaphysics." In *Writing and Difference.* Trans. A. Bass. Chicago: University of Chicago Press.

———. 1974. *Of Grammatology.* Trans. G. Spivak. Baltimore: Johns Hopkins University Press.

Deutsche, Rosalyn. 1996. *Evictions: Art and Spatial Politics.* Cambridge: MIT Press.

Didi-Huberman, Georges. 1985. *La Peinture Incarnée.* Paris: Editions de Minuit.

———. 1984. "The Art of Not Describing: Vermeer—The Detail of the Patch." *History of the Human Sciences* 2, no 2 (June).

Dillon, Michael. 1999a. "The Scandal of the Refugee: Some Reflections on the 'Inter' of International Relations and Continental Thought." In *Moral Spaces.* Ed. M. Shapiro and D. Campbell. Minneapolis: University of Minnesota Press.

———. 1999b. "Another Justice." *Political Theory* 27, no. 2 (April).

———. 1996. *Politics of Security.* London: Routledge.

Dodge, William, ed. 1992. *Boundaries of Identity: A Québec Reader.* Toronto: Lester Publishing.

Doel, Marcus. 1996. "A Hundred Thousand Lines of Flight: A Machinic Introduction to the Nomad Thought of Gilles Deleuze and Félix Guattari." *Society and Space* 14.

———. 1994. "Deconstruction on the Move: From Libidinal Economy to Liminal Materialism." *Society and Space* 26.

Drache, Daniel, and Roberto Perin, ed. 1992. *Negotiating with a Sovereign Québec.* Toronto: Lorimer.

Dufour, Gilles. 1993. *Out of Place.* Vancouver: Vancouver Art Gallery.

Edmonton Art Gallery. 1976. *Changing Visions: The Canadian Landscape.* Edmonton: Edmonton Gallery and AGO.

Elshtain, Jean. 1982. "Aristotle, the Public-Private Split, and the Case of the

Suffragists." In *The Family in Political Thought*. Ed. J. Elshtain. Amherst: University of Massachusetts Press.

Farmanfarmaian, Abouali. 1992. "Did You Measure Up? The Role of Race and Sexuality in the Gulf War." In *Collateral Damage: The New World Order at Home and Abroad*. Ed. C. Peters. Boston: South End Press.

Fermon, Nicole. 1994. "Domesticating Women, Civilizing Men: Rousseau's Political Program." *The Sociological Quarterly* 35, no. 3 (August).

Foucault, Michel. 1989. *Foucault Live (Interviews 1966–1984)*. New York: Semiotext(e).

———. 1988. *Politics, Philosophy, Culture: Interviews and Other Writings*. Ed. L. Kritzman. Trans. A. Sheridon. New York: Routledge.

———. 1984a. "Nietzsche, Genealogy, History." In *The Foucault Reader*. Ed. P. Rabinow. New York: Pantheon Books.

———. 1984b. "Des espaces autres." *Architecture-Mouvement-Continuité* (October).

———. 1982. "The Subject and Power." In *Michel Foucault: Beyond Structuralism and Hermeneutics*. Ed. H. Dreyfus and P. Rabinow. Chicago: University of Chicago Press.

———. 1981. *History and Sexuality, Part 1*. Harmondsworth, England: Penguin Books.

———. 1980. *Power/Knowledge*. New York: Pantheon Books.

———. 1977. *Language, Counter-Memory, and Practice—Selected Essays and Interviews*. Ithaca, N.Y.: Cornell University Press.

Freud, Sigmund. 1955. "The Uncanny." In *The Standard Edition of the Complete Psychological Works of Sigmund Freud*, Vol. 14. London: Hogarth Press.

Gagnon, Michelle, and Martin Allor. 1996. "Québec." In *Public 14*. Public Access.

Gilroy, Paul. 1993. *The Black Atlantic: Modernity and Double Consciousness*. Cambridge: Harvard University Press.

Glassman, Marc. 1995. "Where Zulus Meet Mohawks: Clement Virgo's *Rude*." *Take One* 5, no. 30–31 (fall).

Golding, Sue, ed. 1997. *The Eight Technologies of Otherness*. New York: Routledge.

Gordon, Avery, and Christopher Newfield. 1995. "White Philosophy." In *Identities*. Ed. K. A. Appiah and H. L. Gates Jr. Chicago: University of Chicago Press.

Habermas, Jürgen. 1998. "The European Nation-State: On the Past and Future of Sovereignty and Citizenship." *Public Culture* 10, no. 2.

Halkes-Halim, Petra. 1995. *Changing Concepts of the Sublime and the Landscape: The Landscape Paintings of Eleanor Bond and Jeffrey Spalding*. Ottawa: M.A. Thesis.

Hamacher, Werner. 1997. "One Too Many Multiculturalisms." In *Violence,*

Identity, and Self-Determination. Ed. H. de Vries and S. Weber. Stanford: Stanford University Press.

Harcourt, Peter. 1988. "Politics or Paranoia." In *Documents in Canadian Cinema.* Peterborough: Broadview Press.

———. 1977. *Movies and Mythologies: Toward a National Cinema.* Toronto: CBC Publications.

Hardt, Michael, and Antonio Negri. 2000. *Empire.* Cambridge: Harvard University Press.

Harper, Russell. 1966. *Painting in Canada: A History.* Toronto: Toronto University Press.

Harrison, Charles. 1994a. "The Effects of Landscape." In *Landscape and Power.* Ed. W. J. T. Mitchell. Chicago: University of Chicago Press.

———. 1994b. *English Art and Modernism, 1900–1939.* New Haven, Connecticut: Yale University Press.

Heidegger, Martin. 1990. *Kant and the Problem of Metaphysics.* Trans. R. Taft. Bloomington: Indiana University Press.

———. 1988. *Being and Time.* Oxford: Blackwell.

———. 1984. *The Metaphysical Foundations of Logic.* Trans. M. Heim. Bloomington: Indiana University Press.

———. 1973. "Overcoming Metaphysics." In *The End of Philosophy.* Trans. J. Stambaugh. New York: Harper and Row.

———. 1972. *On Time and Being.* Oxford: Basil Blackwell.

———. 1971. "Building, Dwelling, Thinking." In *Poetry, Language, and Thought.* Trans. A. Hofstadter. New York: Harper and Row.

Hill, Charles. 1995. *The Group of Seven—Art for a Nation.* Ottawa: National Gallery of Canada/McLelland and Stewart.

Hobsbawm, Eric. 1990. *Nations and Nationalism Since 1780: Programme, Myth, Reality.* Cambridge: Cambridge University Press.

Holquist, Michael. 1990. *Dialogism: Bakhtin and His World.* New York: Routledge.

hooks, bell. 1992. *Black Looks: Race and Representation.* Boston: South End Press.

Hoskins, Eric. 1993. *London Free Press* (27 March).

Hroch, Miroslav. 1985. *Social Preconditions of National Revival in Europe.* Cambridge: Cambridge University Press.

Hubbard, R. H. 1963. *The Development of Canadian Art.* Ottawa: National Gallery of Canada.

JanMohamed, Abdul. 1992. "The Specular Border Intellectual." In *Edward Said: A Critical Reader.* Cambridge, Mass.: Blackwell Publishers.

Kaplan, David. 1994. "Two Nations in Search of a State: Canada's Ambivalent Spatial Identities." *Annals of the Association of Geographers* 84, no. 4 (December).

Kawash, Samira. 1998. "The Homeless Body." In *Public Culture* 10, no. 2.

Keohane, Kieran. 1997. *Symptoms of Canada: An Essay on the Canadian Identity.* Toronto: Toronto University Press.

Koh, Germaine. 1998. "Jin-me Yoon." In *Crossings.* Ottawa: National Gallery of Canada.

Kohn, Hans. 1945. *The Idea of Nationalism: A Study in Its Origins and Background.* New York. Macmillan.

Krishna, Sankaran. 1994. "Cartographic Anxiety: Mapping the Body Politic in India." *Alternatives* 19.

Kristeva, Julia. 1993. *Nations without Nationalism.* Trans. L. Roudiez. New York: Columbia University Press.

———. 1991. *Strangers to Ourselves.* Trans. L. Roudiez. New York: Columbia University Press.

———. 1982. *Powers of Horror.* Trans. L. Roudiez. New York: Columbia University Press.

Lacoue-Labarthe, Philippe. 1998. "Transcendence Ends in Politics." In *Typography.* Trans. C. Fynsk. Stanford: Stanford University Press.

Levin, Charles. 1996. *Jean Baudrillard: A Study in Cultural Metaphysics.* London: Prentice Hall.

Levinas, Emmanuel. 1991. "Wholly Otherwise." In *Re-Reading Levinas.* Ed. R. Bernasconi and S. Critchley. Bloomington: Indiana University Press.

———. 1989. *The Levinas Reader.* Oxford: Basil Blackwell.

———. 1987. *Collected Philosophical Papers.* Trans. A. Lingis. The Hague: Martinus Nijhof.

———. 1986. *Face to Face with Levinas.* Ed. R. A. Cohen. Albany: State University of New York Press.

———. 1983. "Beyond Intentionality." In *Philosophy in France Today.* Ed. A. Montefiore. Cambridge: Cambridge University Press.

———. 1981. *Otherwise than Being, or Beyond Essence.* The Hague: Nijhoff.

———. 1976. *Difficult Freedom / Difficile Liberté.* Paris: Albin Michel.

———. 1969. *Totality and Infinity.* Trans. A. Lingis. Pittsburgh: Duquesne University Press.

Lubiano, Wahneema. 1998. "Black Nationalism and Black Common Sense: Policing Ourselves and Others." In *The House That Race Built.* Ed. L. Wahneema. New York: Vintage Books.

MacLaren, Peter. 1994. "White Terror and Oppositional Agency: Toward a Critical Multiculturalism." In *Multiculturalism: A Critical Reader.* Ed. David Theo Goldberg. Oxford: Basil Blackwell.

Magnussen, Warren. 1994. "Social Movements and the Global City." In *Millennium: Journal of International Studies* 23, no. 3.

———. 1990. "The Reification of Political Community." In *Contending Sovereignties*. Boulder: Lynne Rienner Publishers.

Massumi, Brian. 1996. "Becoming-Deleuzian." *Society and Space* 14.

McAfee, Noëlle. 1993. "Abject Strangers: Toward an Ethics of Respect." In *Ethics, Politics, and Difference in Julia Kristeva's Writing*. Ed. Kelly Oliver. New York: Routledge.

Michaels, Anne. 1996. *Fugitive Pieces*. Toronto: McLelland and Stewart.

Michaels, Walter Benn. 1995. "Race into Culture: A Critical Genealogy of Cultural Identity." In *Identities*. Ed. K. A. Appiah and H. L. Gates Jr. Chicago: University of Chicago Press.

Minh-Ha, Trinh. 1996. "An Acoustic Journey." In *Rethinking Borders*. Minneapolis: University of Minnesota Press.

———. 1994. "Other than Myself/ My Other Self." In *Travellers' Tales: Narratives of Home and Displacement*. Routledge: New York.

Mitchell, Timothy. 1998. "Nationalism, Imperialism, Economism: A Comment on Habermas." *Public Culture* 10, no. 2.

———. 1991. "The Limits of the State: Beyond Statist Approaches and Their Critics." *American Political Science Review* 85, no. 1 (March).

Mitchell, W. J. T., ed. 1994a. *Landscape and Power*. Chicago: University of Chicago Press.

———. 1994b. *Picture Theory*. Chicago: University of Chicago Press.

———. 1980. *The Language of Images*. Chicago: University of Chicago Press.

Molloy, Patricia. 1999. "Desiring Security/Securing Desire." In *From the Strategic Self to the Ethical Relation: Pedagogies of War and Peace*. Doctoral thesis, Department of Education, Ontario Institute for Studies in Education of the University of Toronto.

Moretti, Franco. 1998. *Atlas of the European Novel, 1800–1900*. London: Verso.

Morrison, Toni. 1998a. "Home." In *The House That Race Built*. Ed. W. Lubiano. New York: Vintage Books.

———. 1998b. "Strangers." *The New Yorker* (October 12).

———. 1990. "Unspeakable Thoughts Unspoken." *Michigan Quarterly Review* 32 (fall).

Moruzzi, Norma Claire. 1993. "National Abjects: Julia Kristeva on the Process of Political Self-Identification." In *Ethics, Politics, and Difference in Julia Kristeva's Writing*. Ed. K. Oliver. New York: Routledge.

Mouffe, Chantal. 1995. "Democratic Politics and the Question of Identity." In *The Identity in Question*. Ed. J. Rajchman. New York: Routledge.

———. 1992. "Feminism, Citizenship, and Radical Democratic Politics." In *Feminists Theorize the Political*. Ed. J. Butler and J. Scott. New York: Routledge.

Murray, Joan. 1984. *The Best of the Group of Seven*. Edmonton: Hurtig.

Nairn, Tom. 1977. *The Break-Up of Britain: Crisis and Neo-Nationalism*. London: N.L.B.

Nancy, Jean-Luc. 1997. *The Sense of the World*. Trans. J. S. Librett. Minneapolis: University of Minnesota Press.

———. 1996. "Being With." In *Centre for Theoretical Studies: Working Papers*, no 2. Colchester: Essex University Press.

———. 1991. *The Inoperative Community*. Trans. P. Connor, L. Garbus, M. Holland, and S. Sawhney. Minneapolis: University of Minnesota Press.

Nancy, Jean-Luc, and Philippe Lacoue-Labarthe. 1997. *Retreating the Political*. Ed. S. Sparks. New York: Routledge.

———. 1989. "The Unconscious Is Structured Like an Affect." In *Stanford Literature Review* 6, no. 2 (fall).

Nasgaard, Roald. 1976. *Changing Visions: The Canadian Landscape*. Edmonton Gallery and AGO.

Nemiroff, Diane. 1998. "Crossings." In *Crossings*. Ottawa: National Gallery of Canada.

Nietzsche, Friedrich. 1990. *Werke in Drei Bänden*. Kettwig: Phaidon Verlag.

———. 1980. *On the Advantages and Disadvantages of History for Life*. Trans. P. Preuss. Indianapolis: Hackett Publishing Company.

———. 1978. *Thus Spoke Zarathustra*. Trans. W. Kaufmann. New York: Penguin Books.

———. 1968. *The Will to Power*. Trans. W. Kaufmann and R. J. Hollingdale. New York: Vintage Books.

Norris, Andrew. 1998. "Carl Schmitt on Friends, Enemies, and the Political." In *Telos* 112 (summer).

Osborne, Harold. 1983. *Oxford Companion to Art*. Oxford: Oxford University Press.

Perin, Roberto. 1992. "Answering the Québec Question: Two Centuries of Equivocation." In *Negotiating with a Sovereign Québec*. Ed. D. Drache, R. Perin. Toronto: James Lorimer and Company.

Pevere, Geoff. 1988. "The Rites (and Wrongs) of the Elder or The Cinema We Got, The Critics We Need." In *Documents in Canadian Film*. Ed. D. Fetherling. Peterborough: Broadview Press.

Rancière, Jacques. 1999. *Disagreements: Politics and Philosophy*. Trans. J. Rose. Minneapolis: University of Minnesota Press.

———. 1992. "Politics, Identification, and Subjectivization." *October* 61 (summer).

Reed, John. 1993. *The Post-Colonial Landscape*. Saskatoon: The Mendel Art Gallery.

Reid, Dennis. 1973. *A Concise History of Canadian Painting*. Toronto: Oxford University Press.

Rodowick, D. N. 1997. *Gilles Deleuze's Time Machine.* Durham: Durham University Press.

Romney, Jonathan. 1995. *Sight and Sound* 5, no. 5 (May).

Rose, Jacqueline. 1996. *States of Fantasy.* Oxford: Clarendon Press.

Russell, Harper. 1966. *Painting in Canada: A History.* Toronto: Toronto University Press.

Russell, Peter, ed. 1966. *Nationalism in Canada.* Toronto: McGraw-Hill.

Rybczynski, Witold. 1986. *Home: A Short History of an Idea.* New York: Penguin Books.

Sack, Robert. 1986. *Human Territoriality: Its Theory and History.* Cambridge: Cambridge University Press.

Said, Edward. 1994. "Reflections on Exile." In *Altogether Elsewhere: Writers on Exile.* Ed. M. Robinson. London: Harcourt Brace and Company.

———. 1993. "Nationalism, Human Rights, and Interpretation." *Raritan* 12, no. 3.

———. 1984. "Reflections on Life in Exile." *Harper's Magazine* no. 269 (September).

———. 1983. *The World, the Text, and the Critic.* Cambridge: Harvard University Press.

———. 1979. *Orientalism.* New York: Random House.

St.-Exupéry, Antoine de. 1946. *Le Petit Prince.* Paris: Gallimard.

Sassen, Saskia. 2000. "Spatialities and Temporalities of the Global: Elements for a Theorization." *Public Culture* 30, no. 1.

Scott, Joan. 1995. "Multiculturalism and the Politics of Identity." In *The Identity in Question.* Ed. J. Rajchman. New York: Routledge.

Severin, Timothy. 1970. *The Golden Antilles.* London: Hamish Hamilton.

Shadbolt, Doris. 1990. *Emily Carr.* Vancouver: Douglas and McIntyre.

Shapiro, Michael. 2001. "Sovereignty, Dissymmetry, and Bare Life." In *Moral Ambiguity: National Culture and the Politics of the Family.* Minneapolis: University of Minnesota Press.

———. 2000. "National Times and Other Times: Re-thinking Citizenship." *Cultural Studies* no. 1 (January).

———. 1997. *Violent Cartographies.* Minneapolis: University of Minnesota Press.

———. 1994. "Moral Geographies and the Ethics of Post-Sovereignty." *Public Culture* 6, no. 3.

———. 1992. *Reading the Postmodern Polity.* Minneapolis: University of Minnesota Press.

Shaviro, Stephen. 1993. *The Cinematic Body.* Minneapolis: University of Minnesota Press.

Shields, Rob. 1991. *Places on the Margin: Alternative Geographies of Modernity.* London: Routledge.

Soguk, Nevzat. 1999. *States and Strangers: Refugees and Displacements of State-craft*. Minneapolis: University of Minnesota Press.

Sparks, Simon. 1997. "Politica Ficta." In *Retreating the Political*. New York: Routledge.

Stammelmann, Richard. 1993. "The Strangeness of the Other and the Otherness of the Stranger: Edmond Jabès." *Yale French Studies* 82.

Taylor, Charles. 1992. *The Politics of Recognition*. Princeton: Princeton University Press.

Teitelbaum, Matthew. 1991. "Sighting the Single Tree, Sighting the New Found Land." In *Eye of Nature*. Ed. D. Augaitis and H. Pakasaar. Banff: Walter Phillips Gallery.

Théberge, Pierre. 1998. *Crossings*. National Gallery of Canada: Ottawa.

Walcott, Rinaldo. 1997. *Black Like Who?* Toronto: Insomniac Press.

Wald, Priscilla. 1995. *Constituting Americans: Cultural Anxiety and Narrative Form*. Durham: Duke University Press.

Walker, R. B. J. 1997. "The Subject of Security." In *Critical Security Studies*. Ed. K. Krauss and M. C. Williams. Minneapolis: University of Minnesota Press.

———. 1995. "International Relations and the Concept of the Political." In *International Relations Theory Today*. Ed. K. Booth and S. Smith. University Park: Pennsylvania State University Press.

———. 1993. *Inside/Outside: International Relations as Political Theory*. Cambridge: Cambridge University Press.

———. 1991. "On the Spatiotemporal Conditions of Democratic Practice." *Alternatives* 16.

———. 1990. "Sovereignty, Identity, Community: Reflections on the Horizons of Contemporary Political Practice." In *Contending Sovereignties*. Ed. R. B. J. Walker and S. Mendlovitz. Boulder: Lynne Rienner Publishers.

Walker, R. B. J., and Saul Mendlovitz, ed. 1990. *Contending Sovereignties*. Boulder: Lynne Rienner Publishers.

West, Cornel. 1998. "Afterword." In *The House That Race Built*. Ed. W. Lubiano. New York: Vintage Books.

Wigley, Mark. 1995. *The Architecture of Deconstruction: Derrida's Haunt*. Cambridge: MIT Press.

Williams, Dorothy. 1992. "Blacks in Montreal." In *Boundaries of Identity: A Québec Reader*. Ed. W. Dodge. Toronto: Lester Publishing Ltd.

Williams, Patricia. 1998. "The Ethnic Scarring of American Whiteness." In *The House That Race Built*. Ed. W. Lubiano. New York: Vintage Books.

Wilson, Robert, and Wimal Dissanayake, ed. 1996. *Globallocal: Cultural Production and the Transnational Imaginary*. Durham: Duke University Press.

Wood, David. 1992. "Reading Derrida." In *Derrida: A Critical Reader*. London: Basil Blackwell.

Wulf, Christoph. 1987. "La voie lactée." *Traverses* 41.

Xenos, Nicholas. 1996. "Civic Nationalism: Oxymoron." *Critical Review* 10, no. 2 (spring).

Yack, Bernard. 1996. "The Myth of the Civic Nation." *Critical Review* 10, no. 2 (spring).

Yoon, Jin-me. 1998. *Before the Land, Behind the Camera*. Museum of Contemporary Photography, Ottawa, Ontario.

————. 1991a. "Touring Home: Jin-me Yoon." In *Constructing Cultural Identity: Jin-Me Yoon, Bob Boyer, Liz Magor*. Edmonton Art Gallery.

————.1991b. *Souvenirs of Self (Postcard Project)*. Walter Phillips Gallery, Banff, Alberta.

Index

Erin Manning lives in Montreal and teaches at McGill University and Carleton University. She is an artist and author of the novels *The Window Dresser* and *The Perfect Mango*.